Pakistan: 1992

EDITED BY
Charles H. Kennedy

Routledge
Taylor & Francis Group
LONDON AND NEW YORK

First published 1993 by Westview Press

Published 2019 by Routledge
52 Vanderbilt Avenue, New York, NY 10017
2 Park Square, Milton Park, Abingdon, Oxon OX14 4RN

Routledge is an imprint of the Taylor & Francis Group, an informa business

Library of Congress ISSN: 1061-6101

ISBN 13: 978-0-367-28212-7 (hbk)
ISBN 13: 978-0-367-29758-9 (pbk)

Pakistan: 1992

Published in cooperation with
the American Institute of Pakistan Studies

Contents

Preface

Pakistan: 1992 is the inaugural volume of a prospective series of biennial assessments of contemporary events and issues in Pakistan affairs. In general, the series will cover issues relevant to Pakistan's domestic politics, foreign policy, and economy. This volume contains special chapters on the 1990 elections, Islamization, health policy, Afghanistan, and Kashmir. Each of the contributors to this volume is a specialist on Pakistan, and each has had recent research experience in the state relevant to their respective contributions. *Pakistan: 1992* is published in affiliation with the American Institute of Pakistan Studies, a non-profit, non-partisan educational organization in its nineteenth year of operation, which is dedicated to encouraging and supporting research on issues relevant to Pakistan and the promotion of scholarly exchange between the United States and Pakistan.

I wish to express deep appreciation to all of the authors of *Pakistan: 1992* for their hard work under rigorous deadlines. Special thanks is also owed to those scholars who agreed to serve as discussants at the 1992 Annual Convention of the Association for Asian Studies in March, where earlier versions of the chapters included in this volume were presented. Those scholars were: Rafiq Afzal, University of Massachusetts; Larry Goodson, Campbell University; Shafik Hashmi, Georgia Southern University; Sikandar Hayat, Embassy of Pakistan; Rasul Rais, Columbia University; and Mohammad Waseem, Columbia University. Their thoughts helped to revise and enrich the manuscript. I am also grateful to Susan McEachern and her colleagues at Westview Press who agreed to undertake this project. It should be noted that Afak Haydar, author of Chapter 5, was also instrumental in the preparation of the glossary.

Closer to home, financial assistance for this project was provided by the Research and Publication Fund of the Graduate School and by the Archie Fund for Faculty Excellence, both of Wake Forest University. Elide Vargas of the WFU Department of Politics proved helpful throughout, as always. Ata Khan, administrative assistant of the American Institute of Pakistan Studies, was indispensable during every phase of the project. Finally, very special thanks is owed to Patricia Poe, who, with the help of Guilford Publishing Company and Lisa Merschel, coaxed the manuscript into its final form.

Charles H. Kennedy
American Institute of Pakistan Studies
Wake Forest University

Map of South Asia. *Source:* Ashok K. Dutt and M. Margaret Geib, *Atlas of South Asia* (Boulder: Westview Press, 1987).

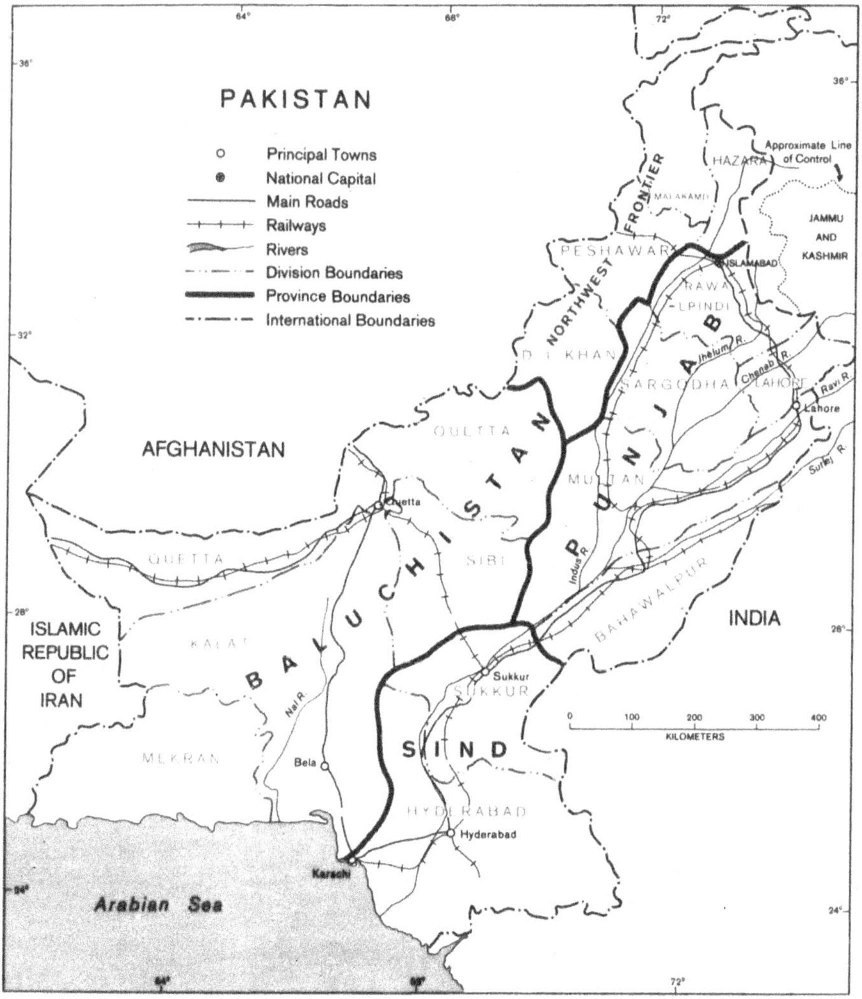

Map of Pakistan. *Source:* Shahid Javed Burki, *Pakistan: The Continuing Search for Nationhood* (Boulder: Westview Press, 1991).

1

Dilemma and Challenge in Nawaz Sharif's Pakistan

Lawrence Ziring

The year 1991 was transitional for the world, and no less so for Pakistan. In many respects it was a defining year for Pakistan's political system and for the central government led by Nawaz Sharif. Never before did international events have a deeper impact on the domestic scene, and by the same token, never before was the country's foreign policy so clearly an extension of its national condition. The time had passed when internal and external matters could be compartmentalized. The intertwining of the one with the other gave new emphasis to holistic doctrine, and indeed Pakistan was called upon to reexamine its basic ethos and to determine the course it would pursue in light of the cataclysmic changes generated by the collapse and disintegration of its giant neighbor, the Soviet Union.

The task of leading the nation during this uncertain period fell upon two personalities, one with his roots in the emergence of the Muslim state, the other, a man half his age, more conditioned by the urban growth and entrepreneurial development of the third world nation.

The relationship between President Ghulam Ishaq Khan and Prime Minister Nawaz Sharif offered more synergism than that between the president and Nawaz Sharif's predecessor, Benazir Bhutto. Whereas division, rivalry, and conflict framed the relationship between Benazir and Ghulam Ishaq, there was relative compatibility in the way in which Ghulam Ishaq interacted with Nawaz Sharif. Such sharp contrast was also discerned in the character of the support that Benazir and Nawaz Sharif received in buttressing their administrations. Benazir led a curious coalition, the most striking feature of which was her inability to carry the Punjab or to find a place within her government for the forces led by Nawaz Sharif. She failed to sustain a coalition with the Karachi-based MQM (Muhajir Qaumi Mahaz), and her tactics prevented alliance with frontier leaders in Balochistan and the NWFP (Northwest Frontier Province). Nawaz Sharif, on the other hand, proved more adept at forming coalitions. As the dominant political figure in the Punjab, he was successful in bringing the Sindhi Muhajir organization into the fold, while heretofore rival provincial and ideological camps joined with him in the creation of a harmony of interests not experienced since the earliest years of the country's independence. And, although Benazir assumed the role of leader of the political opposition, many of her former PPP (Pakistan People's Party) stalwarts opted for a place within the ruling IJI (Islamic Democratic Alliance).

The Intertwining of Domestic and Foreign Policy

But as much as domestic developments caused Pakistanis to reassess their political performance, it was the world beyond Pakistan that provoked the nation to respond to combinations of challenges that demanded reappraisals of its status and role in a rapidly changing global environment. The year began with an American-led international force, of which Pakistan was a token member, assaulting Iraq. The success of Operation Desert Storm forced Baghdad to retreat from Kuwait, which it had invaded, occupied, and annexed only months before. The Pakistani troops that were despatched to Saudi Arabia, however, were stationed distant from the war zone, and their services were neither contemplated nor used by the alliance that planned and prosecuted the action. Moreover, although volunteering forces for the international coalition, Islamabad itself officially proclaimed that they only were to be used to protect the most sacred of the Islamic holy places in Saudi Arabia.

With Pakistani troops distant from the war zone, the government had little difficulty in coping with public sentiment. Nevertheless, a vocal segment of the population left little doubt it favored Baghdad's claim to speak for revolutionary Islam. There was considerable street support for the ouster of the Kuwaiti monarch, and the demonstrators voiced particular approval for Saddam Hussain's defiance of Washington and the U.S.-led coalition. Furthermore, once the American field commander ordered an all-out attack on Iraq and quickly humbled the war-making capability of the Arab world's most formidable military presence, Pakistanis in and outside the armed forces registered their concern that the "real" purpose of the action was to prevent the emergence of a substantial Muslim power. Hence, no less a figure than General Mirza Aslam Beg, Pakistan's Chief of the Army Staff, condemned the United States for what he described as the use of vengeful force. He also had harsh words for the Saudi royal family, as well as the other monarchs in the region. Thus, despite the placing of Pakistani forces in Saudi Arabia, none other than the leader of the Pakistan Army appeared to side with those of his vocal countrymen who unambiguously supported the Iraqi ruler. The episode proved a considerable embarrassment for the government of Nawaz Sharif as well as President Ghulam Ishaq, but their management of state affairs was never in jeopardy. Although publicized as a normal sequence of events, Beg's retirement from the army and the transfer of the command to General Asif Nawaz Janjua was also judged as the government's way of balancing its domestic and foreign needs.

Beg's reaction to the Gulf War was mirrored in the expression of his demonstrative countrymen, but his concern was more broadly geopolitical and strategic. The elimination of Iraq as a major actor in the Middle East seemed to signal a more aggressive American posture in the area. On its face, a formidable Arab state, dedicated to the destruction of Israel, had been seriously damaged by Zionism's principal supporters. Pakistanis spoke of a "Pax Americana" being imposed upon a world no longer balanced by a Soviet presence. Moreover, strains in Washington-Islamabad relations had been aggravated earlier when President Bush failed to certify to the U.S. Congress that Pakistan was not engaged in a nuclear weapons program. In October 1990, the Bush administration suspended military transfers to Pakistan. Under the terms of the Pressler amendment even non-military American aid had been put on hold. From a Pakistani viewpoint, the damage inflicted on Iraq by the Washington-led coalition was serious, but not nearly as vital as the dramatic change in U.S. policy or the threat the Americans seemed to pose to Pakistan's nuclear program.

In the absence of the Soviet Union, let alone a communist threat to the region, Islamabad perceived a different United States, particularly one less inclined to assist the Muslim nation, and even more intimate with India. Indeed, if there were to be ongoing relations of a positive character between the two states, another not immediately apparent raison d'etre would have to be found. In addition to their perception of American "overkill" in Iraq, Pakistanis were clearly ill at ease with a powerful globally involved country no longer restrained by heretofore countervailing influences.

Thus, the passing of the Cold War and the changing American attitude toward Pakistan compelled Islamabad to reevaluate its position vis-a-vis Washington. The Nawaz Sharif government also found it necessary to steer a difficult course between those who demanded a total break with Washington and others who continued to emphasize the utility of a sustained association.

Sino-Pakistani relations never appeared more important, and the visit to Islamabad by China's president was answered by visits from the highest-ranking Pakistani officials. Perhaps the most notable was General Asif Nawaz's journey to Beijing to discuss mutual security interests in the changed conditions. Although agitated over Li Peng's visit to India, Islamabad claimed China remained an important friend and expressed pleasure that the Chinese leader had called upon India to accept Pakistan's overture for a nuclear-free weapons zone in South Asia. And, while new arms agreements were entered into with China, there was ample recognition in Islamabad that the changed world conditions offered new prospects for a Chinese-Indian detente. The full impact of such activity demanded increased vigilance in the Pakistan Foreign Office.

Nor was government unmindful of the need to develop new policies with the Arab Middle East, where the divisions between the monarchies and non-monarchies had become more pronounced; or with Iran, which had emerged stronger from the 1991 Gulf War and with a new pragmatic diplomatic style. Islamabad was also intrigued by developments in Central Asia, and in order to better adjust to the new conditions there, a way needed to be found to harmonize Islamabad's interest in the region with those of Turkey, Iran, and Saudi Arabia.

Islamabad also observed developments within the European Community and was provoked by the global significance of a unified Germany. The organization of the new European Charter and the expansion of the Conference in Security and Cooperation in Europe was recognition that the Cold War was truly over and that a new framework of worldwide relationships was already well advanced.

Islamabad acknowledged the need to bring a final resolution to the struggle in Afghanistan, and the prospects for a satisfactory, compromise solution were much improved in the new global environment. Moreover, the ouster of Najibullah, the collapse of his government, and the seizure of Kabul by factions of the resistance in April 1992 forced Pakistan into a difficult mediator's role. The success or failure of Islamabad's diplomacy would determine whether the Afghan refugees returned to their homeland or remained indefinitely in their Pakistani surroundings. A final and durable settlement of the Afghan conflict, and the establishment of a stable government in Kabul, were essential keys to Pakistan's policy in Central Asia.

But if the Afghanistan problem at least seemed tractable, the same could not be said for Pakistan's continuing difficulties with India. The Kashmir problem generated considerable heat, but efforts at turning down the burners were largely unsuccessful. Conflict between Pakistan and India remained a constant, barely influenced by the disappearance of the Soviet Union or the opening of a new era in East-West relations.

Management and Reform

Although the government was called upon to do some delicate balancing, the principal burden rested on the backs of the higher administration, the professional core within Pakistan's steel frame that combined the talents of the public administrators with that of the civil-military bureaucracy led by Ghulam Ishaq. It was its combined sense of reality that enabled the

Nawaz Sharif government to weather what could have been a far more turbulent period.

Within months of his embarrassing statements, General Beg had been ushered into retirement. Contacts with the Arab oil producers, notably Saudi Arabia and Kuwait, were reinforced. The government also sought to mend fences with the United States, but there was no mistaking the changed circumstances of that relationship or that the Americans were perceived differently, particularly by the Pakistani literati who sought to articulate a new view of the Pakistan condition.

That condition was not something to celebrate in 1991. Pakistan's economy had ceased to expand and the burden placed upon the country by its returning citizens, long domiciled in the Gulf states, was further exacerbated by the loss of a major source of foreign exchange. Pakistanis working in the Arabian peninsula states had remitted huge sums of money to Pakistan. That flow was drastically curtailed by the war and its aftermath, and no less important from a political as well as economic vantage point, the returned laborers could not find employment in Pakistan.

The government nonetheless aggressively tackled some of the country's more long-standing problems. The Water Apportionment Accord which had remained unresolved since independence was concluded despite the continuing criticism of the opposition. The Kalabagh Dam project was suspended pending the development of a compromise formula acceptable to all the provinces. The Water and Power Development Authority, however, was permitted to proceed with the non-controversial Bhasha and Skardu dams. The National Finance Commission (NFC) accepted a formula for a proportional distribution of funding among the different provinces and other funds were reserved for the so-called backward areas. The NFC action, like the Water Accord, was made possible by the dominance of the IJI in each of Pakistan's four provinces.

Nawaz Sharif also used his business experience in an effort aimed at transforming the way Pakistan conducts its commercial affairs. The prime minister cited the changed conditions in the world marketplace that placed new emphasis on the private sector. Restrictions on Pakistani business practices were reduced significantly in order to prepare the country for the competition that it had heretofore neglected. The promotion of exports and new attempts to attract foreign investors were given higher priority. The introduction of foreign currency accounts also was aimed at Pakistani entrepreneurs, some of whom seized the opportunity to expand their activities and increase holdings. Nevertheless, the economy was seriously affected by the worldwide slowdown in economic forces, as well as the new, more cautious attitude of former external benefactors in the Arab world as well as in the West. Pakistan's significant law and order situation also played havoc with the economy, causing both domestic and foreign investors to question the viability of possible ventures.

In spite of strenuous measures, government programs aimed at controlling the violence in Sindh province proved unsuccessful. Lawlessness was so generalized that the citizenry lost what little confidence it had in government's capacity to correct the situation. Incidents of robbery, home invasion, kidnappings, and rape were more numerous than at any other time in the nation's history. Even foreign engineers and technicians could not escape the grasp of the *dacoits*, and development projects in the interior regions of Sindh were seriously affected by the government's inability to guarantee the safety of on-site workers. Moreover, police officials, including officers, were implicated in criminal acts or simply corrupted by the prevailing conditions. Nor was the mayhem isolated to Sindh alone. A massacre of residents in Islampura and Sheikhupura in the Punjab forced Nawaz Sharif to cancel an important trip to Japan, and the attention given to the event raised anew the question of investing in Pakistan's economic future. In the Punjab, citizens were quick to point out that many of the violent assaults on persons and property were perpetrated by unemployed youth from relatively well-to-do families. The easy availability of firearms and an intensifying drug problem were described as causes for an escalating countrywide crime wave.

The government responded to the dilemma by forcing the national parliament to adopt the Twelfth Amendment to the Constitution. The vote was taken before a debate could be mounted by the opposition, and the most contentious aspect of the law was the establishment of Speedy Trial Courts, which were charged with dispensing summary justice almost immediately following the apprehension of suspects. Legal scholars argued that the amendment effectively diminished the powers of the conventional judiciary, created a parallel judiciary with extreme powers, and buttressed the latter by linking it with investigative and prosecuting agencies. Few among the legal community believed the Speedy Trial Courts were the answer to the country's crime problem, and the vast majority concluded that the powers conferred would only strengthen the arbitrary will of the government. Fearing abuses of power, several judgments decided in the new courts were overturned at the appellate level.

The Shariat Bill also was passed in 1991, arousing the concerns of those who feared the government was yielding to Islamic fundamentalists. The legislation, its critics said, destabilized the long-established socio-legal order, and would stand as a barrier to foreign investment in the country. Nawaz Sharif hesitated in fully implementing the legislation with the politician's hope that its mere passage would achieve the desired results. In the end, however, the Shariat Bill failed on all counts. It neither placated the Islamic fundamentalists, nor did it calm the fears of the more secular-minded members of Pakistani society. The increasing alienation of the Jamaat-i-Islami was traced to the failure to enact and enforce a rigid Shariat bill, but the government apparently believed its fortunes remained with those members of society who staunchly opposed providing the *ulema* with powers that could drastically alter their lifestyle. As in the days of Zia ul-Haq, the Pakistan government promoted the notion of an Islamic state, but the actual portrayal of a state governed by theological teaching was judged out of time and substance.

Nevertheless, in January 1992, a Working Group on *Nifaz-i-Shariat* (Islamic legal order) was constituted on a directive of the prime minister. It was called upon to monitor and recommend measures for the enforcement of Islamic laws in the country. Convened under the chairmanship of Maulana Abdus Sattar Khan Niazi, Federal Minister for Religious Affairs, the meeting brought together prominent *ulema* from all schools of Islamic thought, as well as the Federal Minister for Parliamentary Affairs and a number of MNAs. The charge given to the group included an examination of the process of Islamization, and its impact on the individual and the society as a whole. The Working Group adopted a nineteen-point scheme, which it claimed would lead to a pious life for Pakistan's citizens in addition to enhancing their material wellbeing. Among the nineteen points were calls for piety among Pakistan's political leaders; the implementation of all Islamic legislation, especially that body of laws creating the Shariat Courts; increased attention to the work of the Council of Islamic Ideology; the enforcement by central authority of all Shariat rules; the full transformation of the educational system to represent Islamic teaching; controls on the electronic and print media to assure a morally sound Islamic way of life; uniform and enforced prayer schedules for all citizens, including members of the armed forces and civil servants; the total abolition of interest; an Islamic banking system with prohibitions on the acquisition of income in the absence of appropriate labor; and the creation of a women's university. Perhaps more significant in the long term was the recommendation that the political system be brought into greater conformity with Islamic requirements.

The conference also used the occasion to cite its concern for the plight of Muslim fundamentalists in Algeria and called upon the Algiers government to accept the results of the electoral process. Before adjourning, the Working Group addressed the changed conditions in Central Asia and urged the despatch of a delegation of *ulema* to the new Muslim republics of the former Soviet Union. The objective of the delegation would be to interact with the citizens of the new states and to ascertain their needs and concerns. The delegation also was urged to identify Central Asian students who could be brought to Pakistan for religious training. It was most doubtful, however, that the administration was prepared to address all of these issues in the foreseeable future.

Overall, the IJI did not suffer from its go-slow approach to Islamization. Most important, it sought to avoid taking extreme ideological or religious positions. Acceptance of this approach was demonstrated by the Senate elections, wherein the IJI won 28 of the 39 contested seats. The IJI also retained its hold on the lower house and effectively sustained its preeminence in the provincial assemblies. The Local Bodies elections also went in favor of the administration, and the prevailing governmental order was essentially undisturbed by the problems which otherwise afflicted the nation.

Azad Kashmir, the only remaining stronghold of the PPP, also yielded to the IJI in the 1991 elections. The dissolution of the Azad Kashmir Assembly had necessitated the call for new elections, and although the opposition cried fraud, Sardar Abdul Qayyum Khan, in league with Nawaz Sharif, took control of the state's administration.

Nawaz Sharif's success was perhaps less a matter of satisfying the material needs of his constituents and more a question of denying Benazir's re-emergence. Pakistan's disparate and regional political leaders preferred Nawaz Sharif over Benazir Bhutto because they believed he would better serve their interests. A good portion of the Pakistani electorate had obviously drawn the same conclusion. Benazir attempted to provide the opposition with the necessary leadership in the parliament, but she was under increasing pressure from the number of legal cases that had been brought against her. Similarly, her husband and associates were cited with abuses of power as well as criminal acts, and they had considerable difficulty in organizing an effective defense, let alone providing the leadership to challenge the government.

The opposition was highly critical of the government's selection of Jam Sadiq Ali to be Sindh's chief minister. Ordered to deal ruthlessly with Sindhi hooligans and terrorists, Sindh province had been transformed into something resembling a police state. Jam Sadiq was accused of adopting fascist methods, and not only the political opposition, but the country's intelligentsia also voiced the view that the remedy for the region's unrest was worse than the malady. The general fear was raised that the totalitarian actions observed in Sindh would more than likely spread over the entire country if not challenged.

In a desperate attempt at neutralizing the excesses of the Sindh regime, the political opposition forcefully supported the claim of Veena Hayat, a daughter of the elder Sindhi politician, Sardar Hayat Khan, that her home had been invaded by Jam Sadiq's "storm troopers" and that she had been assaulted and raped by them. President Ghulam Ishaq's son-in-law was an advisor to Jam Sadiq in the Sindh Home Ministry, and both he and the Sindh chief minister were alleged as culpable in the alleged rape. Moreover, the opposition claimed that Irfanullah Marwat, the president's son-in-law, had actually engineered the act. According to the opposition, the attack had been ordered to intimidate anyone who might contemplate challenging the government of Jam Sadiq.

A judicial enquiry was opened to investigate the alleged rape, but before it could issue a finding, demonstrations were organized in Islamabad. On the very day that the president was scheduled to address the National Assembly, a riot broke out in front of Parliament House. But the embarrassment caused the president by the unruly demonstrators outside the assembly paled when compared with the opposition's intemperate interruptions of Ghulam Ishaq's speech to the assembled legislators. The president was called upon to address the issue of the alleged rape, and under extraordinary pressure, he was forced to make an emotional defense of his son-in-law. Moreover, although the judicial enquiry had not yet completed its work, the president felt compelled to exonerate his relative. Seldom had the nation seen Ghulam Ishaq yield to his emotions, and clearly the opposition's tactics were geared to disorient the aging statesman. Although Ghulam Ishaq's capacity to lead the nation was brought into question, it was clear that Benazir Bhutto, who led the verbal assault on the president, earned few credits from the episode.

Moreover, the sudden death of Jam Sadiq lowered the level of the debate and focused attention away from the Veena Hayat case. Jam Sadiq's successor, Syed Muzaffar Hussain Shah, seemed to promise a firm but less arbitrary administration. Still, the anarchical conditions prevailing in the province were hardly relieved. Thus, in mid-April 1992, the new Sindh government announced the formation of a village defense system. The new system was intended to mobilize the rural population for purposes of self-defense. Skeptics, however, wondered whether this new province-wide arrangement would actively reduce the threat posed by the itinerant bands of gangsters and terrorists that indiscriminately targeted the province's innocent inhabitants. Indeed, they pointed out, this was not the first time such defense schemes had been planned and authorized.

Critical Issues

The attentive public, however, wanted to see more attention given to social issues and less time spent in political squabbling. Indeed, global events had demonstrated the increasing importance of information and its correlation to public awareness and increased political consciousness. Mass movements were no longer so difficult to organize, nor could societies be insulated from one another. Pakistan's social needs could no longer be ignored with impunity. Nevertheless, the country's educational sector continued to suffer from neglect and lack of vision. The malaise in the educational system was all-pervasive. Teachers would not or could not teach, and students could not or would not learn. Material resources for education were always in short supply, but even IJI policies did little to correct the condition. Education continued to receive low priorities.

Unchecked lawlessness within the schools and universities burdened successive Pakistani governments, no less so the government of Nawaz Sharif. The confusion over direction and mission was compounded by government indifference. This in turn created an angry student body, eager to take issue with the prevailing political forces, yet at the same time exploited by those same forces. As a consequence, violence swamped the campuses, and law enforcement was ill-equipped to meet the challenge. In contemporary Pakistan, the universities and colleges have become armed camps. Teachers are abused, pedagogy has only limited purpose, and examination systems are suspect. In the latter instance, student intimidation of examiners has made a mockery of efforts aimed at establishing reasonable academic standards. Hence, teachers are more cynical about their tasks and objectives and only a few are provoked to engage in professional discourse or in serious intellectual pursuits. In an ambiance of siege, teachers find it virtually impossible to conduct research or expand the horizon of knowledge. In 1992 the government declared its intention to install a National Testing Service. Minister for Education Syed Fakhar Imam called for cooperation among teachers, students, and parents, repeating the oft-heard statement that without a thoroughly educated population the country could never compete with other nations, let alone achieve the goals of progress and prosperity.

The youth problem, particularly among that element with an education, was aggravated further by the economy's failure to offer employment opportunities. Moreover, the country's booming birthrate, among the highest in the world, projected an even more dismal outlook. The flawed census of 1990 was abandoned as a useful reference; nevertheless there was ample reason to conclude that the Pakistani population had topped 125 million by 1992, the vast majority of which subsisted far below the poverty level. At a 3.2 percent rate of increase per annum, cataclysmic Malthusian projections demanded limits to growth. Indeed, the population explosion, slated to double every twenty years, had already resulted in the loss of virtually all development progress achieved during the previous decade. The Nawaz Sharif government was not unmindful of the problem, but religious prohibitions on birth control and family planning, as well as the difficulty in reaching the illiterate masses with adequate information, did not provide much hope that the dilemma could be effectively addressed. The government announced its goal was to reduce the rate of population growth to 2.8 percent, but even that modest reduction would take years to accomplish, and it was by no means certain the government program would affect that section of the population that most needed assistance.

Still another area of concern involved the country's financial institutions. The Pakistan cooperatives and Bank of Credit and Commerce International (BCCI) scandals threatened to wipe out the holdings of small savers. A judicial commission was organized to examine the corrupt practices of those money managers who had discredited their calling with the most unseemly business transactions. And although the Nawaz Sharif government parried assaults linking it to the scandalous activities, its negligence could not be denied. Some observers believed the prime minister, one of the country's supreme businessmen, could not escape responsibility.

Nawaz Sharif was forced to go on public record declaring he would resign if the enquiry found he or his government was implicated in wrongdoing. In fact, the BCCI scandal, with its base in Pakistan, extended around the world. Reports that BCCI had not only misused depositor funds, but also had engaged in or assisted those involved in the drug trade or gun running, did not serve to enhance the reputation of the Nawaz Sharif government. An urgent call to the Gulf emirates, among the principal investors in the bank, by the highest officers in the Pakistan government, met with a positive response when millions of dollars were made available to satisfy the demands of shaken small depositors.

Still another commission was organized to enquire into the affairs of the cooperative finance corporation societies. An executive order called upon the Registrar of the Cooperative Department to initiate legal action against the previous management of the Punjab Industrial Development Corporation for allegedly violating banking rules. The corporation's officers were accused of embezzling public money running into the millions of rupees. Currently supervised by an administrator, the corporation was said to bear a liability of Rs. 10.4 crore (one crore equals 10 million.) The corporation was accused of advancing security-free loans in its 108 branches, and the disclosure opened the entire national banking and financial community to public scrutiny. None of the government enquiries, however, were geared to restore financial equilibrium, let alone depositor confidence.

In these circumstances, even President Ghulam Ishaq was imposed upon to emphasize the need for a new Pakistan, which he said would be based upon a progressive, enlightened, and dynamic society resting upon the eternal teachings of Islam. Only spiritual revival was deemed an answer to the profligate character of the prevailing society. In an address at the laying of a foundation stone for the new Federal Shariat Court Building, the president noted that the common good and welfare of society was Islam's basic objective. The positive enforcement of the *Shariah* (Islamic law), he declared, would be the government's primary consideration in the years ahead. It was unclear, however, if this was real or simply declaratory policy.

U.S.-Pakistan Relations

The Pakistan-U.S. relationship was forged in the early years of the Cold War. The United States knew little about Pakistan other than its geopolitical position astride the eastern flank of the Middle East. Pakistan was the gateway to India and became the rimland anchor of western alliance systems in near proximity to the southern perimeter of the Soviet Union. Pakistan was to be Washington's most "allied ally" during the 1950s, and when Field Marshal Ayub Khan ruled Pakistan, Americans were a large and omnipresent force in the country. In addition to the many civilian advisors scattered over the country, Pakistan was the principal base for American military reconnaissance aircraft overflying Soviet territory.

Pakistanis experienced mixed emotions over this American intrusion. Some benefitted from the association, others saw long-term dangers in the sustained connection. But successive Pakistani governments acknowledged the utility of the relationship and, despite difficult moments in 1962 and 1965, a curious intimacy was sustained.

Americans, however, were for the most part unaware of their government's actions, or if they did ponder the association, were even more bewitched by an alliance which seemed to complicate relations with New Delhi. Although thousands of U.S. citizens assumed tasks in Pakistani political, social, and economic life through private as well as public agencies in the 1960s, most showed little real understanding of the Pakistan scene. The World Bank and International Monetary Fund played important roles in Pakistan's development. They assisted the country in promoting its economic well-being and in meeting its needs for international financial liquidity, but even the work of these institutions was left to a few experts, and a more prescient awareness of Pakistan's national needs seldom received serious attention. Private American investment in Pakistan was never significant, and Islamabad's attempts to woo such capital failed more often than they succeeded. The Fulbright Program and other cultural exchange activities, both publicly and privately funded, were perhaps the most successful in drawing the two nations into reasonable proximity. But few American scholars were prepared to commit their professional lives to the study of Pakistan, and those that did had minimal if any impact on policy makers in either country. Thus, in spite of a long-term association, U.S.-Pakistan relations failed to develop serious dimensions beyond those established by the Cold War.

Pakistanis accused the United States of imposing a dictatorship on the country in 1958. They were especially disturbed by American military support for India in its 1962 border clash with China. But it was the 1965 war with India that strained relations almost to the breaking point. President Lyndon Johnson imposed an embargo on weapon shipments to India and Pakistan, but the impact of that decision fell hardest on Pakistan, forcing Islamabad to accept a ceasefire it was otherwise determined to avoid. That embargo on arms transfers extended into and through the Nixon administration, and it was only during the brief presidency of Gerald Ford that it was officially lifted. While official business continued during the decade of the embargo, the ambiance of the association was never what it had been before its imposition. Even President Nixon's earlier gesture of support to Pakistan during the Indo-Pakistani War of 1971 had not reversed the overriding condition. Nor did Pakistan's role in assisting Washington to normalize its relations with Beijing reverse the negative aspects of the Washington-Islamabad connection.

It was in this changed environment at official levels that the most serious threat to American-Pakistani relations occurred. The assault on the American Embassy in 1979 and its razing by an uncontrolled mob threatened to terminate all efforts at improving the relationship. The world was confronted with what was journalistically described as an Islamic renaissance. The key event provoking this reaction centered on Pakistan's immediate neighbor, Iran. The fall of the Shah and the emergence of Ayatollah Khomeini prompted a revolutionary form of Islam espousing the cause of ridding the Muslim world of its western nemesis, and especially its dominant force, the United States. Targeting American installations and personnel in Muslim countries was one element in an Islamic resurgence that freely publicized its violent character. The attack on the American Embassy, unprotected by the Pakistan government, caused Washington to seriously reappraise its purpose in Pakistan. President Jimmy Carter was shaken by the intensity of the assault and ordered the suspension of American projects in the country. He also called for reducing the size of the American community in the country, as well as the downsizing of American commitments to Islamabad. Only the Cold War sustained U.S.-Pakistan relations during that period, and it was only the superheating of that condition that drew the Americans to reconsider their position. The Soviet invasion of Afghanistan appeared to be timed to the American retreat from the region. Be that as it may, the Soviets miscalculated Washington's response, and although Jimmy Carter's offer of help to defend Pakistan was rejected by Zia ul-Haq early into that crisis, Ronald Reagan's more generous offer of assistance to Islamabad in 1981 was seized with alacrity by Pakistani officialdom. The Reagan administration revived the period of the 1950s when Pakistan was made a principal recipient of American military assistance. The 1981 agreement had two purposes: First, it made Pakistan the conduit for the transfer of sophisticated weapons to the Afghan mujahadin; second, it promised to modernize Pakistan's military establishment through the sale of state-of-the-art weaponry, particularly advanced fighter-bombers.

Another aspect of the agreement, though understated, was Washington's attempt to steer Pakistan away from a course established by Zulfikar Ali Bhutto whereby Pakistan sought to develop nuclear weapons capability. Pakistani nuclear programs took on greater significance after India's detonation of a nuclear device in 1974. Pakistanis believed they could do nothing less than match the Indian example if they were to protect their territorial integrity and national existence. The United States, for its part, clung to the view that Pakistan might yet settle for a conventional deterrent, which bolstered the Reagan government's decision to improve Pakistan's defenses and strike force. With the conflict raging in Afghanistan, Pakistan was identified as a frontline state, and the war material flowing into the country was at times awesome in its magnitude. Indeed, Pakistan became the third-largest recipient of American aid after Israel and Egypt. The protracted nature of the Afghan war required the U.S. president to seek congressional approval to waive specific legislative restrictions on the transfer of aid to countries judged to be engaged in nuclear weapons programs. Pakistan accepted the American rules of the game and insisted its purpose was the peaceful use of nuclear energy. With such official representations, President Reagan certified Islamabad's peaceful intentions to the American Congress, and that body in turn waived the restrictions on assistance to the frontline state. This policy and response became routine until the Soviet Union's decision to withdraw from Afghanistan.

Once the Soviets abandoned their adventure in Afghanistan, the United States was less eager to sustain an action that no longer seemed to merit American involvement. The passing of the Cold War and the retreat of the last Soviet soldier from Afghanistan occurred in 1989. The transformation of the Soviet Union into a less bellicose international actor dramatically altered U.S. interest in rimland Asia. And as the Cold War receded, and with it the Soviet Union itself, it was all too apparent that Washington wanted a final settlement in the region. The decision to cease all assistance to the Afghan resistance was taken in concert with Moscow before the Soviet Union self-destructed in the summer of 1991. The Cold War was not only officially over, the Soviet Union had ceased to exist. In its place were the various republics that heretofore had been integral members of the union, but now declared their independence. Lesser changes may not have exposed the Pakistan nuclear program to public view.

During the Benazir Bhutto interregnum, U.S.-Pakistan relations had entered a twilight zone. Benazir charmed official Washington in all its branches and at all levels. Benazir was able to convince the United States to make a sizeable weapons transfer to her nation's armed forces. The positive American response was in no small way a consequence of American perceptions that Prime Minister Bhutto's longevity was dependent on her capacity to insulate her military establishment from Pakistani politics. Therefore, when Benazir was ousted in the summer of 1990, Washington concluded that her efforts had failed and that the country had again slipped under military control. Moreover, the question of Pakistan's nuclear weapons activity could not be ignored.

Pakistan's nuclear program had remained within the purview of the Pakistan Army, and the removal of Benazir appeared to herald an acceleration of nuclear weapons development. Moreover, Benazir's passing came at a time when the United States-led coalition was mounting its operation against Saddam Hussain's Iraq and was about to unleash Desert Storm. The purpose of the military campaign was ostensibly the reclaiming of Kuwait's sovereignty, but a major aspect of the attack centered on the destruction of Baghdad's capacity to produce weapons of mass destruction. Iraq's nuclear weapons program, therefore, was a prime target. The United States had earlier displayed special concern that Pakistani-Indian hostility, essentially over Kashmir, might erupt into another war. Moreover, if the two antagonists were nuclear armed such a conflict held out the prospect of escalating into a nuclear exchange.

Special missions to Pakistan and India in 1990 were aimed at averting a war. But the apparent success of that venture did not diminish the concern with nuclear proliferation. Washington took a harder position on the nuclear weapons issue, and when President Bush refused to certify that Pakistan was not engaged in nuclear weapons production, American assistance ceased to flow to the Muslim country.

The suspension of aid, including technical assistance, was greeted somewhat defiantly in Pakistan. The nuclear program was a popular issue and coming as it did in the midst of the Gulf crisis, it aroused deeper sentiments among the body politic. The Pakistan government publicized its intention to hold to its original course. National honor as well as the country's security was said to be at stake. The disintegration of the Soviet Union had also stirred the Pakistanis in ways not heretofore contemplated. What was United States policy in the region, given the absence of Soviet countervailing power? Suddenly, Pakistanis began to sense that the United States, heretofore a perceived friend, might be metamorphosizing into a serious foe. Heightening Pakistani concerns was the obvious shifting about of the New Delhi government. Having lost its major patron in the Soviet Union, India was now more inclined to do business with Washington. Pakistan, therefore, concluded that New Delhi was seeking to isolate Pakistan.

Pakistanis pointed to the defeat of the Burton Amendment in the American Congress, which called upon the U.S. government to support a U.N. sponsored plebiscite in Kashmir. They were also mindful of Congressman Stephen Solarz's defense of the Indian position, particularly his recorded comment that "forty years of history clearly established Kashmir as part of India." The passing of Solarz's substitute amendment in 1991 calling for the resolution of the Kashmir dispute within the "framework of the 1972 Simla Declaration" was not what Pakistanis wished to receive from the American legislators.

Pakistanis were again exercised by Senator Larry Pressler's visit to India and Pakistan in January 1992. During his tour, Pressler was quoted as approving India's "peaceful" nuclear program. On the other hand, Pakistan's development of the atom, according to Pressler, was geared for weapons production. Nor did Pressler confine his comments to nuclear questions. The senator also focused attention on the new Central Asian Muslim republics, noting that India had cause for apprehension if they were linked to the Muslim states of the northern tier, and especially to Pakistan. Improvements in U.S.-Pakistan relations, Pressler noted, were dependent on Pakistan's willingness to yield in these areas. The American legislator had chosen to identify the two questions that Pakistanis were most unified upon, and the criticism he aroused prevented the Pakistani president and prime minister from giving him an audience during his brief stay in the country.

The Pressler affair raised the level of the already passionate debate within the country. Writing in *The Muslim*, Shireen Mazari cited America's dire fear of Islam. If the Americans, she wrote, wish to understand the ideological threat to the region, they would do better to center their attention on Hindu fundamentalism. It was Indian stubbornness and Indian intransigence that stymied diplomacy and prevented solutions to South Asian dilemmas. She concluded with the thought that Pakistani officials had agreed to meet with their Indian counterparts and were more than willing to entertain a larger conference, which would include the United States, Russia, and China, to declare the region a nuclear free zone. India, not Pakistan, had rejected Nawaz Sharif's call for just such a meeting. Indeed, it was India that had refused to join with Pakistan in agreeing to sign the Non-Proliferation Treaty. Mazari voiced opposition to Pressler's call for a Camp David meeting, noting that Camp David represented Muslim capitulation to U.S.-Zionist designs and that there would be no more such displays of servility.

Despite the intensity of the debate within Pakistan, the Nawaz Sharif government was determined to sustain its association with the United States. The foreign office sent the country's leading female politician, Syeda Abida Hussain, to Washington as its ambassador in February 1992. With her presence Pakistan's foreign policy assumed a new frankness and candor. In March, Pakistan's Defense Minister, Syed Ghous Ali Shah, declared that Pakistan had achieved nuclear capability, but sought to assure the world that it would be used solely for "peaceful" purposes. The defense minister tried to strike a reassuring note in citing the establishment of a more credible balance of power in the region. In Washington, Ambassador Abida Hussain acknowledged that U.S.-Pakistan relations were at a "crossroads," that the nuclear issue was the major "obstacle," but that the problems between the two countries could be addressed if the United States was prepared to recognize that "small states" continue to be threatened and that armed conflicts "fester in various regions of the world." Pakistan, she said, would feel more secure if all nations, large and small, abided by the principles of the United Nations and agreed to settle their disputes peacefully.

In an effort to demonstrate its goodwill, Pakistan's paramilitary forces were ordered to block the passage of Pakistani militants seeking entry to Kashmir. The foreign office also let it be known that the country's nuclear program was to be understood as a "posture" aimed at convincing India it was time to settle their differences at the conference table.

Pakistan did not want another war with India, but in the face of the continuing American arms embargo, Islamabad was determined to develop "defense autarky." In April 1992, Nawaz Sharif declared that the Pakistani nation was prepared to forego economic development in order to strengthen the country's armed forces.

The New World Order

It was more than fear of India, however, that drove Pakistan to search for ways to gain advantages from the changes in Central Asia that spawned the establishment of the new independent Muslim republics. Although the latter agreed to associate with the new Commonwealth of Independent States, and their orientation was still in the direction of Moscow, their Muslim character also drew them toward the Muslim nations of South and Southwest Asia.

Pakistan was keen to find ways to interact with the new states, and although only minimal commercial or financial involvement was contemplated for the near future, prospects for a spreading association were seriously envisaged. Among the more aroused Pakistani elements were the fundamentalist Muslims who saw significant opportunities for spiritual renewal after decades of religious denial. Moreover, Iran and Saudi Arabia were both active in promoting versions of Islamic practice in the region. Furthermore, both countries had the material means to attract would be followers. In the latter arena, Pakistan could not hope to compete.

Pakistan's interest in Central Asia was both cultural and strategic. Describing historical continuities and traditional ties, Pakistanis, both official and unofficial, stressed the need to follow the trail to Central Asia. Among the Pakistani geopolitical strategists, especially those who projected a different world in the wake of the disappearance of the Soviet Union, Islamic union, or even association, seemed appropriate in meeting the challenge of a new world order, especially the "order" vaguely described by the U.S. president following the conclusion of Operation Desert Storm. But Central Asia offered little of material benefit to Pakistan for the foreseeable future. And, if Islamabad was to find a place for itself under the new global economic conditions, it was likely to find more benefit in associating with the contemporary economic titans on the Pacific Rim and within the European Community.

Nawaz Sharif was Pakistan's first business leader to head a Pakistani government, and it was his task to lead the country in the transitional period that now lay before it. An important goal of the Pakistan government was to promote business with the commercially advanced world. A key to this effort lay in Islamabad's association with Japan and the other Pacific Rim nations. Pakistan, therefore, played host to a seventy-person delegation from Japan in January-February 1992, led by the Advisor of the Bank of Tokyo. The purpose of the delegation was declared to be an exploration of ways and means to promote trade and investment between Japan and Pakistan. Pakistan had much to learn and draw from the Japanese. The dominant questions were Japan's perception of Pakistan and the character of the business association. By the same token, Islamabad looked to South Korea and Taiwan as well as Germany and the European Community for a source of economic activity that would provide it with the needed leverage to relate more fully to the emerging global economic order. Nawaz Sharif had a significant role to play in allaying foreign investor fears that Pakistan's law and order situation was not manageable. He also had to confront the efforts by Islamic fundamentalists to introduce a banking system based solely on Islamic principles, a system not likely to dovetail with the practices of the world's banking community.

Japan's willingness to provide Pakistan with most favorable terms for large-scale loans, including interest rates not to exceed 2.75 percent and a grace period of ten years with a thirty-year maturity, could prove of significant benefit in tackling Islamabad's balance of payments problems. The Nawaz Sharif government was in no position to ignore cementing ties with the more progressive commercial nations of the Pacific Rim.

The new frankness that pervaded Pakistani foreign policy in 1992 reflected the thinking and attitude of the country's prime minister, less so its president. Nawaz Sharif was Pakistan's man of the hour. More so than President Ghulam Ishaq, Nawaz Sharif was able to avoid the more vituperative criticism of the country's political opposition. And, despite the many financial scandals plaguing the country, Nawaz Sharif still carried significant weight in the world's financial circles. He seemed the proper agent to represent Pakistan's cause in the unfolding new world order. He also has gained the attention, and to a large extent the admiration of the Americans, who in 1992 began to take him and his government more seriously. Nawaz Sharif does not have the charisma of Benazir, but his calmness under adversity, his capacity to relate to the civil bureaucracy and armed forces, as well as his realism in a country driven by traditional yearnings, could not be ignored in Washington. A turn in U.S.-Pakistan relations was forecast, a new more mature association was possible between the two long-time allies, but much of this and more appeared to depend on the resiliency of Prime Minister Nawaz Sharif.

2

The 1990 General Elections in Pakistan

William L. Richter

The October 1990 general elections in Pakistan were both a crucial milestone and a controversial political event for the country. The holding of democratic elections has been a relatively rare and underdeveloped practice in Pakistan, the consequences of which have included weak representative institutions and frequent reversion to martial law. In more than four decades of independence, Pakistan has held general elections only four times. Each general election has been held under "unusual" circumstances, and the first two led to disastrous consequences. It can be argued that the 1990 elections were most notable for providing a relatively orderly transition of civilian leadership and a new public mandate. From another perspective, however, the elections can be seen as a reassertion of arbitrary executive power by President Ghulam Ishaq Khan, and an undermining of the democratic course of Pakistan's politics following the death of General Zia ul-Haq in 1988 and the 1988 general elections.

The October 1990 elections were controversial both because of the way in which they came about -- through President Ghulam Ishaq Khan's dismissal of the Benazir Bhutto Government in early August -- and because of the diverse assessments over how free and fair they were.

This study analyzes the elections with respect to three categories of issues: (1) the *circumstances* of the elections, including the questionable dismissal of the Benazir Bhutto government and the characteristics and conduct of the interim government which was in power during the intervening ten week period; (2) the *conduct* of the elections themselves, including both the campaign and the events on election day; and (3) the *consequences* of these events for both the balance of political forces in Pakistan and deeper questions concerning the viability and stability of the political system.

Background and Circumstances

Ideally, popular elections serve many positive ends in a democratic political system. They select leaders and policies in accordance with the general will of the electorate; they socialize citizens to political participation and reinforce public support for representative institutions and officials; they strengthen political parties as linkages between the people and their government; and they are a mechanism for peaceful change.

Unfortunately, Pakistan's experience with elections has been less than ideal. The failure to hold national elections during the first decade of independence (1947-1958), due in part to the political dominance of groups who had no appreciable support base in the new country, dissipated popular support for civilian institutions and paved the way for the imposition of martial law in 1958. During the Ayub Khan decade (1958-1969) the country did manage to hold nationwide presidential elections, but did so under the indirect, "Basic Democracy" system, in which locally elected "Basic Democrats" served as electors for the presidency and all other higher offices. Consequently, it was not until December 7, 1970 -- twenty-three years after becoming an independent country -- that Pakistan was able to hold its first nationwide elections on the principle of one person one vote.

Although the 1970 general elections are generally regarded as having been conducted fairly by the martial-law government of General Yahya Khan, the refusal of the army and of dominant elements in West Pakistan to accept and honor the election's results led to civil war and, ultimately, to the independence of East Pakistan as the Republic of Bangladesh, in December 1971.[1]

Zulfikar Ali Bhutto, whose maneuvering had helped to bring about the Bangladesh War and the breakup of Pakistan, inherited leadership of what remained of the country. He managed several monumental tasks during the early 1970s, including adoption of the 1973 Constitution which, though shelved by martial law during 1977-1985 and heavily modified by presidential ordinance and amendment, remains the basic framework of government today. However, by January 1977, when Bhutto announced that elections would be held the following March, he had become as authoritarian as any of his predecessors.

The 1977 general elections, the first to be conducted under a civilian government, were immediately labeled as "rigged." Opposition leaders mounted a protest movement which brought the country and its economy to a virtual standstill by mid-April. Although the Bhutto government was able to engage the opposition in negotiations, the army stepped in on July 5, before any agreement could be finalized. General Zia ul-Haq deposed Bhutto and announced that fresh elections would be held the following

November, but subsequently had to cancel the elections when it became clear that Bhutto still retained a lot of popular support.[2]

Zulfikar Ali Bhutto was charged with involvement in a murder and subsequently was tried and executed, in April 1979. General Zia again attempted to hold elections, in November, but these too were aborted at the eleventh hour. Martial law became much more stringent, strict censorship was imposed, and political parties were formally banned, although informally they continued to operate. In 1980, Bhutto's Pakistan People's Party (PPP) joined with several of its former adversaries in a Movement for the Restoration of Democracy (MRD) which called for Zia's removal, the lifting of martial law, free elections, and a return to the 1973 Constitution.

In August 1983, Zia announced a plan to return gradually to civilian government. Violent demonstrations erupted, especially in Sindh Province, because the plan was perceived to prolong Zia's martial law. However, the protest was contained and the government's "civilianization" process proceeded, though with some strange twists and turns. Zia called a snap referendum in December 1984, for instance, in order to reinforce his own position before proceeding with any establishment of civilian authority. Then, in February, he held new parliamentary elections. The elections were held on a non-party basis and were sufficiently controlled that the PPP and its MRD partners chose to boycott them.[3] Nonetheless, the elections did permit the creation of a civilian government, under veteran Pakistan Muslim League (PML) politician Muhammad Khan Junejo. Moreover, in ensuing months, Junejo's government managed to create the conditions for the formal termination of martial law (December 1985) and the reestablishment of political parties as legal entities.

However, Zia and the military still remained dominant players. When Junejo's encroachment on military interests became too aggressive, Zia dismissed him and his government in May 1988. After some delay, Zia announced that new, non-partisan elections would be held the following November. Before that point, however, Zia was himself removed from the scene by the August crash of his military transport plane in Bahawalpur, an event that also took the lives of more that two dozen top Pakistani military personnel as well as the American ambassador and military attache. Acting President Ghulam Ishaq Khan and the new Army Chief of Staff General Mirza Aslam Beg gave vigorous public support to the holding of the elections as scheduled, and Pakistan's Supreme Court agreed to their being held on a partisan basis.

More than the formal end of martial law or any of the other events of 1985, or even the death of President Zia, the elections of 1988 seemed to herald a new beginning in Pakistan's search for a viable democratic order. The Pakistan People's Party won a plurality of 93 (of 215 contested) National Assembly seats, and on December 1 President Ghulam

Ishaq invited the PPP's leader, Benazir Bhutto, to become prime minister. The Islami Jamhoori Ittehad (IJI), or Islamic Democratic Alliance, won 55 National Assembly seats to become the major opposition, and also secured sufficient support in Punjab, Pakistan's largest province, to form the government there under Chief Minister Mian Muhammad Nawaz Sharif. The report of the international observer mission called the November 16 elections "an historic event for the citizens of Pakistan" and declared, "These events -- the pre-election period, the elections itself, and the smooth post-election transition -- bode well for the establishment of a stable democracy in Pakistan."[4]

Given the euphoria and high hopes which surrounded the November 1988 elections, the ensuing months brought increasing disappointment, disillusionment, and frustration for everyone, including Prime Minister Bhutto, President Ghulam Ishaq, General Beg, and Chief Minister Nawaz Sharif. From one perspective, Benazir Bhutto found herself confronted on all sides -- by the president, whose enhanced powers under the amended Constitution seriously limited her scope of authority; by the military, which insisted on retaining authority over Afghan policy and other sensitive subjects; by the IJI opposition in the National Assembly, which sought to remove her through no-confidence motions; by the IJI majority in the Senate; and by Nawaz Sharif, who attempted to strengthen Punjab and the other provinces at the expense of the central government. From the perspective of Benazir's adversaries, it was she who was instigating confrontation, seeking to undermine and topple Nawaz Sharif in Punjab, and attempting to expand her power and authority far beyond the limits of either the existing constitution or the conditions established in private conversations with the president prior to her becoming prime minister.

Whichever interpretation one prefers, it is clear that the twenty months of Benazir Bhutto's government was not a period of great accomplishment. No legislation, other than the annual budget, was passed. The political coalition between the PPP and the Muhajir Qaumi Mahaz (MQM), an ethnic party based in urban Sindh (Karachi and Hyderabad), soon broke down and Sindh became an increasingly unmanageable ethnic and political battlefield. The prime minister, her family, and her associates came under increasing attack for corruption. What had begun as a period of high hopes and expectations ultimately deteriorated into an all-too-familiar pattern of frustration, suspicion, anger, and rumor of military takeover.

On August 6, 1990, President Ghulam Ishaq ended the impasse, dismissed the Benazir Bhutto government, dissolved the National Assembly and the NWFP and Sindh Provincial Assemblies, and appointed a caretaker government in Islamabad under Ghulam Mustafa Jatoi, leader of the Combined Opposition Parties (COP) in the National Assembly. In accordance with the constitution, he scheduled national and provincial elections for October 24 and 27, respectively.

Several controversial questions surrounded the dismissal of Benazir Bhutto and hence the elections which flowed from that dismissal: (1) Was the dismissal justified? (2) Was the appointment of the caretaker government fair? (3) Were other governmental actions, particularly the use of tribunals to pursue corruption charges against the deposed PPP rulers, unfair harassment? (4) Did control of the media and other perquisites of incumbency bias the 1990 elections against the PPP? Certainly the reaction of most observers outside Pakistan was negative on all these points. The American news media treated the dismissal as a thinly disguised military coup, and the American Congress expressed concern over the way in which an elected government had been thrown from power. In the wake of the dismissal, it was uncertain (given past experience in Pakistan) whether elections would actually take place and whether Benazir would be allowed to compete.

Justification

President Ghulam Ishaq Khan justified his dissolution of the National Assembly, and the corresponding removal from office of Benazir Bhutto and her cabinet, with reference to clause (2)(b) of Article 58 of the constitution. He took the decision, he argued, "after cool, dispassionate, and careful consideration and with full sense of responsibility, when all other efforts to correct the situation had failed to produce results despite a long and agonizing wait."[5] Among the several aspects of the "situation" Ghulam Ishaq sought to remedy, he cited the "political horse-trading" in the National Assembly; the "procrastination" and incompetence of the National Assembly, including the failure of most of the ministers even to attend; the repeated undermining of the dignity of the Senate; the release of convicted criminals under the rubric of freeing political prisoners; neglect of the Election Commission; manipulation of the bureaucracy; confrontation between the center and the provinces; use of official machinery to promote partisan interests; failure to maintain law and order in Sindh; and widespread corruption ("misuse of power to accumulate and multiply personal fortunes and dole out favours").[6] He stressed that he had allowed these problems to go on for some time despite public urgings that he "fulfil his constitutional obligations."[7] He reminded his national TV and radio audience that he had held fair elections in 1988 and that he had named Benazir prime minister even though she had not had a clear majority in the National Assembly. Finally, he summarized his justification for his actions as follows:

> This decision of mine is not against any individual, any group or any party. If anything, it is directed:
> - against unconstitutional, unlawful and undemocratic practices;
> - against the policies of conflict, confrontation and obstinacy;
> - against the tendencies of opportunism, expediency and selfishness;
> - against the prevalence of rank corruption, incompetence and inaction;
> - against the growing apprehensions about the future of democracy; and
> - against anti-democratic ways in the name of democracy and anti-people practices in the name of populism.[8]

Not everyone took the president's explanation at face value. In particular, many saw the military as the major instigator of his moves. According to one account, the events leading up to the August 6 disbanding of elected governments, "for the fifth time in Pakistan's history," had begun roughly two months earlier, "when the top brass of Pakistan's powerful military decided that enough was enough and Bhutto had to go. Against the background of growing differences ... the military apparently conveyed to the president ... its decision to remove Bhutto if the president did not act to do so. Reliable sources say the deadline of August 14 was also given."[9] The army's objections included some of those cited by the president in his August 6 address, but also included several foreign policy and specific military issues: corruption, Kashmir, Afghanistan, army promotions, control of intelligence agencies, the Sindh situation, and the confrontation between Islamabad and the Punjab provincial governments.[10]

To argue that the army was actively involved behind the scenes is not necessarily to deny the legitimacy of the president's justification for his actions. As Maleeha Lodhi notes:

> Although Bhutto was ousted because she stepped on the army's toes, there is little doubt that she herself made it easier for the military and the president to move against her. Many of the charges that the presidential order laid at her government's door rang true. The Bhutto government had in large measure contributed to its own downfall. During its twenty months in power her government lurched from one mini-crisis to another, lacking any firm political direction, uncomfortable with sharing power and unable to provide effective and coherent rule. The new dawn promised by her administration failed to materialise.[11]

The Caretaker Government

In his August 6 address, President Ghulam Ishaq stated his high regard for the new caretaker prime minister, Ghulam Mustafa Jatoi, as well as his hope that the caretaker government would "discharge its duties efficiently, honestly, impartially and sincerely."

> The Care-taker Government will fix its own priorities. I expect that it will pay special attention to the restoration of law and order and the provision of equal security and justice to all citizens without discrimination. I also expect that it will try to check corruption and root out crime and restore the credibility of institutions responsible for establishing the rule of law. It is obvious that in its limited tenure, the Care-taker Government may not be able to accomplish much. I do, however, hope that it initiates a process of setting good traditions of upholding the supremacy of the constitution and the Law, and creating examples of decency, honesty, justice and fairplay for others to follow.[12]

Justice and fairplay were not necessarily hallmarks of the Jatoi caretaker government. The appointment of the leader of the opposition to replace a deposed prime minister was itself indicative of the bias of the caretaker government.

There were other ways in which Jatoi and his colleagues demonstrated a rather cynical sense of fair play. Some of the Pakistan People's Party politicians whose reputations for corruption were most notorious, indeed including some who were mentioned in the press as examples of PPP corruption, switched sides as soon as Benazir was out of power and joined the Jatoi cabinet.[13]

Accountability

Pakistan has a long tradition of accusing deposed or defeated opponents of corruption and wrongdoing, by means of proceedings which have come to be referred to as *accountability*. The Public and Representative Officers (Disqualification) Act (PRODA), passed in January 1949, was used to disqualify selected individuals from public office in the early years of Pakistan. After the imposition of martial law in 1958, Ayub Khan promulgated an Elective Bodies (Disqualification) Order (EBDO, 1959). Z. A. Bhutto enacted similar acts in 1977, and President Zia also issued Presidential Orders in 1977 and 1978 to accomplish similar ends.[14]

Under the authority of both the 1977 Bhutto laws and the subsequent 1977 Zia Presidential Orders, the caretaker government set up eleven special courts or tribunals to handle accountability cases. One set of courts was given authority to award punishment of up to ten years imprisonment for corruption; the other courts could exclude former legislators from participation in politics for up to seven years.[15] Such arrangements could quite possibly be a useful antidote for corruption in Pakistan if they were utilized fairly, impartially, and consistently. However, such fairness has never been the case and 1990 was no exception. Several features of the arrangements were notable. The time frame for accountability was limited to the twenty months in which Benazir Bhutto's government was in power, despite urging from several quarters that it be extended back to 1985 or even to 1977.[16] Even during this time frame, the government turned a deaf ear to PPP demands that Nawaz Sharif's Punjab provincial government be subjected to similar scrutiny. Although judges were appointed to preside over the tribunals, the persons authorized to send references (that is, bring cases) were the president and the provincial governors, in the case of punishment for misconduct, and the prime minister and provincial chief ministers for disqualifications.[17]

Despite these clear biases against the PPP, the president and members of the caretaker government asserted that the process was fair and neutral.[18] The caretaker Minister for Information and Broadcasting denied that the accountability proceedings were designed to eliminate Benazir Bhutto from the electoral arena, but she did make it clear that the targets were those "who were in power during the last 20 months and misused powers and took illegitimate advantage of their position." She added, "It is our right to initiate accountability against the previous government as we are in power now."[19]

In some respects, President Ghulam Ishaq and the caretaker government found themselves in a dilemma. Having deposed the Bhutto government on grounds of corruption, they were criticized for failing to come forward very quickly with specific charges or evidence. On the other hand, if they were too vigorous in their prosecution, they would appear to be undermining the very legitimacy of the October 24 elections. In the end, they brought several charges against Benazir Bhutto but did not prosecute them very effectively.[20] Consequently, although she had to appear before tribunals in Lahore and Karachi during the campaign period, she remained free to lead her party in the October elections. However, her husband, Asif Ali Zardari, was arrested on charges of taking an unlawful bank loan. Charges were also filed against his father, Hakim Ali Zardari.

The Media

Government ownership of television and radio provides a powerful perquisite of office. During the 1990 election campaign, the government no longer had a monopoly over television news, since a second network, People's Television Network (PTN), had been started under Benazir's government, and PTN brought Cable News Network (CNN) to Pakistan. Although the caretaker government considered eliminating PTN, pressure to keep CNN proved a powerful deterrent.

However, the official television channel Pakistan Television (PTV) provided a solidly pro-government and anti-Bhutto line. Prime Minister Jatoi and other cabinet members were given high positive visibility and the alleged misdeeds of the ousted government, especially of Asif Ali

Zardari, were also frequently featured themes. As one election observation report noted, "The extensive coverage of IJI campaign events also contrasted sharply with the extremely limited coverage state-owned radio and television gave to PDA (the Pakistan Democratic Alliance, the coalition of which the PPP was the major component) events. Yet three days before the election, the Lahore High Court rejected a complaint filed by the PDA regarding biased PTV election coverage."[21]

The print media provided somewhat more balanced coverage. Government-controlled papers tended to voice the same anti-Bhutto line as the official TV and radio media, but the much larger private sector of print journalism provided a much greater diversity of opinion. Some of the newer publications, particularly news magazines like *The Herald*, displayed a significantly higher quality of journalism than has been typical in Pakistan.

Summary

As in 1988, the 1990 general elections were held as a result of the abrupt dismissal of a government which had not formally lost the confidence of the National Assembly. In both instances, the actions of the president were sufficiently questionable to require judicial solution of major questions. There were some important differences between 1988 and 1990, however. Because of Zia's death in August 1988, those who held authority during the period of the elections (i.e., Ghulam Ishaq and Beg) did not have nearly as much of a stake in who won as in demonstrating their capability to conduct free and fair elections. They were cautious to install Benazir as prime minister, but were willing to do so as long as she accepted their conditions. By August 1990, they were much less neutral. The question became increasingly less one of being a neutral arbiter of elections and increasingly more one of what could be done within the letter of the law to ensure that the series of events which culminated in the elections would have the desired outcome, that is, the replacement of Benazir Bhutto with a more effective and acceptable government.

In these circumstances, the question of whether the elections were fair may be answered in two different ways, depending upon how one interprets "fair." If fair means the following of legal procedures, the Pakistan courts have answered the question in the affirmative. If fair means neutral, then the answer would have to be negative. One can argue that elections are seldom if ever entirely neutral. Incumbency, differential resources, and other factors give unfair advantages to one side or another in most democratic elections. Benazir would have used the advantages of incumbency had she been able to, but at least she would have been incumbent through dint of her success in the 1988 elections.

Did the August 6 dismissal save or undermine democracy? Surely it was better to have followed constitutional (or even pseudo-constitutional) procedures than to have gone through the trauma of another military coup. Just as certainly, however, it would have been better to have removed Benazir (if indeed she had to be removed) through less questionable means. The fabric of Pakistan's democracy was stretched and stressed, if not actually torn. How strong it would be in the future would depend not only upon the outcome of the 1990 elections but also upon how the post-election government would function.

The Elections

The formal structure of elections in Pakistan is fairly well established. A three-member Central Election Commission (CEC), made up of three members of the superior judiciary, supervises the preparation of the electoral rolls, the conduct of the elections, the processing of complaints, and the issuing of reports. The laws governing the elections were largely the same in 1990 as they had been in 1988.[22] A total of 207 general (Muslim) seats and 10 minority contests for the National Assembly were scheduled for October 24. A total of 460 general provincial assembly races were scheduled for October 27: 240 in Punjab, 100 in Sindh, 80 in NWFP, and 40 in Balochistan. Minority provincial seats brought the total number of provincial races to 483. Nomination papers were filed by 2,442 candidates for National Assembly seats and 6,806 for provincial contests, an increase from 1988. Large numbers of these withdrew, however, leaving 1,347 national and 3,593 provincial candidates on election day.[23]

Political Parties

Although Pakistan has a large number of political parties, some of which represent no more than one person and a small coterie of followers, the 1990 elections were dominated by two broad electoral coalitions. On one side was the Pakistan Democratic Alliance (PDA), created during the campaign by the joining of Benazir Bhutto's Pakistan People's Party (PPP), Asghar Khan's Tehrik-i-Istiqlal, and two smaller parties. The PPP remained the dominant component of the PDA, but the alliance lent credibility to the PPP's charges that it had been unfairly treated by President Ghulam Ishaq and the caretaker government.

Ranged against the PDA was the Islami Jamhoori Ittehad (IJI), the coalition which had competed strongly with the PPP in 1988 and had been in power in Punjab during 1988-1990. Within the IJI, the Pakistan Muslim League (PML) held a central position, somewhat comparable to the role of the PPP within the PDA.

Within the IJI, and specifically within the PML, there was some internal competition for leadership, from which Mian Muhammad Nawaz Sharif, the former chief minister of Punjab, emerged as top person. In doing so, he overcame challenges by former Prime Minister Muhammad Khan Junejo and Ejaz ul-Haq, the son of the late President Zia ul-Haq. All three of these men, in one way or another, were beneficiaries of the late president. Nawaz Sharif had been appointed Punjab's chief minister and Junejo prime minister under the Zia regime in 1985. Junejo's bid for IJI leadership reflected his past experience as prime minister, as well as his feeling that he had been wrongly dismissed in 1988. Ejaz ul-Haq's popularity drew largely on nostalgia for his father. Although his supporters sought to picture him as the chief rival to Benazir (as the offspring of a "martyred" leader of Pakistan) and Junejo awarded him with the party position of Chief Organiser, Ejaz's relative lack of political experience precluded his being a very serious contender to Nawaz Sharif.

The prominence of these three within the IJI reflected some of the key social elements aggregated under that party's banner. Junejo, from a Sindhi landed family, represented the "feudal" classes which have been dominant in the PML, and in Pakistan generally, for decades. Ejaz, with a graduate degree in business from the United States and banking experience in the Gulf, appealed especially to his father's fundamentalist following. As one account noted, "He expresses himself in strong Jamaat-i-Islami jargon. ...But Ejaz is not a Jamaati; he seems to be too ambitious and too impatient to accept the Jamaati version of party discipline."[24] Nawaz Sharif, as a successful industrialist, represents the newer wealth and emergent political power of the business classes of Pakistan.

An additional aspirant to the prime ministership was the caretaker prime minister, G. M. Jatoi. If the Combined Opposition Parties (COP), the coalition of anti-PPP parties in parliament which included the IJI, had remained together as an electoral coalition, Jatoi might have had some realistic expectation to remain in power. However, the IJI opted to contest the elections outside the COP and Jatoi's National People's Party (NPP), a 1986 split-off from Benazir's PPP, had no significant electoral base of its own. In fact, Jatoi was himself dependent on his friend Ghulam Mustafa Khar for the safe seat of Muzzafargarh from which to get reelected.

A third major political party, but one with its electoral base limited to the urban centers of Karachi and Hyderabad, was the Muhajir Qaumi Mahaz (MQM), under Altaf Hussain. Having emerged in the late 1980s as the champion of the Muhajir (refugee) community in urban Sindh, the MQM won the third-highest number of National Assembly seats in 1988, following the PPP and the IJI. After the breakdown of the post-election PPP-MQM alliance in 1989, the MQM and PPP became bitter enemies, with conflict often erupting into open warfare. In the 1990 election campaign, the IJI agreed not to contest against the MQM in Karachi and Hyderabad, although one of the IJI components, the Jamaat-i-Islami, went ahead and ran candidates in some of the constituencies anyway. The other notable party with a regional/ethnic base was the Awami National Party (ANP) of Khan Abdul Wali Khan. Based in the Pakhtun areas of NWFP and northern Balochistan, the ANP also allied itself with the IJI in the 1990 elections.

In Pakistan's three largest provinces the 1990 elections, therefore, became essentially a contest between the PDA, led by Benazir Bhutto's PPP, and a broad alliance of anti-Benazir forces led by the IJI. Several smaller parties fielded candidates, but did not play much of a role in Punjab, Sindh, or NWFP. The picture in Balochistan was more complex:

> Unlike other parts of Pakistan in the 1990 elections, Balochistan was not polarized politically between the two major coalitions. The greater fragmentation of political forces and the continuing influence of powerful tribal leaders perhaps made for a less tense and confrontational atmosphere in most of the province than in the rest of Pakistan. The two major national alliances -- the IJI and PDA -- had only a limited presence in Balochistan, equalled or surpassed by regional or religious parties: the Jamhoori Watan Party (JWP, an IJI-affiliate, led by former Chief Minister Nawab Akbar Bugti, leader of the Bugti Baloch tribe); and the Jamiat-ul-Ulema-i-Islam Fazlur Rahman Group (JUI-F, based in the Pakhtun areas of NWFP and northern Balochistan). Other regional contenders included the Awạmi National Party (ANP) and Pakhtoonkhwa Milli Awami Party (PMAP), both also based in the Pakhtun areas.[25]

Issues were not particularly evident during the election campaign, other than those which surrounded the occasion for the elections itself. As one commentator noted,

> Like 1985 and 1988, this too has become an issueless election. With platitudes and exhortations ("work harder," "make Pakistan prosperous") posing as policy, and rhetoric ("we are committed to removing poverty") parading as programme, the parties and candidates seem singularly devoid of any concern, much less imaginative solutions, for the country's myriad problems. Few if any ideas or proposals have been offered to resolve Pakistan's outstanding problems either in the political realm (the issues of regional autonomy, ethnic particularism) or the economic domain (a narrow tax base, the chronic and growing gap between government expenditure and revenue, income inequalities).[26]

For the IJI, the central issue was the Bhutto government's alleged misdeeds and corruption in office during the previous twenty months. For the PDA, the main issue was the alleged unconstitutionality of the August dismissal and the caretaker government's alleged wrongdoings and mistreatment of Benazir, her family, and her political associates.

Public opinion polls, published in September, indicated sharp partisan differences on each of these questions. Two-thirds of all respondents voiced approval of Ghulam Ishaq's dissolution of the national and provincial assemblies, including 91 percent of IJI respondents.[27] Twenty-seven percent of PPP voters approved, which is perhaps less remarkable for being so different from the IJI voter opinion than for the fact that more than a quarter of those who identified with the PPP did not agree with Benazir on this key point. Equally revealing was the partisan distribution of responses on questions concerning the validity of corruption charges against the former PPP government. These opinion data reflect polls conducted in August, shortly after Benazir Bhutto's removal from office. The PDA appeared to gain credibility as the campaign progressed in September and October, in part because of the ineptness of the caretaker government, but the disaffection of a significant portion of PPP voters was probably a handicap that was not entirely overcome by election day.

The election campaign period "was marred by incidents of violence and harassment. The most serious incidents involved random acts of violence, partisan clashes and the kidnapping of supporters from opposing political camps."[28] The problem of violence was particularly prevalent in Sindh. In National Assembly constituency 91 (Sialkot, in Punjab), the IJI candidate was killed on the eve of the election, forcing postponement of the election in that constituency.[29]

Expectations and Results

Both the PDA and the IJI anticipated victory with increasingly greater confidence as the elections approached. Attendance at rallies provided encouragement to each side, and predictions in the press were sufficiently diverse to reinforce either coalition's expectations. The public opinion data already noted gave a clear edge to the IJI. A *Newsline* opinion poll, however, revealed a different picture. *Newsline*'s poll, conducted by a Lahore market research firm, found that only one-third (34 percent) of the respondents nationally felt that the dismissal of Benazir's government was justified. Although 60 percent of the respondents judged Benazir's husband, Asif Zardari, to be corrupt, only 27 percent thought Benazir herself to be so. Moreover, 52 percent of the *Newsline* sample thought Nawaz Sharif, the IJI leader, was corrupt.[30] The *Far Eastern Economic Review's* correspondent observed that both parties were "claiming to be beneficiaries of a major change in the electorate's mood in Punjab, the home province to 63 percent of Pakistan's population," but predicted that these shifts would "cancel each other out, resulting in a repeat of the

TABLE 2.1 Opinion on Allegations Against Bhutto Government (in percentages)

	Voting Intentions:				
	All	*PPP*	*IJI*	*Other*	*Undecided*
Corruption					
Correct	73	38	7	83	65
Wrong	17	55	1	9	15
No Opinion	10	7	2	8	20
Horse-Trading					
Correct	73	38	95	86	65
Wrong	16	52	3	11	12
No Opinion	11	10	2	3	23
Nepotism					
Correct	69	31	94	85	58
Wrong	18	61	4	9	14
No Opinion	13	8	2	6	28
Failure to Establish Order in Sindh					
Correct	74	38	95	88	67
Wrong	16	53	3	8	15
No Opinion	10	9	2	4	18

Source: Compiled from Gallup Pakistan, *Gallup Political Weather Report* (September 1990), pp. 9-10.

1988 election, which saw a hung parliament and deadlocked relations between the federation and two of its four provinces.[31] *The Herald*, a highly respected news monthly, published a detailed constituency-by-constituency analysis in October that gave a clear edge to the PDA:

> In the forthcoming general elections, the PDA is set to repeat -- if not slightly improve upon -- the PPP's tally of seats in the November '88 polls. While the party may suffer a small setback by losing a handful of seats in Sindh and the Frontier, it will gain some seats in Balochistan as a result of its alliance with the PNP. In the Punjab, the PDA's performance will be much better than in 1988, a consequence, perhaps of a more intelligent allotment of tickets than previously. The IJI, meanwhile, will put up a disappointing showing, capturing less than 60 seats. The alliance will not be able to sweep the Punjab or make a dent in Sindh. Whether it will be able to cobble together a majority with the help of its allies in the MQM, ANP, JUI, JWP, PDP and among independents, remains a moot point.[32]

TABLE 2.2 Election Results by Party and Region

	PDA	*IJI*	*MQM*	*ANP*	*JUI/F*	*IND*	*Others*	*Total*
Punjab	14	92	-	-	-	6	3	115
NWFP	5	8	-	6	4	3	-	26
Sindh	24	3	15	-	-	4	-	46
Balochistan	2	2	-	-	2	-	5	11
TOTAL	45	105	15	6	6	13	8	198

Source: NDI, *The October 1990 Elections in Pakistan*, p. 196.

The results of the October 24 elections contrasted sharply with this prediction. As the figures in Table 2.2 indicate, the IJI swept Punjab and secured a plurality in NWFP to end up with a narrow majority of 105 of the 207 contested seats. The PDA won 45 seats, more than half of them in Sindh, especially in the PPP strongholds of rural Sindh. The MQM, as expected, swept urban Sindh.

In percentages of total votes polled within the country, the IJI only barely edged out the PDA:

> According to the data compiled on the basis of official results consolidated by the Returning Officers, the total number of votes cast for the Muslim constituencies of the National Assembly comes to 2,12,84,085. The number of votes polled by the IJI candidates is 79,08,513, or 37.16 percent and the PDA candidates bagged 77,43,007 votes or 36.38 percent of the total votes polled. The other minor parties polled 32,80,224 votes or 15.40 percent and the independent candidates polled 21,25,284 votes or 9.99 percent of the votes cast.[33]

The IJI credited their victory to their strategy of holding their own coalition together and forming electoral alliances throughout the country in order to ensure head-to-head contests with the PDA.

The PDA blamed their loss on alleged widespread rigging of the elections by the IJI and the caretaker government. During the polling itself, the PDA faxed and hand carried numerous complaints to the Election Commission.

Election Observer Teams

As in 1988, election observation teams were on hand in Pakistan to observe the 1990 elections. Unlike 1990, the observer reports themselves became part of the controversy surrounding the elections. In particular, the preliminary report of the 40-member international observer team, sponsored by the National Democratic Institute for International Affairs

(NDI), was subjected to misinterpretation and attack from both sides. The NDI preliminary statement, issued in a press conference in Karachi on October 26, noted that "the elections, as we observed them at the local level, were generally open, orderly and well-administered" and that the "election personnel involved in administering the process were usually well-versed in the system." However, it continued, "the election process was not without problems," among which were noted: "a highly polarized political environment," "the ongoing tribunal process during the campaign," and "several specific and serious problems" in certain constituencies on election day, including:

- the killing of candidates, party workers and other civilians;
- the kidnapping and arrest of party workers; and
- attacks by armed men on polling officials, polling agents and voters.

Despite its noting of these and other malpractices, the statement concluded, "The delegation does not believe that the above-mentioned problems significantly altered the outcome of the elections."[34]

The IJI, the government, and the official press immediately trumpeted this statement as an endorsement of the elections as "free and fair," while the PDA and much of the independent press labeled it a whitewash.

A sixteen-member team from member countries of the South Asian Association for Regional Cooperation (SAARC) visited some of the same areas as the NDI team and offered conclusions even less critical than, but substantially in agreement with, those of NDI:

> The actual process of polling appeared to be free, fair and orderly in a majority of the polling stations visited by the Mission. In a minority of the polling stations visited, there were serious improprieties and violent incidents. The Mission received other complaints and allegations about electoral malpractices that it was not in a position to verify.[35]

A four-person team from the International Federation for Human Rights (IFHR) issued a statement on October 29 that was much more critical of the elections:

> 1. The election campaign was held in an atmosphere of great tension against Mrs. Bhutto; 2. The electoral proceedings were held with great care, giving the impression of regularity; 3. However, serious irregularities were noticed by the observers at the local level [six examples given]; 4. From explanations provided by PDA, and without the complete official figures more than five days after the General Elections, ... it seems that the results giving a very large majority to IJI, against the deposed Prime Minister Benazir Bhutto, can be partly explained by a mechanism of highly sophisticated rigging which would have occurred between the polling

stations and the offices responsible for collecting results at the constituency level.[36]

Moreover, the IFHR report also judged it to be "unfortunate that the day after the first election [sic] an observer team from NDI deemed it right to hold a press conference stating that, apart from a few incidents, the proceedings were 'regular' and the results 'not at all affected'. This statement had a considerable impact, on the eve of the second elections, being on the front page of the newspapers and destabilizing the balance of forces."[37]

That the NDI statement was issued two days, not one day, after the general election, and that "not ... significantly altered" is not the same as "not at all affected" raise questions concerning how carefully the IFHR team conducted its investigation. The NDI final report contrasted the SAARC Observation Team report, "which reflected a balanced assessment of the election process," with that of the IFHR team, "which denounced the elections despite having no experience in observing elections, arriving in Pakistan on election day, and possessing limited information on the prevailing political situation."[38]

The NDI final report also provided a very careful, cautious, balanced, and thorough consideration of a wide range of allegations of electoral malpractice, particularly the charges made by the PDA. It recounted credible examples of "retail fraud," such as double registration of voters and drive-by shootings, and of "wholesale fraud" such as ballot-stuffing. On the basis of statistical analyses of all National Assembly races, including comparisons between 1988 and 1990 results, the report concluded that approximately 15 percent of the contested constituencies showed questionable results. "In all of these questionable constituencies, the PDA lost at least 15 percent of the vote that it had received in 1988." The IJI won in approximately 70 percent of such constituencies, the PDA in 6 percent, and third parties in 24 percent.[39]

The author's personal observations, before and during the elections, support the general assessments of the NDI final report: that malpractices did occur in several constituencies; and that the conditions under which the elections were held were biased against the PDA; but that the ultimate outcome of the elections was generally in accordance with popular sentiment.

Consequences

How one evaluates the 1990 elections depends to some extent on their immediate and longer-term consequences. The 1970 elections were followed, within four months, by civil war. The 1977 elections resulted in civil disorder and ultimately, within four months, in martial law. The

1990 elections, like those of 1988, brought new governments to power in Islamabad and in most of the provinces. Nawaz Sharif became prime minister and managed, within his first months in office, to accomplish some major initiatives, particularly in areas of economic policy and inter-provincial cooperation.

Like 1988, the system benefitted from the willingness of those who lost the election to accept an opposition role and to continue to participate. Benazir Bhutto became Opposition Leader in the National Assembly. Perhaps the most important consequence was that the transition to new leadership occurred without direct, or at least formal, military intervention.

Interestingly, from a vantage point of more than a year following the 1990 elections, the similarities between the Nawaz Sharif government and that of Benazir Bhutto are perhaps more striking than the differences. Like Benazir, Nawaz Sharif and Ghulam Ishaq have both been implicated in corruption scandals. Like Benazir, Nawaz Sharif has found the powers of the president, under the amended constitution, to be too restrictive. As during the Bhutto era, relations between the president and the prime minister have at times been sufficiently tense to engender rumors of another dismissal.

Conclusions

Elections are turning points in the lives of many nations. They often mark the beginnings and the ends of political eras. In Pakistan, elections are in some ways less significant than in other countries, and in some ways more so, in both respects because of the country's relatively meager experience with elections and the still-shaky foundations of the democratic system. The 1990 elections therefore permit at least some tentative prognoses concerning the future of elections in Pakistan, the future configuration of Pakistani politics, and the prospects for the survival of democratic and civilian government.

Future of Elections in Pakistan

Given the sense of pride (and some degree of surprise) that Pakistan could conduct relatively clean elections in 1988, the 1990 elections engender a more cautious assessment of how far Pakistan has emerged from its well-established traditions of electoral malpractice and, more broadly, corruption. As in other countries, when stakes are high and sanctions are low, corruption will increase. Pakistan has developed a capacity for freer and fairer elections than in the past, but there is obviously much need for improvement. The NDI final report suggested several reforms -- affecting the Central Election Commission, the media, police, army, accountability processes, political parties, polling station procedures, monitoring techniques, processing of complaints, civic education, and more.[40] It would be overly optimistic to expect that all of these recommendations would be implemented sufficiently to guarantee that the next general elections in Pakistan would be entirely free and fair.

Despite the many problems of the 1990 elections, it is important to recognize some of their positive accomplishments. Throughout most of the country, the elections were held fairly and competently. Polling officials, voters, party workers, and others gained experience in the process. The elections played an important role in facilitating change from a government which had largely dissipated its popular mandate to one which the public was willing to accept and endorse (though probably not with as wide a margin as electoral figures indicated). That elections were held, that they were generally conducted well, that they provided for a relatively peaceful governmental transition, that the results of the elections were generally accepted, and that a period of relatively effective governmental performance has followed -- all of these are no mean achievements in a country which has seen so little of any of them in the past.

International observer missions were a more prominent feature of the 1990 elections than at any previous time. The controversy which surrounded the NDI preliminary statement was indicative of both the challenges to election observation teams in a highly charged political atmosphere and the importance which outside observers have been accorded in the electoral process in Pakistan. However much electoral fraud occurred in 1990, it seems safe to assume that no less would have taken place in the absence of outside observers. Just as the task of conducting effective elections is a progressively developing art, so is that of election observation. It would be a serious mistake for Pakistan to reduce its commitment to either in the future.

Future of Politics in Pakistan

Successive democratic elections provide snapshots of the development of politics in a country, especially of the configuration of political parties. Taken together, the 1988 and 1990 elections demonstrate that two broad-based political entities have come to dominate Pakistani politics. In the 1990 national elections, the IJI and the PDA together won 73.5 percent of the votes. The Islami Jamhoori Ittehad has shown that it can maintain continuity over time, resolve internal differences, forge external alliances, and rule in Islamabad as well as in the provinces. These were the first elections since the PPP was formed in 1967 that it has contested elections under any name other than its own. Although it lost power in 1990, it showed that it could remain a major player in the system. The PPP continues to be dominated by the Bhutto family, to the extent that Benazir faces no credible competitor for leadership. That, along with the general absence of internal democracy within the party, has been a weakness.

The 1990 elections also demonstrated the persistence, possibly the expansion, of the importance of regional patterns of politics in Pakistan. The dynamics of the conflicts between the rural-based PPP and the Karachi- and Hyderabad-based MQM in Sindh, the rather distinctive ethnic and political patterns in Balochistan, and the still different patterns in the other two provinces suggest that provincial politics are -- and will remain for some time -- important and interesting in their own right. It is unfortunate that neither Pakistani nor foreign scholars have given adequate attention to these political phenomena.

The 1990 elections also illustrated some changes in the social base of politics. The "feudal" class of landed families who have dominated Pakistani politics for decades -- including the Bhuttos, Jatoi, and Junejo -- have had to make way for those of more "middle-class" origins, including Nawaz Sharif, Ejaz ul-Haq, and the MQM leader Altaf Hussain. Although the lower classes have marginal representation at best, the social diversification of the political elite should be seen as a positive development, and one to which successive elections have made a contribution.

The 1990 elections demonstrated both the weaknesses and the strengths of Pakistan's current democratic set-up. The president's actions revealed the weakness and fragility of representative institutions, but they also showed that serious deadlock in the system could be handled without the intervention of the military. In effect, Pakistan's political system in 1990 worked just as President Zia had intended when he had the Eighth Amendment to the constitution passed in 1985. To a PPP partisan, or indeed to anyone who regards such checks on elected officials as an undermining of democracy, both the Eighth Amendment and its implementation in 1990 were a step backward.

If, on the other hand, one sees the development of democracy as an incremental process of developing and improving the effectiveness of representative institutions, expanding participation, and maintaining and building commitment to constitutional order, the lessons of 1990 are more mixed. Much will depend on the lessons Pakistan's leaders and people draw from 1990, and on the steps they take to strengthen both elections and the democratic system.

Notes

1. See E. Wayne Nafziger and William L. Richter, "Biafra and Bangladesh: The Political Economy of Secessionist Conflict," *Journal of Peace Research* Vol. 13, no. 2 (1976), pp. 91-110. It is worth noting that the post-1971 history of elections in Bangladesh has been at least as dismal as that of Pakistan.

2. Cf. William L. Richter, "Persistent Praetorianism: Pakistan's Third Military Regime," *Pacific Affairs*, Vol. 51, no. 3 (Fall 1978), pp. 406-426.

3. Cf. Ijaz Shari Gilani, *Pakistan at the Polls: Campaign Candidates and Voters: A Study of the 1985 National Elections* (Rawalpindi: Pakistan Institute of Public Opinion, n.d.).

4. Cf. *Pakistan Elections: Foundation for Democracy: International Delegation Report* (Washington, D.C.: The National Democratic Institute for International Affairs, 1989), pp. 1-2.

5. Ghulam Ishaq Khan, "Address to Nation and Dissolution Order" (August 6, 1990), p. 4.

6. *Ibid.*, pp. 6-16.

7. *Ibid.*, p. 17.

8. *Ibid.*, pp. 18-19.

9. Maleeha Lodhi, "Special Report: A Shadow Military State? The Inside Story of Bhutto's Fall," *Newsline* (August 1990), p. iii.

10. Ahmed Rashid, "The Battle for Islamabad," *The Herald* (August, 1990), pp. 26-32.

11. Lodhi, "Special Report: A Shadow Military State?" p. v.

12. Ghulam Ishaq Khan "Address" (1990), p. 20.

13. One of those who jumped to the Jatoi side was Ghulam Mustafa Khar, a former chief minister of Punjab and protege of Zulfikar Ali Bhutto. For a personal expose of Khar's affairs, public and private, see Tehmina Durrani, *My Feudal Lord* (New Delhi: Sterling Publishers, 1992).

14. The historical background of accountability measures is summarized in Sabihuddin Ahmed, "One-Eyed Accountability," *Newsline* (November, 1990), pp. 27-30.

15. Mahmood Zaman, "Tribunals Begin Work Next Week," *Dawn* (August 24, 1990).

16. Then Ambassador Robert Oakley, in a speech before the Asia Society in Washington, endorsed the suggestion that the period be extended back to 1985. The PPP were the major proponents of including all of the Zia period (including Ghulam Ishaq Khan's service therein) in the scope of accountability.

17. Zaman "Tribunals" (1990).

18. Tariq Butt, "Accountability Process Even-Handed: Ishaq," *The Muslim* (September 9, 1990).

19. "Accountability not aimed at PPP, says Abida," *The Muslim* (September 13, 1990).

20. Salamat Ali, "Selective Justice," *Far Eastern Economic Review* (October 4, 1990), pp. 30-31.

21. National Democratic Institute, *The October 1990 Elections in Pakistan* (Washington D.C.: The National Democratic Institute for International Affairs, 1990) p. 50.

22. Between 1988 and 1990, four changes were made in election procedures. First, the manner in which candidacies could be challenged was changed. In 1988, only registered candidates could challenge the candidacy of a prospective opponent; the 1990 law permitted any qualified elector in the district to challenge any candidacy. Second, the period in which such challenges could be made was expanded from two to four days. Third, the number of High Court judges who sit on tribunals that hear appeals to the decisions of returning officers concerning the nomination of candidates was expanded from one to three. Fourth, and most significant, the 1990 law required the president to ask the designee of the party that won the most seats in the relevant assembly to form a new government at the national and provincial levels. *Ibid.*, pp. 27-28.

23. Election Commission of Pakistan, *Elections 90: Facts and Figures Relating to the General Elections 1990* (Islamabad, n.d.), pp. 15-19.

24. Anwar Iqbal, "Candidate Ejaz-ul-Haq," *Newsline* (October 1990), p. 92. Cf. Kaleem Omar, "The Men and Women Who Would be Prime Minister," *Newsline* (October 1990), pp. 87-90; "Party Time," *Herald* (Special Issue: Election 90), pp. 16-29.

25. National Democratic Institute, *October 1990 Elections in Pakistan* (1990), p. 79.

26. Maleeha Lodhi, "Who Cares about the Real Issues?" *Newsline* (October 1990), p. 38. Cf. Tariq Husain, "Taking Issue," *Herald* (Special Issue: Election 90), pp. 30-31.

27. Gallup Pakistan, *Gallup Political Weather Report* (September 1990), p. 6.

28. National Democratic Institute, *October 1990 Elections in Pakistan* (1990), pp. 52-53. The NDI report also noted that more than 60 people were kidnapped between August and mid-October.

29. *Ibid.*, pp. 53-54.

30. "The People's Poll," *Newsline* (October 1990), pp. 42-49.

31. Salamat Ali, "Provincial Attitudes," *Far Eastern Economic Review* (October 18, 1990), p. 26.

32. "The Herald 207," *Herald* (Special Issue: Election 90), p. 91.

33. Election Commission of Pakistan, *Election 90*, p. 33.

34. "Preliminary Statement: International Observer Delegation to the Pakistan National Elections, October 26, 1990," National Democratic Institute, *The October 1990 Elections in Pakistan*, Appendix IX, pp. 159-162. The author was a member of the NDI delegation, participated in the discussions from which the preliminary statement was drawn, and drafted some minor parts of the final report.

35. SAARC Non-governmental Observer Mission, "Interim Statement," reprinted in National Democratic Institute, *The October 1990 Elections in Pakistan*, Appendix XXVI, pp. 235-236.

36. Federation Internationale des Droits de l'Homme, "Press Release," reprinted in National Democratic Institute, *The October 1990 Elections in Pakistan*, Appendix XXVI, pp. 232-233.

37. *Ibid.*, Appendix XXVI, pp. 233-234.

38. *Ibid.*, *The October 1990 Elections in Pakistan*, Appendix XXVI, p. 109. The NDI report responded to the criticism concerning the timing of the preliminary statement by noting that "it was issued on October 26, almost 48 hours after the polls closed and after CEC had released preliminary results from virtually all constituencies. Failure to issue a statement at that time would have been viewed

as a conclusion, *sub silentio* and without evidence, that the elections were fraudulent. Failure to issue a statement could also have created a situation where, potentially, 40 individuals would have offered separate opinions, based on personal observations formed in different regions of the country. Such *ad hoc* impressions would only have added to the confusion prevailing in Pakistan." *Ibid.*, pp. 107-108.

39. *Ibid.*, pp, 90-101.

40. *Ibid.*, pp, 110-117.

3

Economic Policy After Zia ul-Haq

Shahid Javed Burki

This chapter has three parts. The first provides a brief overview of the development of the Pakistani economy by looking at state policies adopted in five years -- 1949, 1958, 1972, 1977, and 1992 -- that were critical for the economic development of the country. The first four have proven to be watersheds, and the last may also prove to be a year which could leave a profound impact on the evolution of the economy. In fact, we will suggest that 1992 may well be a make-or-break year for the country's economy. It is possible for the government to adopt a set of policies that would propel the country toward becoming an "economic tiger" in South Asia. The government's failure to be active in an imaginative way would condemn Pakistan to long-term poverty.

The second part provides an assessment of the economic situation in 1992 and identifies four areas of economic policy-making that invite the government's immediate attention. The third part offers an analysis of the situation faced by the government of Prime Minister Nawaz Sharif and suggests why some of the policy initiatives taken by it may pay rich economic dividends.

Five Critical Years in Pakistan's Economy

Five years stand out as significant milestones on the economic route Pakistan has taken since it achieved independence in 1947. Profound and lasting changes occurred in each of these five years. 1949 was the first turning point for the Pakistani economy. The country was still struggling to handle the chaos created by the partition of British India when India dealt a further blow by halting trade with its neighbor, thus bringing to an end the customs union that had tied the two nations economies since independence. The Indian action was prompted by Pakistan's decision not to follow the "sterling area" and devalue its currency with respect to the U.S. dollar. This decision changed the rate of exchange from parity to 144 Indian rupees for 100 Pakistani rupees. India refused to accept the new rate and halted the flow of goods and commodities between the two countries. This was a crippling blow for the fledgling state of Pakistan, which responded by inviting its private sector to quickly set up consumer goods industries in the country.

The series of decisions that emanated from the Indian action had great significance for Pakistan's economic history.[1] They established the private sector as the leading sector of the economy at the time India was allowing the state to climb the "commanding heights of the economy." Having placed the private sector at the center of the economic stage, Pakistan could not resort to serious central planning as a way of allocating national resources. Consequently, planning did not acquire the type of prominence that was assigned to it in India and several other newly independent countries. With central planning downplayed in favor of the market, Pakistan put the development of the social sectors in the lap of the market. The assumption was that rapid economic growth would first help those who possessed physical assets by returning large profits to them. The rich, in turn, would allow incomes to "trickle down" to the less privileged segments of the population by providing increased employment to the poor and by increasing the consumption of the goods and commodities the poor produced. The poor would use the additions to their incomes not only for increasing the consumption of daily necessities but also for buying education, health, and better shelter for their families. "There exists functional justification for inequality of income that raises production for all and not consumption for a few. The road to eventual equalities may inevitably lie through initial inequalities,"[2] wrote Mahbubul Haq in support of the strategy Pakistan adopted in the Second Five Year Plan (1960-65). Haq at that time was the chief economist of the Planning Commission and as such was one of the principal authors of the Second Plan.

The second important year for the Pakistani economy was 1958, when General Ayub Khan established the first military government and introduced new ways of doing economic business. Under Ayub Khan the government became a much more important actor on the economic stage. By assigning an important economic role to the state, Ayub Khan was responding to strong popular perceptions. One of these was the belief in the country that the political turmoil that preceded army intervention was the result of the failure to establish institutions that could mediate between the leadership groups and those they sought to govern. Such mediation was required for healthy economic development to take place. For nearly a decade Pakistan had struggled to provide a constitutional basis for governance. When the

1956 Constitution was finally enacted, it did not immediately bring about a truly representative government. Ayub Khan watched this situation from the sidelines and became convinced that the country needed a new form of political management which allowed the government a firmer control of the instruments of power than was permitted by the constitution. Democracy, he believed, did not suit the "genius of the Pakistani people."[3] Ayub Khan's conviction that developing countries needed strong, central management was reinforced by some development economists who argued that the colonial rulers had handed over the reins of government to "soft states." Gunnar Myrdal was the most influential of these thinkers and his analysis of the economic, social, and political backwardness of the developing societies was to have a profound impact on the attitudes of the generation of politicians and administrators who held power in the developing world in the 1960s and 1970s.[4]

Although the model of economic development adopted by Ayub Khan[5] allowed the state a much more important role in economic management and although Ayub Khan instituted central planning for allocating public sector resources for development, he did not abandon the two guiding principles for economic development that were adopted in 1949: that the private sector would lead the economy and that the market would be allowed to take care of poverty alleviation and social development.

In 1972, Zulfikar Ali Bhutto, by beginning the process of nationalization, redefined the role of the state in economic management. Like Ayub Khan, Bhutto also was reacting to a series of perceptions about the Pakistani economy. The most important of these was the one articulated once again by Mahbubul Haq. Haq had changed his previous thinking, now believing that the model of economic development practiced during the Ayub period had done little to improve the well being of the common man; that the "trickle down approach to development," of which he himself had been a strong proponent,[6] had only served to concentrate economic wealth in the hands of "twenty-two industrial families;" and that the state had to intervene strongly to correct the natural tendency in unguided markets to concentrate wealth in the hands of those who possessed physical assets. The question of the failure of the market, even with government prodding, to address social development also was being addressed by some international institutions at the time that Haq gave his "twenty-two family" speech. The International Labor Office (ILO) had launched its world employment program to find ways of addressing this failure of the market to lift the poor out of poverty. Zulfikar Ali Bhutto took counsel from these findings and, starting on January 1, 1972, introduced a series of measures that were to alter completely the structure of the economy.[7]

The failure of the state to provide for the welfare of the underprivileged was as profound under Bhutto as was the failure of the market during the Ayub Khan period. Under Bhutto the state also failed to run the economy efficiently. During the Bhutto years the increases in the output of the agricultural and industrial sectors were below the rate of growth of population. In other words, for the first time in the economic history of Pakistan, there was a decline in net real industrial and agricultural output per head of the population. Bhutto's approach to economic management succeeded in neither increasing the country's aggregate wealth nor in improving the lot of the poor. A correction was clearly needed. That correction came in 1977, the fourth most important year in Pakistan's economic history. The civil bureaucracy, working under the overall guidance of the military, decided to return the country to the Ayubian model of economic management. Private entrepreneurs were called out once again to take the lead and the development of the social sectors was left once more to the mercy of the marketplace. President Zia ul-Haq also decided that the time had finally arrived to fulfill what he believed was the promise Pakistan's founding fathers had made to the citizens of the new country at the time of its birth. In his view Pakistan had been created not only as a homeland for the Muslims of British India but as a country in which the state would be run according to the principles laid down in the Quran and followed by the Prophet. Accordingly, under his watchful eye Pakistan began the process of Islamization, including the introduction of Islam into the economy.

The decision to go back to the Ayubian economic model produced the desired results. During the Zia period, Pakistan's economy returned to the rate of growth it had achieved during the days of Ayub Khan. The full impact of the decision to Islamize the economy remains to be felt, however, as Pakistan has still to fully assimilate and absorb the Islamization measures introduced by President Zia.[8]

Pakistan's economic history has left a number of loose threads. In 1949, the country opted for *laissez faire* economics, placing faith in private initiative to produce growth as well as to alleviate poverty. In 1958, while not discarding *laissez faire* economics, the first generation of Pakistan's military leaders chose to use the state to guide and channel private initiative. They believed that a weak state of the type that operated in the country during the first post-independence decade was not good for economic development. In 1972, Pakistan went socialist. The private sector was distrusted and discarded and the state became all powerful. In 1977, the second generation of military rulers, while not markedly reducing the role of the state, returned some respectability to private initiative. They also began, albeit uncertainly, the process of Islamizing the economy.

With such twists and turns occurring over a relatively short period of time, it is extraordinary that Pakistan has managed a high rate of economic growth throughout its 45 years of existence. However, the time may have arrived when it no longer has the luxury to experiment, to continuously adopt new models for managing the economy. Before 1992 ends, Pakistan will need to settle down and select an economic system that suits its circumstances.

If it does, 1992 may well stand out as the fifth important year in Pakistan's brief economic history; it could be a make or break year for the economy. In 1992, Pakistan could begin the process of economic restructuring that could move the country out of the ranks of the poor nations and into those of the middle income ones. Failure to take appropriate actions in 1992 could bring Pakistan back into line with other countries of South Asia that remain mired in poverty.

Why should one year matter so much in the life of a country's economy? Why should we consider 1992 to be so critical for Pakistan's economic future? Why should we equate 1992 with 1949, 1958, 1972, and 1977, attaching to it the same amount of significance that these earlier years undoubtedly deserve?

There are two answers to these questions. First, now is the time to tie the loose ends left by Pakistan's economic history; to develop a broad political consensus on how the economy is to be managed. Without such an understanding the country will begin to drift.

Global economic and political uncertainties are the second reason why 1992 could be a make-or-break year for the Pakistani economy. The world events of 1990 and 1991 have changed Pakistan's external environment to such an extent that the country must redefine very clearly its approach to economic development. The external environment matters more for Pakistan's economy than it does for most other developing countries because Pakistan has relied more on external assistance and external capital flows than is normal for the developing world. Pakistan also has a very large number of its citizens living abroad. Perhaps two to three percent of the country's population is now working in the Middle East, Europe, and North America. The fate of this Pakistani diaspora will be determined to some extent by the way its homeland accommodates itself to the world of 1992. The country's economic policies will also influence the amount of remittances these expatriate Pakistanis send to their families back home. In the past, these remittances have helped to finance Pakistan's perennially large external account deficit. Pakistan is now even more dependent upon them than in the past. Savings by expatriate Pakistanis could also become an important source of foreign direct investment for the country.

Pakistan does not have the luxury of time within which to rearticulate its external position. It must be done before 1992 ends. The present administration appears to have sensed that. Its willingness to be more pragmatic about the situation in Afghanistan no doubt contributed to the demise of the Najibullah regime in Kabul. It has also begun to see a role for the country in Central Asia.

The administration of Prime Minister Nawaz Sharif has begun to address some of the country's major problems. These include defining a new role for the public sector. Since the Bhutto nationalizations of 1974-

1976, the state extended its reach well beyond its legitimate functions and started to intrude into the productive parts of the economy. The public sector mostly failed in this new role and, consequently, became a enormous drain on the country's resources. Another problem requiring an urgent solution is that of finding a resource base on which the country could rely for economic and social development. With the dramatic changes in its geopolitical situation in the last couple of years, Pakistan seems to have lost the luxury of passing the burden of financing development onto its foreign friends. The Nawaz Sharif administration has also been obliged to articulate in unambiguous terms the role of Islam in economic matters.

There are several other problems that will need to be addressed soon and with political determination, including a very high rate of population growth, an increasing rate of unemployment, a possible increase in the incidence of absolute poverty, a very low level of social development, and a rapidly deteriorating physical infrastructure. The list is a long one, but the window of opportunity available to the Pakistani leadership is narrow in terms of time. If the government does not take advantage of it soon, Pakistan will be condemned to an economic future similar to the one faced by the poor countries of South Asia and Africa.

Pakistan's Economy in 1992

Pakistan's economy in 1992 has reached the point at which it could begin to make the transition to the middle-income state. It already possesses many attributes of a middle-income country. Only one-quarter of its gross domestic product comes from the agricultural sector. The norm for low-income countries is between two-fifths and one-half. Manufacturing is now an important part of the economy, contributing about 18 percent to national output. In poor countries, the manufacturing sector has a much smaller presence. Several parts of the economy have achieved technological sophistication not normally seen in poor countries. This is true of the sectors of agriculture, manufacturing, transport, communications, and general services. Trade now has a significant role in the economy; exports and imports combined are equal to nearly a third of the gross domestic product. Again, there is a fair degree of technological sophistication in the product composition of both imports and exports. More than a third of the population lives in urban areas, and the urban population is distributed over a number of cities. Half a dozen cities have populations of more than one million. In poor countries, the proportion of urban population is much smaller and normally concentrated in one city, usually the capital of the country. Pakistan's economy, therefore, resembles in many ways the economies of middle-income countries.

TABLE 3.1 GNP Per Capita According to PPP Methodology

Country	*Methodology*		*Ratio*
	Atlas	*ICP*	*ICP/Atlas*
Bangladesh	210	1050	5.0
India	350	1150	3.3
Pakistan	380	1770	4.7
Kenya	370	1120	3.0
Philippines	730	2320	3.2
Turkey	1630	5020	3.1
South Korea	5400	7190	1.3

Note: The data is for 1990.

Source: The World Bank, *World Development Report 1992* (Washington, D.C., 1992), Tables 1 and 30, pp. 218-219 and 276-277.

In fact, according to one way of estimating gross national income, Pakistan is already a middle-income country. The "purchasing power parity" (PPP) method for estimating national income measures more accurately the level of economic well-being in a country.[9] According to this method, Pakistan's per capita income in 1990 was on the order of $1770, while the line that divides poor from middle-income countries is estimated at $1200. According to this method of accounting, Pakistan made the transition into the ranks of the middle income countries several years ago. It is useful to point out that the adjustment in the level of income required to move from the conventional to the purchasing power parity method is much greater for Pakistan than for most other poor countries. For instance, according to the PPP method, India's per capita income is estimated at about $1150, still below the poverty line.

Pakistan does not have to draw comfort that it has done well in the past merely in terms of a different method of estimating national income. Even in terms of the conventional measurement of national income, Pakistan could make the transition before the end of this decade if the stage is set in 1992.

But there are a number of problems that will have to be addressed before Pakistan can achieve the status of a middle-income country in terms of the conventional national income measurement criteria. Four of these problems need to be underscored. First is the absence of a robust legal framework within which economic transactions should be carried out. Economic laws and regulations exist, but they are largely ignored.

The result is large-scale corruption, which, apart from being moral repugnant, also creates serious economic distortions. Economists call corruption a rent-seeking activity; those who can dispense favors charge "rents" from those who need them. President Ghulam Ishaq Khan dismissed the government of Prime Minister Benazir Bhutto on grounds of corruption.[10] The president in his speech, and the government later in the several references made to the special courts, charged that members of the government and Asif Zardari, the husband of the prime minister, had dispensed licenses for the establishment of industries, provided access to government-owned financial institutions, and had allotted plots of government owned land to scores of people in return for large sums of money. The administration of Prime Minister Nawaz Sharif also has been accused of financial impropriety. The prime minister himself and Chaudhury Shujaat Hussain, one of his cabinet ministers, were accused of using influence to obtain large loans from a number of privately owned cooperative banks. The Privatization Commission set up by the Nawaz Sharif administration to sell state-owned enterprises was also accused by the media for irregularities. Widespread corruption of the type reported in Pakistan is economically wasteful in the sense that it creates opportunities for returns that may be considerably higher than those that can be obtained from legitimate economic activities. Corruption also deflects the attention of entrepreneurs away from activities that are socially beneficial toward those in which individual profit is very high.

Pakistan's second serious problem is its very low level of social development. A number of social indicators suggest that Pakistan is more backward than the countries at its own level of per capita income. The gap is much larger when we compare the situation in Pakistan with that of middle-income countries. Life expectancy at birth and the rate of infant mortality are two powerful indicators of social development. The two indicators are related in the sense that a high rate of infant mortality translates into low life expectancy. In 1990, Pakistan's infant mortality rate was estimated at 103 per thousand live births compared with 92 for India, 29 for China and a 48 average for middle-income countries.[11] Life expectancy at birth for the people of Pakistan in 1990 was 56 years compared to 59 for India, 70 for China, and 66 for middle-income countries. Pakistan is particularly backward in terms of the economic and social wellbeing of its women. In 1985, the latest year for which this information is available, maternal mortality in the country was estimated at 600 per 100,000 births compared with 500 for India and only 44 for China. In 1989, 27 percent of the school-age girls were attending primary schools compared with 82 percent for India and 135 percent for China.[12] A low level of social development usually translates into a high rate of population growth. Pakistan's current population is estimated at 115 million; in 2000, its population will reach 150 million. According to a World Bank estimate, given current trends, Pakistan's population will stabilize at a level of 556 million, at which point it will be the third largest country in the world, after India (1.862 billion) and China (1.835 billion).[13]

Economists and development experts now recognize that without a high level of social development, it is not possible for societies to attain sustainable high rates of economic growth. It is now also well understood that female health, education, and literacy contribute impressively to economic growth.[14] Economic history has a powerful lesson to communicate to the decision-makers in Pakistan: Its economic vision of attaining the status of a semi-industrial country cannot be realized unless they address in a serious way the problem of social backwardness.

The third problem requiring decision-makers' immediate attention is that of a crumbling physical infrastructure and the chronic shortage of electric power. Both are the results of past neglect; these vital sectors of the economy did not receive sufficient investment to keep up with the rest of the economy. They have now emerged as significant bottlenecks for the further growth of the economy.

In order to improve the level of social development and to improve the physical and power infrastructure Pakistan must find additional domestic and foreign resources to increase the amount of investment in these sectors. This is the fourth problem the economy currently faces: a perennial shortage of domestic and foreign resources. With the changes in the geopolitical situation, which have made Pakistan a less attractive country in the political calculations of the western countries and Japan, Pakistan will have to rely increasingly on its own devices. It must pay a larger proportion of its import bill from exports earnings than it has done in the past, it must make the country more attractive for foreign direct investment than it has ever been, and it must encourage its own citizens working abroad to allow their savings to be used for the development of the home country.

Economic Policies of the Nawaz Sharif Government

There are a number of reasons why the administration of Nawaz Sharif could turn 1992 into a historic year for the Pakistani economy. The first and by far the most important of these is political. The government of Nawaz Sharif has the explicit or implicit backing of several powerful socio-economic groups in the country. With the support of these groups it should be possible for his administration to build a broad consensus for instituting the structural reforms which are urgently required. Such a political consensus could be achieved by Nawaz Sharif with less difficulty than would be possible by a leader who was entirely beholden to the landed interests. There is another reason for optimism about the possibility of instituting structural change in 1992. Nawaz Sharif is the first urban leader to become the country's chief executive. His political constituency lies in the heartland of urban Pakistan. Political arithmetic suggests that he is less dependent on the support of Pakistan's durable feudal masters than any other leader in the country's history barring Muhammad Ali Jinnah. As an urban leader, his instincts appear to be those of a modernist desiring rapid economic change.

Another reason why the present government may succeed in introducing long-postponed structural and economic changes has to do with the ease with which the prime minister can deal with the representatives of the modern sectors of the economy. Being an industrialist himself he has been able to regain the private sector's confidence, which was completely lost by the government of Zulfikar Ali Bhutto and was not regained by the various administrations over which Zia ul-Haq presided during his eleven years in office. Despite promises that she made in her manifesto, even Benazir Bhutto was not able to gain the trust of the private sector.

Nawaz Sharif's administration also has been able to attract foreign private attention toward Pakistan. In large part because of his interest in modernizing the economy with the help of the private sector, the prime minister has been able to interest foreign entrepreneurs in investing in the country. If this interest generates significant capital flows and transfer of technology, Pakistan should be able to narrow the gap that has been widening rapidly in the last two decades between itself and the newly industrializing countries of East Asia. Finally, for the first time in Pakistan's history, genuine devolution of power has occurred from the center to the provinces. The groundwork for this was laid in two accords reached between the central government on the one hand and the four provincial governments on the other. These accords covered the distribution of the waters of the Indus River system and the division of the tax revenues collected by the central government.

In order to turn this potential for success into actual success, the administration headed by Mian Nawaz Sharif must take a number of initiatives. The list is long, but there are some obvious candidates for quick and decisive action. To begin with, it was correct for the government to focus its attention in the early days on the privatization of the productive assets brought under government control by Zulfikar Ali Bhutto. The attention given to this matter helped to send a strong signal to the private sector about the government's overall approach toward economic management. However, the process of privatization has been allowed to drag on and has consumed a great deal of the administration's energy. This energy now needs to be re-channelled to the establishment of a regulatory framework within which a revitalized private sector should be asked to operate. This framework should clearly spell out the obligations of the private sector toward its customers. It should not, however, bind the economy in controls and regulations that produce little public good but do create economic rents which are then easily translated into corruption.

As discussed above, the question of finding a durable resource base for financing development can no longer be postponed. The global shortage of capital and the loss of Pakistan's geopolitical importance following the collapse of the Soviet Union suggest that the country cannot hope to be rescued by the outside world as has happened so frequently in the past. There are two sides to the resource question: expenditure and mobilization. Several administrations in the past built their hopes on the basis of generating more resources by streamlining tax administration. While improvements in tax collection would certainly help, what is even of greater significance is a broadening of the tax base. There are five exceptionally dynamic sectors of the Pakistani economy -- agriculture, commerce, small-scale industry, transport, and real estate -- that remain undertaxed. However, to have these sectors yield an appropriate amount of revenue for the government would require more than an improvement in the tax collection system. It would require the type of political consensus referred to above that would convince the new taxpayers to add to the government's revenues in return for the increased services to be provided by it.

The government must also begin to seriously examine the expenditure side of the resource equation. There are a number of areas that deserve careful scrutiny. As a proportion of its gross domestic product, Pakistan spends more on defense than most developing countries. The fact that it faces a difficult strategic situation cannot be questioned. That notwithstanding, the government must recognize that spending on defense is at the cost of spending on development. In the long run, a robust economy provides a better defense against foreign intrusion than an economy that has been weakened by neglect and the shortage of resources. This is also a good time to re-establish the institutions that were used in the 1960s to evaluate priorities among competing claims on limited development resources. These institutions were largely ignored in the 1970s and 1980s. Without a careful review of public sector expenditure the efficiency of resources committed for development cannot be optimized. And without subjecting themselves to discipline, governments can easily succumb to whimsical, ad hoc, and costly decisions. Finally, the government must carefully review its comparative advantage in the provision of basic services to the people. Experience in Pakistan has shown that the state does a poor job in providing higher education and sophisticated medical care, in running public transport, and even in generating and distributing electric power. Some of these services can be handed over to the private sector within a regulatory framework acceptable to private entrepreneurs.

The increases in the government's services which should be offered in return for a greater tax effort should cover at least three areas. By far the most important are the efforts aimed at improving the rate of literacy, particularly for women; increasing the rate of enrollment in schools, again particularly for girls; improving health coverage, particularly in the countryside; and provision of such basic needs as water supply and sanitation. The administration should pass on to the people a strong message that Pakistan will not be able to achieve a high level of economic growth and sustain it over a long period of time unless it improves its human stock. Increased investments alone will not achieve this objective.

The government also should promise that it will develop and enforce a legal framework within which all economic transactions must be carried out. Those empowered to take decisions that affect the economic lives of the citizens must do so not because of personal contacts, *safarish*, *backsheesh*, and bribe but because of the rules they are required to follow. Limiting the role of the government in economic matters reduces the amount of rent its functionaries can extract out of the economic system. However, the government cannot entirely pull out of economic decision-making. As already indicated, it must be prepared to regulate the private sector in order to ensure public welfare and guard against the type of perverse behavior that earned the private sector a bad name and led to excessive state intervention.

The current government must show a combination of imagination and prudence in developing the vital sector of finance. In the months since it has been in power, it has exhibited the former but not a great deal of the latter. Privatization of some of the nationalized commercial banks, permission for new commercial and investment banks to be set up in the private sector, development of capital markets, and permission to float new instruments for financial intermediation are steps in the right direction. However, the widening and deepening of the financial sector must be undertaken within a regulatory framework that promotes prudential behavior.

All this amounts to a long agenda, but it is well within the reach of the government. If the government succeeds in implementation, it would have set Pakistan on the course of sustainable development. If it fails, Pakistan will no longer be distinguishable from the poverty-stricken countries of South Asia. In spite of the adverse changes in Pakistan's external situation, the country could succeed in finally breaking out of ranks of the poor nations. Even on the external side, the collapse of the Najibullah regime and the establishment of a mujahadin government in Afghanistan in April 1992 has had positive implications for Pakistan. The country is now in a region free of ideological conflict. As *The Wall Street Journal* commented in an editorial: "Most important, thanks to the brave resistance of these [Afghanistan] freedom fighters, the country they have now retaken emerges into a more hopeful world. Communist ideology has expired in all but a few backwaters such as China and India's West Bengal. Neighboring Pakistan has found the breathing room to elect a government whose Prime Minister Nawaz Sharif has turned to free market reforms as the road to development."[15]

Notes

1. For an in-depth analysis of the long term impact on the Pakistani economy of the Indian decision to stop trading with its neighbor, see Shahid Javed Burki, *Pakistan: The Continuing Search for Nationhood* (Boulder, Colo.: Westview Press, 1991), pp. 122-126.

2. Mahbubul Haq, *The Poverty Curtain: Choices for the Third World* (New York: Columbia University Press, (1976), p.1.

3. For the way Ayub Khan perceived the political situation in the years before he assumed political power see his political autobiography, *Friends not Masters* (London: Oxford University Press, 1967).

4. See his influential work, *Asian Drama: An Inquiry into the Poverty of Nations*, 3 vols. (New York: Pantheon, 1968).

5. For a discussion of the economic model adopted by the administration of President Ayub Khan, see Gustav F. Papanek, *Pakistan's Development: Social Goals and Private Incentives* (Cambridge: Harvard University Press, 1967). Also see Shahid Javed Burki, "Bureaucratic model of economic decision-making," *The Muslim* (March 23, 1992).

6. See his book, *A Strategy of Economic Planning: A Case Study of Pakistan* (Karachi: Oxford University Press, 1968).

7. For a discussion of economic management during the Bhutto period see Shahid Javed Burki, *Pakistan under Bhutto, 1971-77* 2nd edition (London: Macmillan, 1988).

8. For an assessment of the Pakistani economy under President Zia ul-Haq see Omar Noman, *Pakistan: Political and Economic History since 1947* (New York: Kegan Paul, 1990) and Shahid Javed Burki, "Pakistan's economy under Zia," in Shahid Javed Burki and Craig Baxter, eds., *Pakistan under the Military: Eleven Years of Zia ul-Haq* (Boulder,Colo.: Westview, 1991), pp. 87-114.

9. For a description of "purchasing power parity" see The World Bank, *World Development Report 1992* (Washington, D.C., 1991), pp. 299-301.

10. See President Ghulam Ishaq Khan's speech and the Presidential Order dismissing the government in *The Muslim* (August 7, 1990).

11. Unless otherwise indicated, these and other statistics that follow are taken from The World Bank, *World Development Report 1991* (Washington, D.C., 1992), pp. 209-303.

12. An enrollment rate of more than 100 percent implies that the children who, while they were of school-age did not attend school, are now being educated. A rate of more than 100 percent means that a society is clearing the back-log of illiteracy.

13. See the World Bank, *World Development Report 1990* (Washington, D.C., 1991), pp. 228-229.

14. These arguments are very well summarized in The World Bank, *World Development Report 1990* (Washington, D.C., 1990); and the United Nations Development Program, *Human Development Report 1991* (New York, 1991).

15. "Afghanistan turns a corner," *The Wall Street Journal* (May 1, 1992), p. A14.

4

Judicial Activism and Islamization After Zia: Toward the Prohibition of Riba

Charles H. Kennedy

Islamic activists have long advocated the elimination of *riba*[1] (financial interest) in Pakistan. But their demand has been stymied by the operation of Pakistan's political system. After an agonizing nine-year gestation (1947-1956) Pakistan's first constitution was born, but Islamic provisions in the document were intentionally vague or weak.[2] Article 28 of the 1956 Constitution did call for the elimination of *riba* "as early as possible" and the 1962 Constitution provided in the principles of policy that "usury" should be abolished.[3] Similar provisions were reiterated in the 1973 Constitution.[4] But, in none of these instances were mechanisms introduced designed to realize such objectives.

The Council of Islamic Ideology (CII), established by the 1962 Constitution as an advisory body, made numerous recommendations during the 1960s that *riba* was "forbidden" by Islam and that Pakistan's banking system was "fundamentally based upon *riba*." Such views were unanimously adopted by the CII in its meeting of December 3, 1969.[5] In subsequent meetings the CII drafted a report, submitted to the government in 1971, that *inter alia* recommended the abolition of *riba*.[6] Such recommendations seem to have had no formal public consideration by the regime of Zulfikar Ali Bhutto, nor by the framers of the 1973 Constitution.[7]

It was not until General Muhammad Zia ul-Haq assumed power as Chief Martial Law Administrator in July 1977 that the issue of *riba* gained center stage in Pakistan's policy arena. After reconstituting the CII (the CII had been largely inactive during Bhutto's tenure) he directed the new membership of the Council on September 29, 1977, to consider how best to "eradicate the curse" of interest from Pakistan. The Council responded by appointing a commission of economists and bankers to examine the issue, which duly submitted an "interim report" to President Zia sometime in late 1978. Apparently on the basis of this report,[8] Zia directed that, effective as of July 1, 1979, the affairs of the National Improvement Trust, the Home Building Finance Corporation, and the Investment Corporation of Pakistan were to be run on an interest-free basis through the adoption of profit-loss sharing (PLS). Also, in a nationwide broadcast on February 10, 1979, Zia announced wide-ranging Islamic reforms in Pakistan's legal system including the adoption of the *hudood* ordinances[9] and promised that interest would be completely abolished in the state within three years.

Five months later the CII issued it long-awaited "final" report on the "elimination of interest from the economy." The report, authored by Dr. Tanzil-ur-Rehman, recommended detailed and far-reaching reforms that, if implemented fully, would have resulted in the complete elimination of financial interest in Pakistan by July 1982.[10]

Zia's government responded to the Council's report by replacing interest-bearing savings accounts with PLS instruments in Pakistan's five state banks. Also, the government introduced and encouraged such banks to adopt financing schemes based upon the principles of *mudarabah* and/or *musharaka*.[11] However, the specific implementation of such reforms was left up to the respective boards of the individual banks. In most instances the banks opted to offer alternative financial instruments to their customers -- those that offered fixed interest rates and those that offered a non-interest component.

Such modes of implementation fell far short of the ideals contemplated by the CII. Indeed, the CII's 1980 report had specifically cautioned against creating alternative banking windows as this would be "extremely dangerous [and] likely to entail perpetuation of the interest-based system."[12] Moreover, after Zia had introduced such cosmetic changes, zeal for further reforms of financial practices quickly waned. In part, this was owing to the domestic opposition generated by the dissemination of the Council's report. More important, however, it was linked to Zia's overall strategy to go slow with the pace of Islamic reform.[13] Zia could honestly claim, as he often did during the remainder of his tenure, that he had introduced Islamic reforms that were designed to combat the scourge of *riba*. But, the banking reforms that he implemented did not seriously challenge the operations or the corporate interests of domestic or Pakistan-based multinational banks.

Zia's policy of prudential, incremental Islamic reform was also demonstrated by jurisdictional limitations imposed upon the newly created Federal Shariat Court (FSC). On June 26, 1980, Zia constituted the FSC, empowering the court to declare a "law void if found repugnant to the injunctions of Islam as laid down in the Holy Quran and Sunnah." However, very significantly he excluded from the FSC's jurisdiction:

> ... the Constitution, Muslim personal law, any law relating to the procedure of any court or tribunal, or until the expiration of three years from the commencement of this chapter [3-A, June 25, 1980] any fiscal law or any law relating to the levy and collection of taxes and fees or banking or insurance practice and procedure.[14]

Clearly, Zia's intent was to prevent the FSC from challenging any fiscal laws on the grounds of Islam's prohibition against *riba* until such time as his government deemed appropriate.

Blocked by the political machinations of Zia, Islamic activists have adopted a three-track strategy to gain passage of their policy agenda. The first strategy entails public education in order to gain popular acceptance of the advisability and viability of an interest-free economy. The second strategy seeks to change Pakistan's constitutional structure, through the passage of a "Shariat bill" which would make the Shariah superordinate to Pakistan's constitution. The third strategy, really a refinement of the second, has sought to encourage Pakistan's superior courts (particularly the FSC and Supreme Court) to take an expansive approach in defining their respective jurisdictions to entertain constitutional questions relevant to matters "repugnant to Islam." The details of such strategies and their track records of success and failure are traced below.

Educating the Public on the Merits of an Interest-Free Economy

Advocates of an interest-free economy have two main tasks to accomplish in order to gain popular acceptance of their views. First, they must demonstrate the normative merit of their position. That is, they must present arguments that lead to the conclusion that Pakistan as a Muslim state should abandon an interest-based economy. Second, and perhaps more important, they must demonstrate the feasibility of operating an interest-free economy in modern times. That is, they must present arguments that lead to the conclusion that mechanisms exist or can be devised that will reconcile an interest-free system with the requisites of domestic and international banking. It is generally acknowledged in Pakistan that Islamic activists have made a much more convincing case for the former proposition than the latter.

Fundamentally, the normative case for the abolition of interest in Pakistan relies on a direct reading of the Holy Quran [II. 275]:

> Those that devour *riba* will not stand except as stands one whom the Evil One by his touch hath driven to madness. That is because they say:

> "Trade is like *riba*." But Allah hath permitted trade and forbidden *riba*. Those who after receiving direction from their Lord desist, shall be pardoned for the past; their case is for Allah to judge. But, those who repeat the offense are Companions of the Fire, they will abide therein forever.

Of course, there is no question as to the authority of the Holy Quran but there is a millenial debate concerning what constitutes "*riba*." Islamic activists are of the view that *riba* "stands for interest in all its types and forms."[15] Others are of the opinion that *riba* should be translated as "usury" and the Quran's prohibition, as a consequence, does not extend to state-regulated banking practice. Islamic activists claim that an overwhelming majority of Muslims in Pakistan subscribe to the former view.

Moreover, when it comes to the question of putting this norm into practice there is considerable disagreement, particularly among those who would be responsible to administer an interest-free system -- economists, bankers, politicians, and bureaucrats. Since the late 1970s, as a consequence, numerous symposia have been held dedicated to the task of defining the modalities of an interest-free economy. Most such conferences have been linked to the Jamaat-i-Islami or a like-minded Sunni institution, and many have been funded directly or indirectly through the largesse of Saudi Arabia. One fruit of such conferences has been an extraordinarily vibrant and proliferating literature pertaining to Islamic economics.[16]

Unfortunately for would-be Islamic reformers, such herculean efforts have been rewarded with few conversions from among the mainstream of Pakistan's economists and bureaucrats. For instance, the Pakistan Institute of Development Economics' (PIDE) conference held in Islamabad during January 1992, attended by the author, largely ignored the implications of an interest-free economic system for Pakistan's development process. This omission was particularly notable in light of the then-recent and much-publicized November 1991 decision of the FSC declaring *riba* repugnant to Islam.

The Islamic Challenge to the Secular Constitution: Shariah Legislation

During the period of martial law (1977-1985) there was no mechanism to challenge Pakistan's constitutional structure on Islamic grounds as the constitution stood suspended. However, in 1985, with the lifting of martial law, "restoration" of the constitution, and the election of the National Assembly, a new avenue was opened to would-be reformers. Namely, the National Assembly, with the concurrence of the Senate, had the power to amend the constitution, and perforce possessed the authority to lift constitutional restrictions on the jurisdiction of the superior courts.

Accordingly, less that three months after the Majlis-i-Shura (Parliament) was convened, on July 13, 1985, two *ulema* members of the senate, Qazi Abdul Latif and Maulana Sami-ul-Haq, submitted a bill to the Senate entitled: "The Enforcement of the Shariah Act, 1985."[17] The Senators' bill proposed that: "All the courts of the country shall be bound to decide all kinds of cases, including financial, etc., according to the Shariah, and the cases decided in contravention of Shariah shall be void."

During the next six months three other similar "Shariah bills" -- two introduced by the government and one introduced by Senator Khurshid Ahmad -- were submitted to the Majlis-i-Shura.[18] Therefore, by early 1986, there were four competing versions of Shariah legislation pending before the Majlis-i-Shura. The task of forging a consensus on these matters fell to the weakly institutionalized government of Prime Minister Muhammad Khan Junejo. It soon became apparent that this task would prove too difficult for the regime to accomplish. Three irreconcilable positions emerged in the Majlis-i-Shura. The first, associated with the Jamaat-i-Islami pressed for the passage of either, or both, of the Senate-sponsored bills. The second, gained support from the Muslim League and advocated, albeit unenthusiastically, the government's versions of Shariah legislation. The main point of dispute between these two groups was the former's insistence that any Shariah bill should include provisions that made the Shariah supra-constitutional, and its implementation binding upon the courts. The official government position, at least as expressed by President Zia and some concurring ministers,[19] was that the jurisdiction of the superior courts should expand in order to Islamicize the legal system, but that the newly "restored" 1985 constitution should not be scrapped in the process. A third group, represented at least tacitly by the loyal opposition, Opposition Parliamentary Group (OPG), and quite vocally by the extra-parliamentary Movement for the Restoration of Democracy (MRD), agreed that the passage of any Shariah legislation was neither necessary nor desirable. Rather, advocates of this latter position argued that the debate over Shariah legislation was designed, in part, to bolster the fading legitimacy of an unpopular regime. Further, as the then MRD leader Benazir Bhutto consistently argued, "Zia's Islamization policy" was reactionary, barbaric, and discriminatory to the rights of women.[20] Opposition to the adoption of Shariah legislation was also voiced by members of Pakistan's Shia community. The Tehrik-e-Nifaz-e-Fiqh-e-Jafaria (TNFJ - Association for the Enforcement of the Shia *Fiqh*) contended that the passage of any of the Shariah bills before the legislature would result in the enforcement of Pakistan's majority

Sunni personal law (Hanafi) over the personal law of the Shias. The latter contention was highly publicized.[21]

Prime Minister Junejo's government attempted on several occasions to reconcile the conflicting positions of pro-Shariah bill legislators in order to gain passage of some form of Shariah legislation. But, such attempts proved unsuccessful.

Accordingly, by his own account, President Zia grew impatient with the pace of Islamic reforms, and on May 29, 1988, he dismissed Junejo's government. One of the reasons Zia gave for this action was the slow progress of Islamization, and the inablility or unwillingness of Junejo's government to work for the passage of any Shariah bill.[22] Two weeks after the dismissal of the government, on June 15, Zia took matters into his own hands and promulgated his own Shariah bill -- "The Enforcement of Shariah Ordinance, 1988."[23] Zia's ordinance attempted to effect a compromise on the issues of the supremacy of the Shariah and the jurisdiction of the superior courts to interpret the Shariah:

> 3. Supremacy of the Shariah. Shari'ah shall be the supreme source of law in Pakistan and the *Grund Norm* for guidance of policy-making by the state and shall be enforced in the manner and as envisaged thereunder.
>
> 4. Court to decide cases according to Shariah. If a question arises before a court that a law or a provision of law is repugnant to the Shari'ah, the court shall, if it is satisfied that the question needs consideration, make a reference to the Federal Shariat Court in respect of matters which fall within the jurisdiction of the Federal Shariat Court under the constitution [Article 203-B] and that court may call for and examine the record of the case and decide the question within sixty days.
>
> Provided that, if the question relates to Muslim personal law, any fiscal law or any law relating to the levy and collection of taxes and fees or banking or insurance practice and procedure, the Court shall refer the question to the High Court which shall decide the question within sixty days.[24]

This compromise won few converts. To advocates of Shariah legislation, Zia's ordinance was flawed because it did not specify that the Shariah was supra-constitutional. Clause 4 still exempted the constitution from the purview of the courts. More important, Zia's ordinance assigned jurisdiction for interpretation of matters that fell outside of the purview of the FSC as per Article 203-B with the High Courts, not the FSC. It is generally acknowledged that Pakistan's four High Courts contain few "Islamic judicial activists," nor, for that matter, do they contain many conversant with Islamic law or related matters.[25] Consequently, it was assumed that the pace of Islamization would stall or perhaps even be reversed under the terms of Zia's ordinance. On the other hand, to those who were opposed to the passage of any Shariah bill, Zia's ordinance was considered at best unnecessary, and at worst, obscurantist or anti-democratic.

In any case, Zia's ordinance proved ephemeral. The 1985 Constitution mandates that a presidential ordinance stands repealed if it is not considered for legislation and passed by the National Assembly within four months of its promulgation.[26] Zia's untimely death, in August, effectively eliminated any significant political support for the bill, although President Ghulam Ishaq Khan promulgated a "revised" Shariah ordinance (in fact, identical to Zia's) on October 15.[27] The latter ordinance was presented to the newly constituted National Assembly, headed by Benazir Bhutto, in December 1988. The Assembly took no action on the bill, allowing it to expire with no legal effect on February 15, 1989.

Consistent with its public position, Benazir's government showed no inclination to revive the issue of the adoption of a Shariah bill. Indeed, Benazir took the position that "Zia's Islamization program" should be dismantled, ideally through the repeal of the Eighth Amendment and the restoration of the 1973 constitution.

Nevertheless, by early 1990 sentiment had grown in the Senate, controlled by the opposition Islami Jamhoori Ittehad (IJI - Islamic Democratic Alliance), to disinter Zia's Shariah ordinance. Accordingly, in May 1990, the Senate passed yet another version of the bill, the "Shariat Bill (Senate Version), 1990," which was similar in most respects to Zia's ill-fated ordinance.[28] Those who had opposed Zia's ordinance in 1988 had dropped their objections on two grounds. First, Zia's ordinance, although flawed, was better than no ordinance at all.[29] Second, passage of the Senate bill would force the consideration of a similar bill in the National Assembly. The Senate reasoned that prospective debate on such a bill in the National Assembly would prove very embarrassing to Benazir's shaky coalition government. It would be easy to characterize Benazir's anticipated opposition to the bill as further evidence of her "anti-Islamic" sentiments, which in turn would serve to weaken her government. However, on August 6, the eve of the scheduled debate on the Shariah bill in the National Assembly, President Ghulam Ishaq Khan dismissed Benazir's twenty-month old government and installed an IJI-led coalition government under Prime Minister Ghulam Mustapha Jatoi.[30]

The November 1990 General Elections resulted in an overwhelming victory for the IJI and installed its leader, Mian Nawaz Sharif, as prime minister. Nawaz Sharif, the former Chief Minister of the Punjab, was a close political ally of the late Zia ul-Haq, and he was on record as being both ideologically and emotionally committed to the passage of a Shariah bill. Accordingly, in late March 1991, he established a committee of senators, MNAs, judges, lawyers, and *ulema* to draft another version of Shariah legislation. On May 12, the fruit of this committee was presented to the National Assembly, wherein it rapidly gained passage, on May 16.

Twelve days later it passed the Senate. In both houses support for the legislation divided along partisan lines -- members of the IJI voted overwhelmingly to support the bill; members of Benazir Bhutto's Pakistan People's Party (PPP) voted against the bill in the National Assembly, and abstained in the Senate.[31]

Despite considerable self-serving hyperbole by government officials,[32] the "Enforcement of Shariah Act, 1991"[33] is likely to have only a marginal impact upon the pace of Islamization in Pakistan. First, as an "act" of the Majlis-i-Shura it does not amend the constitutional provisions that limit the scope of the superior courts' jurisdiction. Second, the 1991 Act does not address the jurisdictional issue between the High Courts and the FSC, the main point of Zia's 1988 Shariah bill. It is also important to note that "Shariah" is defined narrowly in the 1991 Act as the "Quran and Sunnah," and further that "with respect to the personal law of any Muslim sect, the expression Quran and Sunnah shall mean the Quran and Sunnah as interpreted by that sect."

The Enforcement of Shariah Act, 1991 also finesses issues relevant to the Islamization of the economy and of the educational system by establishing two independent "commissions" to study the issues and to report back "within a period of three years unless extended by the Majlis-i-Shura."

An obvious conclusion, therefore, is that the primary significance of the 1991 Shariah Act is political, not legal. The political message is that Nawaz Sharif's government was able to deliver a Shariah act when two previous regimes had failed to produce the goods. Moreover, the PPP's opposition to the passage of the 1991 Act was characterized skillfully by the IJI and the pro-government press as proof of the PPP's and Benazir Bhutto's "anti-Islamic sentiments." In this context the content of the Shariah Act became secondary to the symbolic importance of its passage.

Disappointed by the outcomes of the political process and the lack of societal consensus regarding the content and pace of Islamic reform, Islamic activists have grown to place increasing reliance upon the superior courts. Throughout, the key issue has been the courts' posture towards the interpretation of their jurisdiction to consider relevant matters "repugnant to Islam."

The Objectives Resolution and *Riba*

Zia's establishment of the Federal Shariat Court (FSC) and the Shariat Appellate Bench of the Supreme Court (SAB) provided another avenue for would-be Islamic reformers. Among its functions, the FSC was granted extensive jurisdiction to entertain "Shariat petitions" brought by citizens of Pakistan or by federal or provincial governments challenging "any law or provision of law" as repugnant to the Holy Quran. Such powers were circumscribed as discussed above by Article 203-B of the 1985 Constitution. The SAB is the final court of appeal against FSC decisions.

Accordingly, several Shariat petitions[34] were filed with the newly created FSC challenging provisions of various laws which sanctioned the payment of financial interest. The Court as per Chief Justice Aftab Hussain dismissed such petitions on the grounds of lack of jurisdiction. In the Essa E.H. Jafar case, Aftab Hussain found that any law concerning interest was by definition a "fiscal law" and hence was excluded from the FSC's jurisdiction by Article 203-B of the constitution.[35] This finding was upheld in several other cases as well.[36] The exclusion of the FSC's jurisdiction to deal with "any fiscal law" originally was set to expire within three years, that is by June 25, 1983. However, the time limit was extended three times by President Zia -- first, to four years, then to five years, and finally to ten years.[37] Therefore, the FSC was effectively banned from consideration of laws relevant to *riba* until 1990.

However, the doors to judicial review of laws countenancing *riba* were not permanently locked. The key was the "Objectives Resolution." When Pakistan's constitution was "restored" in 1985, the Objectives Resolution, a preamble to the 1956, 1962, and 1973 constitutions, was made a substantive part of the document (Article 2-A). The Objectives Resolution originally had been adopted by Pakistan's First Constituent Assembly in 1949 and is a declaratory statement that provides that Pakistan will be a state: "Wherein the Muslims should be enabled to order their lives in the individual and collective spheres in accordance with the teachings and requirements of Islam as set out in the Holy Quran and Sunnah."[38]

The judicial doctrine developed during 1987 by Dr. Tanzil-ur-Rehman, then judge of the Sindh High Court, was that the Objectives Resolution formed the fundamental basis of Pakistan's constitutional structure, its *grund norm* and consequently that it is supra-constitutional. Therefore, superior courts possess the jurisdiction to examine laws, even if protected by the constitution, on the grounds of violation of the principles of the Objectives Resolution unless the relevant court's jurisdiction is specifically excluded from the consideration of a particular subject. That is, the FSC does not have jurisdiction to examine fiscal laws for repugnancy to the principles of Islam, but the High Courts possess such jurisdiction through the vehicle of the Objectives Resolution.

On the basis of this line of reasoning, Justice Tanzil-ur-Rehman claimed standing for the Sindh High Court to consider three cases in which the validity of *riba* was challenged. In Bank of Oman v. East Trading Co., he granted leave to appeal an impugned decision of a district court pertaining to bank interest on the grounds that the High Court had jurisdiction through Article 2-A to "construe the existing laws in the light of the Holy Quran and Sunnah, as enshrined in the constitution except that when a certain law falls within the exclusive jurisdiction of the FSC."[39] The decision was clarified in the Irshad Khan case. In this case relief was granted the petitioner against interest on a private note.[40] In the course of the decision, Justice Tanzil-ur-Rehman presented a spirited argument supporting the position that *riba* of any kind is un-Islamic. Similarly, in Habib Bank v. Muhammad Hussain[41] Justice Rehman invoked Article 2-A to enable the High Court to examine the question of bank interest; and as before found that its collection was un-Islamic. However, unlike Irshad Khan, the court was bound by precedent, and hence, was unable to grant relief to the petitioner. In the Habib Bank case the petitioner had borrowed money from a commercial bank. As a consequence, the transaction was protected by Article 270-A of constitution as amended by the Eighth Amendment, the legal mechanisms that indemnified actions taken during the Martial Law of Zia ul-Haq (1979-1985). Earlier the Sindh High Court, in a full bench decision, had ruled that Article 270-A was valid legislation and that it could not be challenged by Article 2-A.[42] Similarly, in subsequent cases the Supreme Court found that Article 270-A was valid legislation.[43]

Support for Justice Tanzil-ur-Rehman's findings were subsequently provided by two cases decided in the High Courts. In Shahbazad Chaudhry[44] Justice Khalil-ur-Rehman Khan ruled that Article 2-A gave the courts the right to examine provisions of the Companies Act to ensure that "the affairs of the company are [not] being conducted in a manner prejudicial to the public interest." Accordingly, he directed that the respondent, a private firm, disinvest from ventures that held a fixed rate of return, and re-invest in permissable forms of investment -- shareholding or PLS. That is, he found that *riba* was not in the public interest. Similarly Justice Wajihuddin Ahmad in Aijaz Haroon v. Iman Durrani[45] ruled that provisions in the Negotiable Instruments Act, 1881 that provided for fixed interest rates were "un-Islamic;" and that the courts in Pakistan are precluded from decreeing relief in any form whatever." Accordingly, he granted relief to the petitioner from paying a fixed rate of interest but creatively ruled that the petitioner should repay the lender an amount that would take into account the effects of currency inflation across the term of the loan.

As ingenious as such judicial activism is, the utilization of the Objectives Resolution doctrine is at best an imperfect tool to effect the goal of prohibiting the practice of *riba* in the state. The doctrine cannot be applied to challenge laws indemnified by Article 270-A; and an overwhelming majority of Pakistan's High Court judges are opposed both to the application of the Objectives Resolution doctrine as well as to a total ban on *riba*.[46] Moreover, Justice Tanzil-ur-Rehman, the most active proponent of the doctrine, retired from the Sindh High Court on June 15, 1990.

The Faisal Case: Findings and Implications

However, an unexpected confluence of factors propelled the *riba* issue to center stage in Pakistan's judicial system within the next year. First, Benazir's government "neglected" to extend the date banning FSC consideration of "fiscal law," found in Article 203-B, beyond June 25, 1990.[47] Second, President Ghulam Ishaq Khan, citing widespread corruption, among other reasons, dismissed the twenty-month old government of Benazir Bhutto in August 1990. Third, Ghulam Ishaq called Justice Tanzil-ur-Rehman out of "retirement" (from his professorial assignment at the International Islamic University, Malaysia) and appointed him as Chief Justice of the FSC on November 15, 1990.[48]

As expected, one of the first acts of the newly appointed Chief Justice was to announce, through a decision rendered on January 13, 1991, that the FSC was now in a position to entertain Shariat petitions challenging fiscal legislation.[49] The Court was swamped with such petitions. A total of 115 Shariat petitions were filed between June 30, 1990, and October 24, 1991, challenging twenty separate laws as repugnant to Islam on the grounds that such laws countenanced *riba*. The overwhelming majority of such petitions relied upon the Quran (esp., II: 275-278) to substantiate their arguments.[50] Such petitions found a sympathetic ear in Tanzil-ur-Rehman and among a majority of other justices of the FSC.

Accordingly, in November 1991, the FSC completed a monumental decision, authored by Chief Justice Tanzil-ur-Rehman, that totalled 564 pages including appendices.[51] The decision, Mahmood-ur-Rehman Faisal v. Secretary, Ministry of Law and Parliamentary Affairs, granted relief to the overwhelming majority of the petitioners by declaring provisions of twenty federal and provincial laws dealing with *riba* as repugnant to Islam, and ordered their revision by July 1, 1992.[52] The main findings of the decision are summarized below:[53]

(1) *Riba* means "any addition, however slight, over and above the principal," and includes both usury and interest.
(2) No legal distinction can be made between "productive loans" and "consumption loans." Both are *riba*. The prohibition against *riba* is absolute, there are no exceptions.
(3) Quranic decrees regards *riba* are not allegorical (*mutashabahat*) but constitute part of the clear text (*nass*) of the Quran.
(4) The prohibition of *riba* does not counter the public good (*maslaha*). *Ijtehad* (independent reasoning) regarding the public good is only applicable when there is no textual precedent (*nass*) found in the Quran.

(5) The indexation of loans in order to control for the effects of inflation is prohibited by Islam. In the Quran money is treated like a commodity, it must be exchanged in kind, not value.
(6) Any system of mark-up is repugnant to Islam because it is tantamount to interest.

Throughout, the Faisal decision relies heavily on the Council of Islamic Ideology's views on *riba* as expressed in the CII's 1980 and 1983 reports.[54] Both the latter reports were written by Tanzil-ur-Rehman when he was chairman of the Council. Curiously, therefore, it is often the case that the primary justification of arguments expressed by the FSC in the Faisal decision are the author's own words. That is, Justice Tanzil-ur-Rehman quotes himself extensively in the Faisal decision.

The government of Nawaz Sharif has been shakened seriously by the implications of the FSC's decision. First, Nawaz Sharif's major domestic policy initiative since assuming office in late 1990 has been the liberalization of Pakistan's economy; an initiative which is clearly threatened by the Faisal decision. Second, the government has publicly committed itself to pursuing the goal of Islamization. As described above, Nawaz Sharif personally shepherded the Shariat Bill through the Majlis-i-Shura, and the major base of his government's support has remained the IJI, a party that is ideologically committed to Islamization. Therefore, the government finds itself caught between a rock and a hard place. If the government appeals the Faisal decision (a policy favored by a majority of the Cabinet)[55] it opens itself to the charge that it is being hypocritical relevant to the Islamization process; if it does not appeal the decision Nawaz Sharif's economic policy is likely to fail. Faced with such a difficult decision, the government chose the path of least resistance. It encouraged a semi-government entity, the Agricultural Development Bank, to file an appeal before the Shariat Appellate Bench of the Supreme Court (SAB) challenging the Faisal decision. As of June 1992, the appeal remains pending.

Of course, it is speculative to predict the outcome of the appeal before the SAB. However, it is the considered opinion of this author that the appeal is likely to fail for two reasons. First, the Faisal decision is very tightly argued and it contains direct rebuttals of the arguments that are most likely to be presented by the advocates of the Agricultural Development Bank. Indeed, the Faisal decision rejected the well-prepared plaints of the National Bank of Pakistan, the State Life Insurance Company, and the Banking Council of Pakistan.[56] Second, the current membership of the SAB is very unlikely to overturn the Faisal decision on philosophical grounds. The Court is composed of five justices of the Supreme Court, three of whom (a majority) are well-known for supporting an Islamic activist interpretation of the role of Pakistan's superior courts.[57]

If this prediction proves correct then Nawaz Sharif's government not only faces a dilemma, but Pakistan is rapidly approaching a constitutional crisis as well. Given the Majlis-i-Shura's inability to reach any decision on controversial Islamic matters (1985 -), it is highly unlikely that Pakistan's legislative institutions will be able to draft laws that will meet the objections of the courts, let alone to amend the constitution, in a timely fashion. Alternatively, the Ministry of Justice and Parliamentary Affairs is loathe to craft and to promulgate laws through Presidental Ordinance that would respond to the FSC's order. Therefore, a confrontation looms between the courts and the government. If neither abandons their respective positions, then the only remedies are extra-constitutional (to dismiss the government, or to suspend the operation of the courts). Obviously, neither outcome would be congenial to the further growth of democracy in the state.

Conclusion

This chapter has demonstrated that there is no consensus either in regard to the content or in regard to the desired pace of Islamic reform in Pakistan. Successive governments' attempts to forge such a consensus, through the consideration of various forms of Shariah legislation failed to the extent that the fruit of this process, the Enforcement of Shariah Act, 1991, provoked more questions than it answered. In the absence of such a consensus, the superior courts have "seized the opportunity," or alternatively, "have been forced" to adopt an increasingly activist stance in regard to the Islamization process. In either case, the superior courts have become, largely through default, the primary locus of legislative authority in the state. This is demonstrated forcefully in regards to the *riba* issue. Successive governments have attempted to defer consideration of the *riba* issue, and successive legislatures have given the issue no formal consideration at all. Into this policy vacuum has stepped the FSC, with an activist chief justice who has seized the opportunity to introduce an extremist interpretation of the prohibition of *riba* which arguably threatens the fundamentals of Pakistan's economic system. Despite a near-consensus within the current government opposed to the FSC's decision, the government is powerless to act, a captive of an ideological commitment to Islam; and a lack of political leadership. Unfortunately, the likely victim of this scenario will be Pakistan's fragile democratic system.

Notes

1. *Riba* is most often translated as "usury" in Western sources. However, Islamic activists consider *riba* to apply to all forms of financial interest. Such definitional concerns are a central part of the policy debate concerning this issue. Accordingly, this chapter does not use an English translation of the term.

2. There is a significant literature concerning the role of Islam in the formation of Pakistan's first constitution. Among the most useful sources are: Leonard Binder, *Religion and Politics in Pakistan* (Berkeley: University of California Press, 1961); Herbert Feldman, *A Constitution for Pakistan* (Karachi: Oxford University Press, 1956); Sayed Riaz Ahmed, *Maulana Maududi and the Islamic State* (Lahore: People's Publishing House, 1976); and Manzooruddin Ahmad, *Pakistan: The Emerging Islamic State* (Karachi: Allies Book Corporation, 1961).

3. Number 18.

4. Article 38.

5. Council of Islamic Ideology, *Report of Consolidated Recommendations on the "The Islamic Economic System"* (Islamabad: CII, 1983), pp. 9-10. Hereinafter CII (1983).

6. CII (1983), p. 10.

7. Government of Pakistan, National Assembly of Pakistan, *Report of the Constitution Committee Presented to the National Assembly of Pakistan on 31 December 1972* (Islamabad: Manager, Printing Corporation of Pakistan Press, 1972).

8. This report was not published. A later version of the interim report was submitted to the CII in February 1980. It was published as "Interim Report of the Panel of Economists and Bankers on the Elimination of Interest" and was appended to: Council of Islamic Ideology, *Report of the Council of Islamic Ideology on the Elimination of Interest from the Economy* (Islamabad: CII, 1980). Hereinafter CII (1980).

9. For details see Charles H. Kennedy, "Islamization in Pakistan: Implementation of the Hudood Ordinances," *Asian Survey* Vol. 18, no. 3 (March 1988), pp. 307-316.

10. CII (1980). Dr. Tanzil-ur-Rehman was Chairman of the CII. The other members of the Council were: Maulana Zafar Ahmad Ansari, Khalid Ishaque, Mufti Sayyahuddin Kakakhel, Khwaja Qamaruddin Siyalvi, Maulana Muhammad Taqi Usmani, Maulana Muhammad Hanif Nadvi, Dr. Ziauddin Ahmad, Allama Syed Muhammad Razi, Maulana Shamsul Haq Afghani, and Dr. Khowar Khan Chisti.

11. *Murabaha* is a practice in which the bank purchases, in its own name, goods that an importer or trader wants, and then sells them to him at an agreed mark-up. The technique is used for financing trade, but because the bank takes title to the goods, and is therefore engaged in buying and selling, its profit derives from a real service and entails a certain, albeit minimal, risk. *Musharaka* is a practice in which the bank enters into a partnership with a client in which both share the equity capital -- and perhaps even management -- of a project or deal, and both share in the profits or losses according to their equity shareholding.

12. CII (1980), paragraph 1.32, p. 26.

13. The details of this argument are found in Charles H. Kennedy, "Islamization and Legal Reform in Pakistan, 1979-1989," *Pacific Affairs* Vol. 63, no. 1 (Spring 1990), pp. 62-77.

14. 1985 Constitution, Article 203-B.

15. e.g. CII (1980), paragraph 1.1, p. 7.

16. Perhaps the most influential of such works are those published by the Islamabad-based Institute of Policy Sciences. Their relevant publications include: Ziauddin Ahmad, et. al. eds., *Money and Banking in Islam*; Ziauddin Ahmad, et. al., eds. *Fiscal Policy and Resource Allocation in Islam*; Muhammad Ahmad Khan, *Islamic Economics: Annotated Sources in English and Urdu*; Munawar Iqbal and M. Fahim Khan, *A Survey of Issues and a Programme for Research in Monetary and Fiscal Economies in Islam*; and Khurshid Ahmad, *Towards Monetary and Fiscal System of Islam* (Islamabad: IPE, various dates).

17. Qazi Abdul Latif and Maulana Sami-ul-Haq, "Enforcement of Shariah Act, 1985" (xerox: 1985).

18. Senate Select Committee, "Report of the Select Committee on the 'Enforcement of Shariah Bill, 1989'," Maqbool Ahmad Khan chairman (xerox: 1985); Khurshid Ahmad, et. al. "Ninth Constitution Amendment Bill" in *Dawn* (November 1, 1985); Ministry of Law and Parliamentary Affairs, "Constitution (Ninth Amendment) Act, 1985" (xerox: 1986). A more complete discussion is found in Charles H. Kennedy, "Repugnancy to Islam - Who Decides? Islam and Legal Reform in Pakistan," *International and Comparative Law Quarterly* (forthcoming 1992).

19. Personal interviews with principals. Islamabad, May-June, 1987.

20. See the discussion found in Kennedy, "Islamization" (1990), pp. 71-77.

21. For example see the treatment of this issue in *Dawn* and *The Muslim* during 1987.

22. The text of his address is found in *Dawn* (May 30, 1988). In an important case, Federation of Pakistan v. Md. Saifullah Khan *All-Pakistan Legal Decisions* (*PLD*) 1989 SC 166, the Supreme Court ruled that Zia's dissolution of the National Assembly was un-constitutional, but that no relief could be granted to the petitioners. That is, the National Assembly would remain dissolved.

23. "Enforcement of Shariah Ordinance, 1988 (Ordinance I of 1988), June 15, 1988." *PLD* 1988 Central Statutes 29.

24. "Enforcement of Shariah Ordinance, 1988," p. 31.

25. Cf. Kennedy, "Islamization" (1990), p. 67; pp. 71-77.

26. 1985 Constitution, Article 89(2).

27. "Enforcement of Shariah (Revised) Ordinance, 1988 (Ordinance XXI of 1988), October 15, 1988," *PLD* 1989 Central Statutes 18.

28. The most important modification was that it tightened the wording of Article 3 of Zia's 1988 act to read: "Shariah shall be the supreme law of Pakistan... and shall have effect notwithstanding anything contained in any other law, custom or usage." Like Zia's act it adopted the expedient of assigning jurisdiction to the High Courts in matters exempted from FSC jurisdiction by Article 203-B.

29. Personal interviews, Islamabad, January 1990.

30. The official reasons for the dismissal are presented in "Dissolution of National Assembly by President of Pakistan," *PLD* 1991 Central Statutes 142.

31. For a pro-government view of the debate before the Majlis-i-Shura see *Pakistan Times* (May 10 - May 29, 1991).

32. For example, Ghulam Haider Wyne, Chief Minister of the Punjab, cited the passage of the Shariah Act, 1991 as "one of the most important events in Islamic history." *Pakistan Times* (May 29, 1991).

33. Enforcement of Shariah Act, 1991 (Act X of 1991), *PLD* 1991 Central Statutes 373. For a critical discussion of the act see Topical Studies Group - Islamabad, *Enforcement of Shariah Act, 1991: Text and Topic* (Islamabad: Topical Studies Group, 1991).

34. A total of fifteen Shariat petitions were filed before the FSC between 1979-1987 challenging *riba*.

35. Essa E.H. Jafar v. Federation of Pakistan, *PLD* 1982 FSC 212, pp. 215-216.

36. For instance Md. Sadiq Khan v. Federation of Pakistan *PLD*, 1983 FSC 43; Ibrahim Bhai v. Government of Pakistan, Shariat Petition (SP) 6/K/83; and Sarfaraz Hussain v. Federation of Pakistan, SP 1/K/82.

37. Presidential Order (PO), no. 7, 1983; P.O., no. 2, 1984; and P.O., no. 14, 1985.

38. 1985 Constitution, Article 2-A annex. For a more complete discussion of the historical significance of the Objectives Resolution and of the development of the resultant judicial doctrine see Kennedy "Repugnancy" (1992).

39. Bank of Oman, Ltd. v. East Trading Co., *PLD* 1987 Kar 404; p. 442.

40. Irshad H. Khan v. Parveen Ajaz, *PLD* 1987 Kar 466.

41. Habib Bank v. Muhammad Hussain, *PLD* 1987 Kar 616.

42. Muhammad Bachal Memon v. Government of Sindh, *PLD* 1987 Kar 296. A full bench decision is binding upon a single judge bench.

43. Except where actions taken under martial law were *mala fides*, or without jurisdiction. See Federation of Pakistan v. Ghulam Mustapha Khar, *PLD* 1989 SC 30; Federation of Pakistan v. Md. Saifullah Khan, *PLD* 1989 SC 166.

44. Shahbazad Chaudhry v. Services I.T., Ltd., *PLD* 1988 Lah 1.

45. Aijaz Haroon v. Iman Durrani, *PLD* 1989 Kar 304.

46. See Kennedy "Repugnancy" (1992). It is important to note that support for the Objectives Resolution doctrine, although a minority position, was provided by two prominent jurists -- Nasim Hassan Shah and Gul Muhammad Khan. The former is a senior judge of the Supreme Court, the latter the former Chief Justice of the FSC. See Nasim Hassan Shah, "The Objectives Resolution and its Impact on the Administration of Justice in Pakistan," *PLD* Journal 186; and Gul Muhammad Khan, "Islamization of Laws in Pakistan," *PLD* 1986 Journal 249.

47. There is ample evidence to support the contention that Benazir's government did not give adequate consideration to matters pertaining to the Islamization process. The government was publicly committed to rolling back "Zia's Islamization program" but it failed to take requisite actions to delay the consideration of various issues pending before the superior courts -- e.g. pre-emption, *qisas* and *diyat*, and land reforms. From all available evidence the failure to extend Article 203-B's ban on the consideration of fiscal matters was an "oversight." Source: interviews with relevant officials, Islamabad, January 1992.

48. A biodata of Justice Tanzil-ur-Rehman is found in *PLD* 1991 Journal 3.

49. Dr. Mahmood-ur-Rehman Faisal et. al. v. Secretary, Ministry of Law and Parliamentary Affairs *PLD* 1991 FSC 35. In the decision Justice Tanzil-ur-Rehman defined *zakat* and *ushr* as "Muslim personal laws" and therefore beyond the jurisdiction of the FSC as per Article 203-B.

50. The author examined the relevant Shariat petitions before the FSC in Islamabad during January 1992.

51. Certified court copy of the decision, Mahmood-ur-Rehman Faisal v. Secretary, Ministry of Justice, Law and Parliamentary Affairs SP 30/I/90. Hereinafter Faisal. The decision was unanimous and rendered by a three judge bench consisting of Dr. Tanzil-ur-Rehman, Dr. Fida Muhammad Khan, and Abaidullah Khan. The decision will be reported as *PLD* 1992 FSC 1.

52. Provisions of the following twenty laws were declared repugnant to Islam in the Faisal case: The Interest Act, 1839; The Government Savings Bank Act, 1873; Negotiable Instruments Act, 1881; The Land Acquisition Act, 1894; The Code of Criminal Procedure, 1908; Co-operative Societies Act, 1925; Co-operative Societies Rules, 1927; The Insurance Act, 1938; The State Bank of Pakistan Act, 1956; The West Pakistan Money Lenders Act, 1960; The West Pakistan Money Lenders Rules, 1960; The Punjab Money Lenders Ordinance, 1960; The Sind Money Lenders Ordinance, 1960; The NWFP Money Lenders Ordinance, 1960; The Baluchistan Money Lenders Ordinance, 1960; The Agricultural Development Bank Rules, 1961; The Banking Companies Ordinance, 1962; The Banking Companies Rules, 1963; The Banks (Nationalization) Payment of Compensation Rules, 1974; and The Banking Companies (Recovery of Loans) Ordinance, 1979. The FSC's discussion of these impugned laws is found in Faisal, pp. 215-279.

53. As per the author's reading of the Faisal decision.

54. See CII (1980); CII (1983).

55. Personal interviews, January 1992.

56. The unsuccessful plaints were brought by two of Pakistan's most-renowned barristers, Khalid Ishaque and S.M. Zafar. For the discussion of their relevant arguments and the FSC's rebuttal see the Faisal decision, pp. 68-74; 79-85.

57. The SAB is composed (June 1992) of Chairman, Justice Nasim Hassan Shah; Justice Pir Muhammad Karam Shah; Justice Maulana Taqi Usmani; Justice Shafiur Rehman; and Justice Abdul Qadeer Chaudhry. The first three are well-known Islamic legal activists.

5

The Politicization of the Shias and the Development of the Tehrik-e-Nifaz-e-Fiqh-e-Jafaria in Pakistan

Afak Haydar

The Shias[1] constitute the second largest Muslim school of jurisprudence (*mazhab*) in Pakistan.[2] The *mazahib* of the majority of the Pakistanis are cumulatively referred to as Sunni. The Shias number at least 20 percent of the total population of Pakistan. They played a critical role in the creation of Pakistan: they contributed significantly to its administrative stability, its economic growth, its political evolution, and its social development during its formative phase. They participated in all aspects of life in Pakistan as equal partners with their Sunni compatriots, and did not feel discriminated against during 1947-1977. It was during the Zia period (1977-1988) that the Shias felt it necessary to form a separate organization, with a political agenda.

This chapter is designed to review the fundamentals of the Shia *mazhab*; the contribution of Shias to the creation and to the economic and political development of Pakistan; their disillusionment because of the policies of the Zia regime; and the consequential establishment of the Tehrik-e-Nifaz-e-Fiqh-e-Jafaria (TNFJ - The Movement for the Establishment of the Shia *Fiqh)*, its demands, and its impact on the politics of Pakistan.

The Fundamentals of Shia Belief

The chief differences between the Shias and the Sunnis may be identified in two broad categories: doctrinal differences in belief and jurisprudential differences in interpretation of the Quran and the Sunnah.

All Muslims believe in *Tawheed* (unity of God), *Risalah* (the series of prophets sent by God for the guidance of mankind), and *Qiyamah* (the Day of Judgment, when man will be judged for his acts of omission and commission and be rewarded or punished for life in the hereafter). The Shias have two additional articles of faith: the institution of *Imamat* and the concept of *Adl* as an inseparable attribute of God.

The Shias believe that it is necessary for mankind to continue to receive Divine guidance about the interpretation of the Quran and the Prophet's Sunnah after the death of the (last) Prophet. This Divine guidance is received through Imams, who are, like the Prophet, *masoom* (sinless). They also believe that all Imams, beginning with the first, Ali were named by the Prophet under Divine direction. Ali was succeeded by his oldest son, Hasan, who was succeeded by his younger brother Husain, who was succeeded by his son Ali, and so on, until the twelfth Imam, Muhammad, succeeded his father, Hasan al-Askari, the eleventh Imam. The twelfth Imam went into occultation and will return as the *Mahdi*.[3] The other doctrinal difference lies in the Shia belief in *Adl* (Justice) as an inseparable attribute of Allah: He is not only One; He is also *Adl*, Just.[4]

This belief has a great impact on the Shia attitude in the controversy between predestination and free will. Is everything predestined by God, with man only a mechanical device carrying out the commands with no free will? Or does man have an element of free will? The Shias believe that man may be held accountable for his acts of omission and commission only if he has an element of free will. It would be unfair and unjust for God to hold man accountable for his acts of omission and commission if man had no hand in doing what he did or failed to do. And, since God is Just, He cannot (will not?) ask man to be accountable for acts over which man has no control. The Shias believe that the balance necessary for keeping the cosmos in operation can be maintained only by a Just God.[5]

The jurisprudential differences between the Shias and the Sunnis in the interpretation of the Quran and the Sunnah are numerous but mostly minor. The most important difference between the two groups is the right of a Shia *mujtahid* (scholar) to issue *fatawa* (edicts), to "discover" law in response to developments in science and technology, or to respond to the changing patterns of life. There are differences in the interpretation of family laws: of marriage and divorce (including temporary marriage); about inheritance and wills; about religious obligations; about how much, how, and to whom to give *zakat* and *khums*; about what animals (and seafood) are *halal*, *makrooh*, or *haram* (permitted, preferably avoided, or absolutely prohibited for human consumption, respectively).[6] There are also minor differences about rituals: how to perform ablutions prior to the daily prayers, how to stand (and, whether to cover the head) while saying the daily prayers, when to begin and end the Ramadan fast, how to perform the hajj, and how to bury the dead.[7]

The Contribution of the Shias to the Creation and Development of Pakistan

The Shias contributed to the creation and development of Pakistan not as Shias but as Muslim members of contemporary India. It must be admitted that there were some Shias (just as there were many Sunnis) who worked with the Indian National Congress and were opposed to the creation of Pakistan. But, by and large, most Shias of the Subcontinent worked with the All-India Muslim League, and the Quaid-e-Azam Muhammad Ali Jinnah, himself a Shia. Many prominent coworkers of Jinnah were Shias: His Highness Sir Sultan Muhammad Khan, Agha Khan III (Founder President of the Muslim League); his son, Prince Ali Khan (at one time Pakistan's Ambassador to the United Nations); Maharaja Sir Muhammad Ali Muhammad Khan and Raja Amir Ahmed Khan of Mahmoodabad; Raja Syed Muhammad Mahdi of Peerpur; Mr. M. A. H. Ispahani (at one time Ambassador to the United States); Raja Ghazanfar Ali Khan (at one time Federal Minister, later Ambassador); Mr Justice M. R. Kiyani (at one time Chief Justice of Pakistan); and, Mr Akhter Husain (at one time Governor of West Pakistan). Also, many senior civil servants in the new state were Shias, including Hashim Raza (first Administrator of Karachi, later Chief Secretary, East Pakistan); A. T. Naqvi (Chief Commissioner, Karachi); and Kazim Raza (Inspector General of Police, Karachi).[8] Also crucial was the Shia community's contribution to the establishment of an economic and industrial infrastructure of Pakistan. Prominent among the economic pioneers were the Gokals (shipping lines) the Habibs (banking), and the Ispahanis (airlines and banking).[9]

The Advent of the Zia Regime

From 1947 to 1977, the Shias enjoyed religious freedom, and the community did not feel threatened by the government or by fellow Muslims. There were some Shia-Sunni riots during this period, however, particularly during Moharram, when Muslims in general and Shias in particular commemorate the martyrdom of Imam Husain (the grandson of the Prophet) and his family and friends, under orders of Yazid ibn Muawiya in 61 AH.

During this period three heads of state (Muhammad Ali Jinnah (1947-1948), Iskander Mirza (1956-1958), and General Yahya Khan (1969-1970) were Shias. Zulfikar Ali Bhutto, at one time president, later prime minister (1971-1977), came from a Shia background. Every prime minister from Liaquat Ali Khan to Zulfikar Ali Bhutto had Shia cabinet ministers. The senior civil service that holds key administrative positions in the national and provincial administrations had (and has) numerous Shias. The armed forces had adequate representation of the Shias including numerous flag officers, and at least two commanders-in-chief, Generals Musa Khan and Yahya Khan. The Shias had an adequate share in the economic life of the society: in retail business, in international commerce, in transportation, and in industry. Moreover, those segments of the civil laws of the country that affected the religious aspects of a person's life were developed during the pre-Mughal period, and were incorporated by the British and later by Pakistan into its legal system.[10]

In short, during the period 1947-1977, as a community, the Shias had no reason to feel insecure or threatened. They had adequate representation in the political leadership, in the civil services, in the armed forces, and in business and industry. Most important, their lives as Shias were secure. There were no restrictions on the observance of their religious rites and they were governed by their own personal laws in matters of marriage, divorce, and inheritance. The criminal laws of the society were based on the common law codes developed by the British and were universally applicable to all members of the society without regard to *mazhab*. "None of the governments in Pakistan saw any purpose in changing these practices."[11] The Shias were content with being treated as equal members of the society.

Most Sunni *ulema* had opposed the creation of Pakistan; some had even labeled Muhammad Ali Jinnah a *kafir*. Although the demand for Pakistan was made in the name of Islam, Jinnah had categorically stated that Pakistan was not going to be a theocratic state; it was designed to be a state of and for the Muslims and not a Muslim state.[12] That was the policy pursued by all governments from the government of Liaquat Ali Khan to that of Zulfikar Ali Bhutto.

General Zia ul-Haq, then Chief of the Army Staff, overthrew the Bhutto government in a bloodless coup on July 5, 1977. Soon after taking over as Chief Martial Law Administrator and President, Zia announced his plans for the establishment of *Nizam-e-Mustafa* (the Islamic order). He reconstituted the Council of Islamic Ideology, composed of representatives of various schools of jurisprudence and persuasions. Mufti Jafar Husain, a prominent Shia scholar, was appointed to represent the Shia views. Zia also amended certain criminal laws. On 12 Rabi-ul-Awwal, 1399 AH (anniversary of the Prophet's birth date -- February 10, 1979), he promulgated *hudood* ordinances[13] that provided "Islamic" punishments for certain criminal acts.[14] Mufti Jafar Husain resigned from the Council to protest the promulgation of the ordinances and the Zia government's announcement that the Hanafi *fiqh* was to be enforced in Pakistan.[15]

Tehrik-e-Nifaz-e-Fiqh-e-Jafaria

The resignation of Mufti Jafar Husain precipitated a crisis in the Shia community. The Shia leadership called a meeting of Shias in the city of Bhakkar on April 12-13, 1979, to protest the government's desire to enforce the Hanafi *fiqh*. The meeting was attended by a large number of Shias: intellectuals, scholars, and people from all walks of life. The meeting elected Mufti Jafar Husain to lead the community as it organized and prepared itself to protect the rights of Shias. Soon after his election as the Quaid-e-Millat-e-Jafaria (the leader of the Jafari [Shia] community), Mufti Jafar Husain announced that the Shias would start a nationwide movement -- to be known as Tehrik-e-Nifaz-e-Fiqh-e-Jafaria (TNFJ) -- if the Shia demands were not met by the government.[16]

The Bhakkar meeting adopted a resolution outlining the demands of the Shia community. These demands have since been articulated in greater detail by the TNFJ in its publication *Sabeelena* (Our Path). These demands include:[17]

> 1. All court decisions involving Shias should be made according to their *fiqh* known as *fiqh-e-Jafari.*
>
> 2. All income from Shia trusts should be spent on Shia religious affairs.
>
> 3. The Government should remove all restrictions on *azadari* (mourning commemoration) of Imam Husain. Also, the Government should facilitate the travel of Shias to Shia holy shrines [in Iran, Iraq, Saudi Arabia, and Syria].
>
> 4. Shia scholars and Shia attorneys must be provided representation in Shariat (religious law) courts; Shias should be provided facilities to present their religious programs on [government owned] radio and television.
>
> 5. Prominent *mujtahids* and other [Shia] scholars from Iran should be invited to tour Pakistan just as [Sunni] scholars are invited from Saudi Arabia.
>
> 6. The curriculum for courses on theology for Shia students should reflect the Shia point of view.

On June 30, 1980, General Zia ul-Haq promulgated the Zakat and Ushr Ordinance, 1980, asking banks to deduct 2.5 percent of the holdings in all personal and corporate savings and fixed deposit accounts of

Muslims on the designated date.[18] The Shias objected to the collection of *zakat* by the government as their *fiqh* requires them to handle *zakat* in a different manner.[19] The TNFJ demanded exemption from provisions of the ordinance, but the government did not grant their request.

Discontent grew in the Shia community. It was caused by a combination of several factors: imposition of the *hudood* and the *zakat* and *ushr* ordinances (in both cases the Shia *fiqh* is different from others); Zia's desire to enforce the Hanafi *fiqh* for all the people of Pakistan; some local restrictions about Moharram *azadari*; and the Shia perception that the government was unresponsive to the religious sensitivities of the Shia community. The discontent and disillusionment was exacerbated by the feeling that this was happening in Pakistan, a country that the Shias had helped create and build with their blood and sweat.

The Shias were especially unhappy about the *hudood* ordinances. While all *mazahib* agree on certain acts (including all acts covered by the *hudood* ordinances) as being prohibited, the Shias disagree with the Sunnis about punishment for some of these criminal acts. For example, the Shia definition of theft differs from the common Sunni definition and they prescribe a different punishment for the offense. In Shia theology, the severance of the hand as punishment for theft requires severance of only four fingers and not the severance of the hand from the wrist.[20]

The Shias also hold that the government has no authority to collect *zakat* and *ushr*. The Shias give *zakat* and *khums* on different bases to deserving persons (or, institutions), mostly through the agency of their *mujtahids*. Moreover, the government was not the proper agency to collect the *zakat*; and according to Shia *fiqh*, it was not due on all savings; nor was *ushr* due on all crops. Therefore, they perceived the ordinance as unprecedented governmental interference in the exercise of their religious obligations.

The Shias believed that the government's decision to enforce the Hanafi *fiqh* in Pakistan was made under pressure from the vociferous conservatives of the Sunni community, some of whom argued that since Iran has imposed the Shia *fiqh* on all its citizens, including the Sunnis, Pakistan should impose the Hanafi *fiqh* on all its citizens, including the Shias. The Shias were unwilling to accept the argument. What happened in Iran was Iran's business, not theirs; but what was going to happen in Pakistan was their business.

The Shias of Pakistan are extremely sensitive about the *azadari* (mourning commemoration) issue. This author believes that many Shias seem to exhibit their identification with Islam more through *azadari* than through the fundamental obligations of a Muslim: *salat*, *zakat*, and fasting. Local administrators in Pakistan will tell you that the *azadari* days are some of the most tense days of the year for them. The *azadari* processions are scenes of potential "disturbances" because of the emotional attachment of the Shias to the rituals. Therefore, any restrictions placed by the administration on *azadari* are resented by the Shia community.

The Shias called for a rally in Islamabad in early July 1980 nominally to protest the assassination of Allama Baqar-al-Sadr, a prominent Shia scholar. The rally soon became a protest against the policies of the Zia administration. The government tried to stop the Shias from assembling, but the Shias ignored the ban, gathering in Islamabad in large numbers. The police used tear gas and batons to disperse the crowds, and even fired on the crowds. One person (Muhammad Husain Shah) was killed. The Shia community declared him a martyr and offered to provide other martyrs for the achievement of their objectives.

Ultimately, Zia met with Shia leaders, including representatives of the TNFJ. On July 6, 1980, the government issued a statement, jointly signed by Mahmood Haroon, Minister for Religious Affairs, and Mufti Jafar Husain, the TNFJ leader. This has come to be known as the "Islamabad Agreement."[21] Under this agreement Zia agreed not to impose the laws of any one *fiqh* on the followers of another *fiqh*. The Shias also earned exemption in principle from collection of *zakat* and *ushr*. The formal ordinance exempting the Shias was issued on October 29, 1983.[22]

Did Zia agree to the Shia demands because of the pressure exerted on him by the demands of the Shias? Or was there some pressure on him from within, from his own generals in uniform? Some Shias gave this author to understand that both factors were responsible for the Islamabad Agreement.[23]

Under the exemption granted to the Shias from collection of *zakat* and *ushr*, a Shia has to file a signed, witnessed, and notarized statement to the effect that he is a Muslim, that he is a follower of the Jafari *fiqh*, and that according to his *fiqh*, he cannot pay the *zakat* or *ushr* in the manner prescribed by the government. This must be done at least thirty days before the first day of Ramadan (the ninth lunar month) each year. A declaration once submitted to the collecting agency remains valid until revoked.[24]

The Politicization of the TNFJ Since 1984

Mufti Jafar Husain passed away on August 29, 1983. The post-Jafar Husain era represents a new phase in the life of the TNFJ. We will review the following to understand this new phase: (1) The impact of the Islamic revolution of Iran on the TNFJ, (2) the election of Allama Syed

Arif Husain al-Husaini as the leader of the main branch of the TNFJ, and (3) the split in the TNFJ and the establishment of the Moosavi group.

The Impact of the Islamic Revolution of Iran on the TNFJ

The monarchy of Muhammad Reza Shah, Shahinshah Aryamehr of Iran, was overthrown in January 1979 by a combination of anti-Shah forces. These forces included such diverse elements as the Islamic Marxist Mujahideen-e-Khalq, the secular Fedayin-e-Khalq, the intellectuals, the merchant class, the urban poor, the young students, and the Shia clergy. The common denominator among all anti-Shah forces was their real or apparent Shiaism. Thus, they came to follow the clergy, which was led by Ayotollah Ruhollah Khomeini. Khomeini had lived in exile since 1964, first in neighboring Iraq and later (from October 1978) in Paris, guiding the revolutionary forces from overseas. The Shah left Iran on "vacation" on January 16, 1979; two weeks later, on February 1, 1979, Khomeini returned to Tehran. The Bakhtiar government, appointed by the Shah during his last days, was replaced by a new government led by Mehdi Bazargan. By late April, the Islamic revolution had consolidated its powers, Iran had adopted a new constitution and Khomeini had established his Islamic *Vilayat-e-Faqeeh.*

Khomeini labeled the revolution an "Islamic" revolution, and not an "Iranian" revolution, or a "Shia" revolution. This label contributed to the acceptance of the revolution by Muslims around the world, including Muslims in Pakistan. The Shias of Pakistan (and India) have always looked to Iran for cultural (and quite often for spiritual) leadership and guidance. Like the rest of the Muslims of Pakistan, the Shias were favorably impressed by the revolution in Iran.

But a proper understanding of the impact of the Iranian Islamic revolution on the politicization of the Shias and the operation of the TNFJ in Pakistan demands that we understand two factors. First, like its predecessor Shia organizations in the Subcontinent, the TNFJ in 1980 was apolitical in nature; its plans and demands concerned mostly Shia religious issues. Its leader, Mufti Jafar Husain belonged to the old, traditional school of Shia scholars: strongly religious and equally strongly apolitical. He remained the leader of the TNFJ until his death in August 1983. Second, the Shia mosques, *madaris* (schools attached to mosques), and more important the Shia *majalis* (Moharram lecture-mourning sessions) were dominated by *ulema* of the non-revolutionary, apolitical school of thought. These *ulema* included Mufti Jafar Husain. It may be fair to say that these *ulema* welcomed the revolution in Iran because it replaced an autocratic, secular, anti-*ulema,* monarchy by a government run by the *ulema.* It will be unfair, however, to say that they were influenced by the revolution in the contents of their sermons or their leadership style. They (including Mufti Jafar Husain) remained attached to the old school of thought.

Election and Policies of Allama Arif Husain al-Husaini

After Mufti Jafar Husain's death on August 29, 1983,[25] the TNFJ leadership assembled in Bhakkar in February 1984 and elected as its leader Allama Arif Husain al-Husaini, a young, relatively unknown cleric, a graduate of Shia seminaries in Iran and Iraq, and a disciple of Khomeini.

Allama al-Husaini brought his political as well as religious views to the TNFJ. He was a true follower of the Khomeini school: there is no separation between church and state in Islam; and Islam demands the establishment of a just Islamic order throughout the world, especially in a Muslim country like Pakistan. Such a just Islamic order would not be too unlike the *Vilayat-e-Faqeeh* being implemented in Iran. Al-Husaini was a leader full of zeal and fervor, dedicated to the cause he perceived as the responsibility of the TNFJ. He transformed the TNFJ from a purely religious organization, standing for the security and protection of the rights of the Shias, into an organization demanding the establishment of a pure Islamic social and political order in Pakistan. The new TNFJ was not "sectarian" anymore. It now exhorted the Shias in Pakistan to strive for, to work toward, *Ittahad-bain-al-Muslimeen* (unity among all Muslims). The Shias were being urged to emphasize the commonalities and not the dissimilarities with the other *mazahib* of Islam.

The TNFJ adopted a *manshoor* (constitution) and presented it at the Quran and Sunnat Conference in Lahore on July 6, 1987. The 80-page document, titled *Sabeelena*[26] (Our Way) outlines the proposed line of action recommended by the TNFJ for the establishment of a just Islamic order in Pakistan.

The first section (Introduction) is devoted to stating the universally accepted Muslim belief that as representative of God on this earth, man must act according to His dictates. And that, throughout human history, God has sent a series of prophets to guide mankind to the straight path, but man has persistently strayed away from this straight path; unjust people, unjust nations, have brought innocent people under their control.

The second section (Pakistan on the Path of *Inhiraf* [deviation]) outlines the TNFJ's views about the creation of Pakistan (to be an Islamic state) and how it has strayed away from that path. In so doing, it argues, Pakistan has created problems like the Kashmir issue, political instability, alliances with the superpowers, poverty, an inappropriate educational system, and injustice.

The third section proposes an outline of a total system for Pakistan. It has sub-sections on the executive structure, the legislature, the judiciary, economics, foreign policy, education, *jihad*, fundamental rights, cultural organization, and miscellaneous items.

The fourth section identifies the TNFJ position on various issues: Kashmir, Indian Muslims, Afghanistan, the Islamic Revolution in Iran, Muslim minorities, the nationalities issue, international organizations, the Palestine issue, Muslim unity, American interventions, and the "current" [Zia] government [in Pakistan]. The document concludes as follows:

> This program for the superiority of the Quran and the Sunnat, the deliverance of those who have nothing, and the security and consolidation of the country has been presented by the Tehrik-e-Nifaz-e-Fiqh-e-Jafaria. But, the spirit behind this program suggests that this is not a program for a particular group or a particular school of jurisprudence.
>
> We present this program to followers of all Islamic schools of jurisprudence in Pakistan, to people of all areas, and all political groups, and all the people of Pakistan.
>
> The source of the principles and objectives presented here is the Quran and the Sunnat, which are immutable [sources]. However, we will welcome all suggestions to improve upon the conditions of the present and the general good of the people.
>
> We invite all the people of Pakistan to join us in this journey to end the injustice and exploitation, deliverance from imperialism, and freedom under Divine laws.

The document is not a Shia, sectarian plan of action. It invites all Muslims in Pakistan to work together for the establishment of an Islamic order in Pakistan and for the establishment of a government based on the Quran and the Sunnah of the Prophet. It clearly states that all references to the Quran and Sunnah will assume interpretation of the Quran and Sunnah as given by the followers of different schools of jurisprudence for members of those different groups.

In an interview given to the weekly *Zanjeer* of Lahore, Allama al-Husaini outlined the objectives of the TNFJ as follows:[27]

> The enforcement of the Islamic system in the country in the proper way;
> Struggle against the Western system and culture, particularly to rid the nation of American control;
> Struggle for the establishment of democracy in the country.

Allama Arif Husain al-Husaini was assassinated on August 5, 1988.[28] Allegations were made that he was killed because he was an outspoken critic of the Zia regime; because he was becoming popular among the Shias; and because he was demanding the recognition of the Shia *fiqh* as the only *fiqh* acceptable to the Shias of Pakistan in the Islamization process.

Policies of Allama Syed Sajid Ali Naqvi and the TNFJ, 1992

Allama al-Husaini was succeeded by the current leader of the TNFJ, Allama Syed Sajid Ali Naqvi. This author interviewed Allama Sajid Naqvi at his residence in Rawalpindi on March 21, 1992.[29] The current policies and demands of the TNFJ as explained by Allama Sajid Naqvi are summarized below.

Raison d'etre. Allama Sajid Naqvi emphasized the fact that the TNFJ had ceased to be a purely religious organization soon after the assumption of leadership by the late al-Husaini, who, according to Allama Sajid Naqvi had asked not only for the protection of the rights of the Shias but for the establishment of a just Islamic order. The TNFJ stands for the creation of a just Islamic order in Pakistan. It seeks to achieve this goal with the cooperation of all Pakistanis, not just the Shias.

Political Alliances. The TNFJ recognizes that it is important for the Shias to have their point of view represented in the Parliament. There may be Shia members of Parliament; but there is nobody who represents the Shia point of view. The TNFJ tried to enter into an alliance with the PPP in the 1988 national election. The alliance did not work and the TNFJ had to contest elections as the TNFJ, which they did not want, because it gave the appearance of a sectarian contest. They joined the PPP alliance in the 1990 election. Currently, the TNFJ is in alliance with the PDA. Allama Sajid Naqvi emphasized that the TNFJ is not and does not want to appear to be a sectarian group.

Impact of the Islamic Revolution of Iran on the TNFJ. Beginning in 1984, with the leadership of Allama al-Husaini, the TNFJ did not want to remain confined to Shia demands in Pakistan but wanted to expand its goals to the establishment of a just Islamic society in Pakistan. This is what the TNFJ stands for today. And, in defining this goal, the TNFJ has been influenced by the Islamic revolution of Iran.

Vilayat-e-Faqeeh and Pakistan. On being asked if the concept of *vilayat-e-faqeeh* was applicable to Pakistan, Allama Sajid Naqvi said that the concept is neither new nor novel. It may be known by different names in different parts of the world. For example, it may be known in Pakistan as *khilafat* or "some people may call it the Islamic order under a parliamentary system" of government. Since the circumstances in

Pakistan are different from the conditions in Iran, the *vilayat-e-faqeeh* may not be the same in the two countries.

On being asked if people of the Hanafi *fiqh* were elected as president, prime minister and legislators, and followed not only the constitutional obligations but also Islamic obligations [as they understood these requirements], would they be establishing a *vilayat-e-faqeeh*, Allama Sajid Naqvi said that these people may be fulfilling the requirements of the *vilayat-e-faqeeh* but may not be designated as *vali-e-faqeeh*.

Unity of Muslims. On being asked to explain *ittehad bain-al-Muslimeen*, Allama Sajid Naqvi said that they (the TNFJ) believe that Muslims of all schools of *fiqh* are one nation and should work together. He said that "the Shias and the Sunnis are two branches of the tree of Islam" and they should not fight with each other; they should respect each other.

Summary of TNFJ Demands. On being asked to summarize the TNFJ demands, Allama Sajid Naqvi said that in the political field they were seeking the following:

> Let us open the doors of *ijtehad* and provide *ijtehad* to fit the needs of current society. We should not depend upon *fatawa* of the past.
>
> Let us establish some laws as general laws that are applicable to all Muslims, because 95 percent of all laws would be common to all schools of jurisprudence. Let us create separate "personal" laws for the remaining five percent of the issues: members of each *fiqh* would be governed by laws according to their own *fiqh* in these matters.

On being asked who would be competent to issues *fatawa* according to *ijtehad* (would elected representatives of the people be so competent?), Allama Sajid Naqvi said that he would agree in principle to give this right to the representatives of the people, provided they are competent to do so. And only those who understand the Quran and Sunnah well enough to interpret it properly, would be competent to issue *fatawa* based on *ijtehad*.

The Split in the TNFJ and the Establishment of the Moosavi Group

The bylaws of the TNFJ state that a vacancy in the position of the leader of the TNFJ (caused by death or resignation of the incumbent) may be filled by election of a new leader by the Central Committee. The Central Committee of the TNFJ did not meet immediately after the death of Mufti Jafar Husain to elect his replacement. As stated earlier, the

Shias held a convention in Bhakkar on February 10, 1984, almost six months after the death of Mufti Jafar Husain and elected Allama Arif Husain al-Husaini as their leader. This election seems to have been accepted by a vast majority of the Shias of Pakistan.

In December 1983, Shia *ulema*, leaders of several Shia organizations, and prominent Shias gathered in Rawalpindi to select a leader to fill the vacancy caused by the death of Mufti Jafar Husain. The literature published by the TNFJ (Moosavi Group - TNFJ (MG)) suggests that several names were proposed but the group did not show unanimous agreement on any person. Eventually, someone suggested the name of Allama Syed Hamid Husain Moosavi, a local Shia *alim*, who was not present at the meeting. It is reported that the people assembled there gave unanimous approval to his being selected as the leader of the TNFJ (MG). Allama Moosavi was approached to accept the leadership role. He is reported to have said that he did not want to accept a national assignment at the request of a regional group, suggesting instead that a national convention be called and that the Rawalpindi group might wish to place his name before the national convention. He would be willing to accept the leadership role if he was elected by the entire convention. He is reported to have said that he would support any other person who may be elected by the national convention.

An All-Pakistan Shia Convention was called by the Rawalpindi group to meet at Deena Asadabad, District Jhelum, Punjab on February 9-10, 1984. The plenary session was preceded by a special session of *ulema*, and Shia leadership from different parts of the country on February 9, 1984. Allama Moosavi's name was suggested by the Rawalpindi delegation and numerous persons in attendance spoke at the meeting to support his election. It is pointed out in the TNFJ (MG) literature that no other name was suggested at the meeting of the leadership nor did any person speak against the election of Allama Moosavi as the leader. The national convention met in plenary session on February 10, 1984 and elected Allama Moosavi by unanimous vote.[30]

Ironically, this is the same date on which the Supreme Council of the TNFJ met in Bhakkar (together with another convention of Shias) and elected Allama Arif Husain al-Husaini as the leader of the TNFJ. Like Allama Arif Husain al-Husaini, Allama Moosavi is from the Northern areas of Pakistan. He is also reported to have studied under, among others, Ayatollah Ruhollah Khomeini. The similarities end there. While Allama al-Husaini was a pro-active, politically oriented leader, who followed the Khomeini line and politicized the Shia masses, Allama Moosavi has restricted the activities of the TNFJ (MG) to religious issues only. The demands of TNFJ (MG) are:[31]

1. The Enforcement of the Jafari *fiqh* for the Shias of Pakistan;
2. The introduction of separate courses in Shia theology for Shia students;

3. The establishment of separate faculties of Shia *fiqh* in all universities of Pakistan and representation in the Islamic Research Institute;
4. The appointment of a Shia judge on the Federal Shariat Court;
5. Adequate representation of Shias in higher level courts;
6. Equal representation of the Shia school of jurisprudence in publicly owned media;
7. Abolition of all unnecessary restrictions (such as a need for license) for *azadari* processions;
8. Establishment of a separate Shia *Auqaf* [Trusts] Board;
9. Reconstruction of mausoleums that have been demolished in the *Janat-ul-Baqee* [a cemetery in Medina, Saudi Arabia];
10. Effective representation of the Shias on the Council of Islamic Ideology; and,
11. Repeal of a recent amendment by the Government of the Punjab to section 30 (3) of the Police Act, 1961, empowering District Magistrates to prohibit the taking out of processions of *azadari*.

On assumption of office as President of the TNFJ (MG) on February 10, 1984, Allama Moosavi delivered an extensive Presidential Address,[32] that exhibited his dedication to purely religious issues. He paid tribute to his predecessors who fought for the recognition of Shia rights. These predecessors included Mufti Jafar Husain, who sought and obtained exemption from payment of *zakat* by the Shias to the Government of Pakistan. Allama Moosavi emphasized the need for organizing the Shias to collect *zakat* and disburse it according to the Shia *fiqh*. This, he said, is designed to bring about an equitable distribution of wealth. He said that he recognizes that the Shias have three remarkable institutions that provide them with better opportunities for organization and meeting contemporary challenges: *azadari*, *taqleed* and *ijtehad*. However, he regretted the absence of a central organization to channel all Shia resources and demands. He promised to do his best to help establish such a central organization.

He offered to help the Government of Pakistan in its efforts at Islamization. The following portion of his Presidential Address that deals with Islamization and the TNFJ (MG) position deserves to be quoted:

> The most important question is: When talking about Islamization in Pakistan, which interpretation of Islam does the Government mean? There are only two interpretations of Islam possible, as far as Pakistan is concerned: one is the Hanafi interpretation of Islam; the other is . . . the Shia interpretation. If Islam is enforced in Pakistan it will have to be enforced according to these two interpretations. But, this is strange that all steps taken by the Government of Pakistan about Islamization are not congruent with both of these *taqleedi* interpretations; rather, the spirit of these steps is non-*taqleedi*. It would be up to our Sunni brethren to ask the Government as to why the non-*taqleedi* way has been adopted instead of the Hanafi jurisprudence [for the Hanafis]. We wish to point out that

the Shia jurisprudence has been totally ignored in all steps taken by the Government of Pakistan in the name of enforcement of Islam. We also demand that the Government should rectify past errors and give the *fiqh Jafari* its rightful place in the government and politics of Pakistan.
Before proceeding any further, I wish to explain the term "rightful place." Whenever we talk about the inclusion of *fiqh-e-Ahl-e-Bait* [the *fiqh* of the Prophet's Household, that is the *fiqh Jafari*] it is always correlated to the percentage of Shias in the population of Pakistan, and it is said that the Shia demands cannot be granted since the Shias are not in a majority. I want to make it clear that this way of thinking is absolutely wrong and unprincipled. The percentages should be referred to only when the subject of discussion is a minority community of Pakistan. Please remember that the Shias are not one of the minority communities of Pakistan, nor is any of their demands a demand for the rights of a minority. When the Shias place a demand [before the Government], it is a demand made by equal partners and first class citizens for the removal of difficulties in the exercise of their responsibilities. Our demand for the enforcement of *fiqh Jafaria* is not a demand for a certain percentage in the national affairs; it is a demand for the total enforcement of the *fiqh Jafaria*. Please note that this is not a demand for distribution of certain offices or seats in an assembly; nor is it the issue of proper representation of different provinces. Our demand is an ideological demand; and an ideology is always a unit by itself. It is not possible to have a certain part of the national political system to be Hanafi and certain other parts to be Shia. On the contrary, an Islamic system in Pakistan can only be one in which the *fiqh-e-Ahl-e-Bait* [Shia] and the *fiqh* Hanafi are enforced simultaneously and fully. In more clear words, we are saying that any law enforced in Pakistan in the name of Islam will have to be according to the Hanafi *fiqh* for the Hanafis and according to the Shia *fiqh* for the Shias.

After this explanation of our position, it should be clear that when we talk about representation of Shias on the Council of Islamic Ideology, we do not suggest that the number of Shia members of the Council be increased from one to two or three. Rather, we demand that the current method of decision-making by majority vote by the Council should be replaced by a system that whenever a decision is made according to some other school of jurisprudence, the Shia interpretation should constitute an integral part of the decision-making process.

The government has taken numerous steps in the name of Islam. What is the degree of representation given to the Shia school of thought? An Islamic university has been established in the country, where courses of study include three to four other schools of jurisprudence [*fiqh*] that are not even followed in Pakistan. But, the *fiqh-e-Ahl-e-Bait* is not listed even as an item.

The government has opened an Institute for Islamic Research. The Institute brings out a monthly journal and has published more than sixty books. Not even one page of these publications is devoted to the Shia school of jurisprudence.

The government has established the Federal Shariat Court to Islamize the laws. The court has representation not only of religious schools of thought but also political points of view. However, there is nobody to represent the Shia point of view.

Special arrangements have been made to train persons with backgrounds in law for appointment to the Qazi courts. But, it was not deemed necessary to keep these prospective Qazis informed about the Shia laws.

Special educational courses are organized to introduce current members of the judiciary to Islamic laws. You may look at the syllabi for these courses; you will find no mention of the Shia laws in these syllabi.

Recently, one year was added to the course of studies for the law degree. The syllabus prepared by the Islamic University, Islamabad does not include any reference to *fiqh-e-Ahl-e-Bait*.

Azadari of Imam Husain is an important part of our worship [*ibadat*]; it is a part of our belief [*iman*]; it is our identification. It is a non-violent protest against untruth; it is a peaceful expression of dislike for injustice and love for the wronged. *Even this innocent activity of ours is subjected to licenses and permits.*

This author interviewed Allama Hamid Husain Moosavi at his residence in Rawalpindi on March 21, 1992. It was a very cordial interview. The staff of the TNFJ (MG) recorded the interview on video tape. Allama Moosavi reiterated the stand of his group as primarily a religious organization, dedicated to the preservation and protection of the rights of the Shias *as* Shias in Pakistan. He read from a published brochure the demands of his group that have been listed above.[33]

Notes

1. There are five major schools of jurisprudence (*mazahib*) in Islam: Jafari; Hanafi; Maliki; Shafaee; and Hambali. Each school is named after one of the five great Imams (jurisconsults) who have given their interpretations to the Quran and the Sunnah of Prophet Muhammad. The first of these (Imam Jafar As-Sadiq) is the founder of the Shia *mazhab*; the other four are the great jurists of the Sunni *mazahib*: Imam Noman Bin Thabit Abu Hanifa; Imam Malik Bin Anas Bin Malik; Imam Muhammad Bin Idrees Shafaee; Imam Ahmed Bin Hambal.

The term *mazhab* (pl. *mazahib*) is used here to mean school of jurisprudence. The transliteration of Arabic words in the Roman alphabet in this paper follows the pronunciation of the Arabic words used in the South Asian Subcontinent. The term Shia refers to the second largest *mazhab* in the Muslim world. The Shias may be sub-divided into several sub-groups: Athna-Ashari (the twelvers), Ismailis (followers of the Agha Khan), Bohras (followers of Syedna Burhanuddin), Zaidis, and others. The largest Shia group in the world is the Athna-Ashari. Although there are quite a few Ismailis and Bohras in Pakistan, most of the Shias in Pakistan belong to the Athna-Ashari group and are generally referred to as Shias or sometimes as followers of the Jafari *fiqh*. It must be emphasized that the followers of each of the five *mazahib* treat the followers of the other *mazahib* as Muslims in all respects.

2. See Saleem Qureshi, "The Politics of the Shia Minority in Pakistan," in Dhirendra Vajpeyi, and Yogendra K. Malik, eds. *Religious and Ethnic Minority Politics in South Asia* (Riverdale, Md: Riverdale Press, 1989). Also see, Munir Ahmed, "The Shi'is of Pakistan," in Martin Kramer, ed., *Shi'ism, Resistance, and Revolution* (Boulder, Colo.: Westview Press, 1987).

3. See, among others, Karl Henerich Gobel, "Imamate," and Allamah Sayyid Muhammad Husayn Tabatabai, Jassim M. Hussain, and Abdulaziz A. Sachedina, "Messianism and the Mahdi," in Seyyed Hossein Nasr, Hamid Dabashi, and Seyyed Vali Reza Nasr, eds., *Expectation of the Millennium* (Albany: State University of New York Press, 1989).

4. See Ayotollah Shaykh Muhammad Husain, *Aal-e-Kashiful-Ghita, Aslush-Shiate-wa-Usooleha* (in Arabic) [The Fundamentals and the Principles of the Shias]; translation in Urdu by Syed Ibn-e-Hasan Najafi, *Asl-o-Usool-e-Shia* (Karachi: Idara-e-Tammadun-e-Islam, n.d.) This publication is hereinafter referred to as Najafi, *Asl-o-Usool-e-Shia*.

5. See Muhammad Husain Behishti and Javaid Bahonar, *Philosophy of Islam* (Salt Lake City: Islamic Publications, n.d.), pp. 181-211.

6. Najafi, 159; and 186 ff.

7. Ibne Hasan Najafi, *Masala-e-Khums* (in Urdu) [The Issue of *Khums*] (Karachi: Idara-e-Tammadun-e-Islam n.d.), p. 249. Also see *Tawzeeh-al-Masail* (in Urdu) (Lahore: Iftikhar Book Depot, n.d.), pp. 242-269. The title of this book may be translated as "The Explanation of Problems;" it is a compendium of *fatawa* regarding religious issues according to the *fatawa* of Ayatollah Abulqasim al-Khoiee. It has been translated into Urdu by Syed Karamat Ali Najafi and is hereinafter referred to as *Tawzeeh-al-Masail*.

This section of the chapter was read by the author to Allama Syed Muhammad Razi, the most prominent *mujtahid* (scholar) of Shias in Pakistan, on March 15, 1992 at his residence in Karachi, Pakistan. He suggested some minor modifications and approved of the contents of the section in the revised form as being in consonance with Shia doctrine and *fiqh*. The author alone is responsible for the contents of the section; he is grateful to Allama Syed Muhammad Razi for his time and valuable suggestions.

8. For detailed description, see Muhammad Wasi Khan, *Tashkeel-e-Pakistan Men Shian-e-Ali Ka Kirdar* (in Urdu) [The Role of the Shias of Ali in the Creation of Pakistan] Volume I, (Karachi: Idara-e-Mehfil-e-Haidari, 1982); and *Tashkeel-e-Pakistan Men Shian-e-Ali Ka Kirdar* (in Urdu) [The Role of the Shias of Ali in the Creation of Pakistan], Volume II: (Karachi: Idara-e-Mehfil-e-Haidari, 1983). These works are hereinafter referred to as Wasi Khan, Vol. I, or Wasi Khan, Vol. II. Also see Qureshi, pp. 113-115.

9. See Wasi Khan, Vol. II.

10. Asaf A. A. Fyzee, *Outlines of Muhammadan Law* (London: Oxford University Press, 1964), pp. 47-48.

11. Rashida Patel, *Islamisation of Laws in Pakistan* (Karachi: Faiza Publishers, 1986), p. 36.

12. Mr. Jinnah's address to the Constituent Assembly of Pakistan on August 11, 1947, quoted among other works in Afzal Iqbal, *Islamization of Pakistan* (Lahore: Vanguard Books, 1986), pp. 34-37; 106-107.

13. These ordinances were: Prohibition (Enforcement of Hadd) Order 1979; The Offense of Zina (Enforcement of Hadd) Ordinance 1979; The Offences Against Property (Enforcement of Hadd) Ordinance 1979; and The Offence of Qazf (Enforcement of Hadd Ordinance) 1979. These ordinances are collectively known as the *hudood* ordinances or the *hudood* laws.

14. See Afak Haydar, "From The Anglo-Muhammadan Law to the Shariah: The Pakistan Experiment, *Journal of South Asian and Middle Eastern Studies* Vol. X, no. 4, (Summer 1987), pp. 33-50.

15. Syed Shahaid Husain Naqvi, "*Tehrik-e-Nifaz-e-fiqh-e-Jafari: Mazi, Haal, Aur Mustaqbil Key Aaieeney Men*" (in Urdu) [Tehrik-e-Nifaz-e-fiqh-e-Jafari: In the Mirror of the Past, the Present, and the Future], *Nida-e-Islam*, Vol. 4, no. 1, (January 1-7, 1992), pp. 2-3.

16. *Ibid.*, p. 2.

17. *Ibid.*, p. 2; and *Sabeelena: Azadi Aur Nejat Key Safar Men Hamara Rasta* (in Urdu) [Our Path in Our Journey for Independence and Salvation], (Karachi: Tehrik-e-Nifaz-e-fiqh-e-Jafaria, 1987). The Urdu text has been translated by this author. This document will hereinafter be cited as *Sabeelena*.

18. For details see Patel, pp. 62-77. *Zakat* is the 2.5 percent "charity tax" mandated by Islam on certain savings; ushr is the 10 percent tax on agricultural produce.

19. Najafi, *Asl-o-Usool-e-Shia*, pp. 243-44.

20. Najafi, *Asl-o-Usool-e-Shia*, pp. 243-44.

21. Government of Pakistan Press Note, photocopy reproduced in"*Ham Keya Chahtey Hain*" (in Urdu) [What Do We Want?] in *Tehrik-e-Nifaz-fiqh-e-Jafaria Ka Tareekhi Tajzia* (in Urdu) [An Historical Analysis of the Tehrik-e-Nifaz-e-fiqh-e-Jafaria) (Karachi: *Fiqh-e-Jafaria* Rabita Committee n.d.), p. 16.

22. The Zakat and Ushr (Third Amendment) Ordinance, 1983: Ordinance No. XXVI of 1983, published in *The Gazette of Pakistan* (October 29, 1983). For details also see Iqbal, p. 108; Patel, pp. 63-64.

23. During personal interviews with several Shias who are active in the TNFJ and its affiliated student organization, the Imamia Student Organization (ISO), at least two persons gave this author to understand that there were some Shia flag officers close to Zia who exerted influence on (demanded of) Zia to accept the Shia demands. One of these persons is a physician, Dr Muhammad Ali, whom this author met in Lahore on March 18, 1992. A manuscript transcript of the notes of the interview is on file in this author's library.

24. See sample of the proforma prepared by the Fiqh-e-Jafaria Rabita Committee and published as a printed leaflet, showing the form to be used under provisions of the Zakat and Ushr (Third Amendment) Ordinance, 1983 and Rule 20 of the Zakat (Deduction and Refund) Rules, 1981.

25. Ghazanfar Kazmi, *Marhoom Mufti Jafar Husain: 1914-1983: Ayyam-e-Rafta Par Mukhtasar Nazar* (in Urdu) [the Late Mufti Jafar Husain: 1914-1983: A Review of the Days Bygone]. (Lahore: Maktabat-al-Reza, 1983), p. 58.

26. *Sabeelena.*

27. Interview of Allama Arif Husain al-Husaini given to Akram Shaikh, published in fortnightly *Zanjeer* (October 1987), pp. 18-27. Selected portions of the interview are reproduced in *The Weekly Razakar* (August 16-24, 1988), p. 219.

28. Syed Muhammad Raza Jafari, "*Mulki Aur Bain-ul-Aqwami Umoor Per Tehrik-e-Nifaz-e-fiqh Jafaria Ka Mawkaf*" (in Urdu) [The Stand of the TNFJ on Domestic and International Issues], *Haftroza Nida-e-Islam*, (September 8-15, 1991), p. 2.

29. The interview was conducted in Urdu. A translation of the transcript is on file with this author. A copy will be placed in the Dean B. Ellis Library of Arkansas State University.

30. Among numerous TNFJ (Moosavi Group) publications, see Allama Syed Raza Husain Shah (Office Secretary, TNFJ (Moosavi Group) Interview With Anjuman-e-Muhibban-Ahle- Bait (in Urdu), dated October 2, 1987, published in the form of a pamphlet by Shaikh Muhammad Akbar, 128 Shipley Fields Road, Shipley, Bradford 18, England.

31. *Shia Mutalibat* [Shia Demands], (Rawalpindi: The Mukhtar Force, n. d.)

32. Hojjat-ul-Islam Syed Hamid Ali Shah al-Moosavi al-Najafi, *Khutba-e-Sadarat* (in Urdu) [Presidential Address] delivered at the Kul-Pakistan [All-Pakistan] Shia Convention, Asadabad, Mangla Road, Jhelum 10 February, 1984 (Rawalpindi: Tehrik-e-Nifaz-e-fiqh-e-Jafaria, Pakistan, 1984).

33. The interview was conducted in Urdu. A translation of the transcript is on file with this author. A copy will be placed in the Dean B. Ellis Library of Arkansas State University.

6

Healing Power and Medical Practice in Pakistani Society

Anne T. Sweetser

Investment in medical institutions is one way that a government in Pakistan can -- and is perceived to -- support or solicit support from constituencies within the country. In the early 1980s, comments concerning the politically motivated opening of numbers of medical schools under the administration of Zulfikar Ali Bhutto were common. Occasionally one heard that these were in excess of national requirements and had been planned and located to appease or appeal to local political figures. Other times the disparaging tone with which the comment was made suggested a similar evaluation.

Under the succeeding administration of Zia ul-Haq, support for *Yunani-* or *Islami-Tibb* (Galenic medicine resystematized and developed by Muslim scholar-physicians) seems to have taken the place of support for biomedicine as a political tool. President Zia convened a conference on *Tibb* on December 21, 1978, and thereafter directed the federal and provincial governments to establish *Tibbi* hospitals and dispensaries.[1] This meeting occurred less than eighteen months after Zia assumed leadership of the country and roughly coincided with his announcement that the government would Islamicize the nation, including the judicial and legal systems. In the decade ending in early 1992 the number of *Tibbia* colleges nearly doubled from ten to eighteen.[2] This suggests that medical policy can be manipulated for ideological as well as strictly political purposes in Pakistan and raises many questions about the interaction among these social domains.

The key to understanding the interrelationships among medicine, politics, and religion in Pakistan, and thus the scope and effectiveness of health policy, lies in appreciation of the fact that healing power, much like political power, is conceptualized in religio-moral terms by the overwhelming majority of Pakistani citizens (excepting some of the most Westernized, biomedically oriented elite). While many forms of medical theory and practice co-exist in the plural medical system, they are unified by this fundamental construction of healing power that conduces to trusting relationships between practitioners and patients and facilitates efficacious treatment. Similarly, the capacity for healing and the opportunity to be in a position to exercise political power, mediated by such factors as genealogy, piety, generosity, and prior success, are both ultimately understood to be refracted from a single religious source. It is these symbolic linkages among supposedly distinct domains of social action that permit politicians to mobilize widespread support through the manipulation of fiscal allocations for health care and training. In succeeding pages the structure of Pakistan's plural medical system; popular constructions of healing, empowerment and efficacy; and the relationship between healing and political power are examined in depth to clarify this argument.

The Plural Medical System of Pakistan

The visitor who associates primarily with English-speaking Pakistanis in major urban areas hears about some very sophisticated hospitals of biomedicine when inquiring about medicine in Pakistan. The institutions which Pakistanis praise to outsiders, however, represent only a small part of a complex system of health care based on several distinct theories of health and illness that are employed by divergent types of practitioners who work in widely varying settings and recommend differing forms of treatment. In short, Pakistan has a pluralistic medical culture.

If pressed by someone who is aware of this pluralism, the typical elite, urban Pakistani will acknowledge that the non-biomedical forms of therapy still persist in some remote corners of the country inhabited by very poor, uneducated people. He or she will most likely explain that when literacy reaches all citizens these remnants of other systems will disappear as they have in the "advanced" parts of the country. As an anthropologist who has associated with lower ranked and poorly educated urban residents as well as members of the elite and conducted extensive research among some of the poorest and most remote of rural Pakistanis, my understanding of healing in Pakistan contrasts sharply with that perceived by many well-educated, outward-looking, upper-class citizens. I observe great vitality in the traditional forms of belief and practice related to illness and healing. This vitality has deep ideological and social structural roots, for it depends upon a pervasive, religiously constructed and experientially grounded understanding of healing power. Further, directly or indirectly, this perspective is shared by the overwhelming majority of Pakistanis. Ultimately even the practice of biomedicine, thought by many of the elite to be separate from its traditional social context, is in fact considerably influenced by indigenous notions of health and illness and the social and religious context in which these exist.

In addition to biomedicine, the plural medical system of Pakistan includes *Yunani-* or *Islami-Tibb*, developed from Galenic humoral medicine (of ancient Greece); and several forms of religious healing. *Ayurveda* (ancient Sanskrit medicine) and homeopathy are both practiced on a smaller scale. When asked to compare these systems people generally refer to the power of one in contrast with that of another. Because they employ a science-based notion of power in an essentially evolutionary idiom, secularized elites tend to dismiss non-biomedical healing as powerless, a remnant of pre-literate society, and hence, as described, the vast majority of Pakistan's citizens. Across society more broadly, it is common for people to think of homeopathy as a second-rate (i.e., less powerful) Western medicine for those too poor to afford biomedical treatment.

From a different perspective, others point out that *Yunani Tibb* is a practice based on *hamdardi* or human sympathy rather than on greed for financial gain and social position, referring to a stereotype about the practice of biomedicine (and the Westernized elite with which it is associated). They note that this form of practice addresses the entire person and his or her situation holistically, not just the physical problem that brings the patient to the clinic, and reiterate that a patient gets individualized attention and treatment. Stress is placed on a moral rather than on a scientifically conceived notion of power, and the integrity and value of the less privileged members of society is simultaneously affirmed. *Ayurveda* is much less well known than *Yunani Tibb* but popularly recognized as a similarly ancient therapy associated with a "different," (i.e., Hindu) religious tradition. Both are administered by the same sub-unit of the Ministry of Health as established under the Unani, Ayurvedic and Homeopathic Practitioners Act, 1965.

Religious Healing

The conception of moral power involved in validation of the legitimacy of *Yunani Tibb* by many Pakistanis is, as mentioned above, the key to understanding their view of healing power most broadly. All Muslims would agree that absolutely no medicine or other form of therapy is capable of saving a person whose divinely determined time of death has arrived. To doubt this would indicate probable insanity, and to seriously argue against this position would invite accusations of heresy and thus, in certain contexts, possibly even threats against one's life. It is this belief that constitutes the predominant frame for thought concerning health and illness and the outcome of sickness or treatment for the great majority of Pakistanis. It is the basis for a variety of forms of religious healing, Prophetic to popular.

Prophetic Medicine. Within religious healing, as in medicine generally, a number of sub-categories are found, and the relative rank or power and acceptability of these within Islam is the subject of considerable debate. Prophetic medicine is based upon pronouncements made and deeds undertaken by the Prophet and recorded in the *hadiths*.[3] Among the principles expounded is the notion that good health is the greatest of treasures, and the apparently contradictory idea that illness is a form of blessing, for a person who is not cleansed of sins through suffering during life will experience great pain in the process of dying or in the grave. Cleanliness, from performing ablutions before prayer and protecting the purity of water and food, to proper management of urine, feces, and all manifestations of sexuality is emphasized. Nursing the sick is stipulated to be the religious duty of each individual or entire communities, depending upon the circumstances. Quarantine in the event of epidemics is also required.

The Prophet consumed honey regularly and had blood drawn periodically to maintain internal balance and purity and thus his own good health. He recommended these plus moderation in consumption of food and level of activity for others as well. He prescribed "sea of costus" and "black nigella" (black cumin?)[4] for a variety of illnesses for which others sought his advice. He also cured by holding his outstretched hand over a suffering patient and reciting the following blessing: "O Lord of men! remove this trouble; and heal, O Thou Healer. There is no cure except Thy cure, a cure which does not leave any ailment."[5]

Advocates of Prophetic medicine dispute among themselves the degree to which an individual should adhere to the principle of *tawakkul* or strict and sole reliance upon prayer. Some condemn even the use of honey and venesection as excessively material actions that connote imperfect faith. Others propound the acceptability of only those herbs suggested by the Prophet to help others. The most liberal argue that since the Prophet employed the herbs of which he had knowledge to cure others, and since all medicinal substances were created by Allah even if they were only recently discovered, employment of all material medicines whatsoever is acceptable within Islam.

Popular Religious Healing. Popular religious healing depends upon a view of the cosmos which is rooted in the description of Creation portrayed in the Quran. In this hierarchized domain, angels were first created by Allah from pure light to be his associates and to worship Him. Though lofty, they were unable to understand Allah's purpose when He decided to create other beings and thus revealed the limits of their wisdom as compared with His. Next to be fashioned, from smokeless fire, were the jinns. Clearly subordinate to Allah, they were given the opportunity or the responsibility of choosing between good and evil, but still were very powerful. In practice, among widely divergent communities throughout Islamdom, a variety of pre-Islamic beings are typically placed in this category and ranked among themselves. Mankind is the third, lowest, and least powerful of Allah's creations. Made from quintessentially mundane clay, we are burdened not only with choosing between good and evil, but with such limited vision that only the most highly blessed, the initiated among us, and the controversial "friends of god" or saints, can begin, generally through intermediaries, to peer across the barrier that delimits the world we can see from the rest of Creation.

Our blindness leads us into considerable folly: we may step on jinns or cut their children with our pruning tools; we may break their dishes or stumble through their homes; or we may dislodge rocks from hillsides that fall on their drying clothes or even urinate on their possessions. An angel sitting on our right shoulder may distract us momentarily and prevent us from committing such outrages, but otherwise they don't intervene.

In response, the jinns are attributed with motivations that reflect human society. Already capricious, those angered by human stupidity frequently take revenge by causing a variety of health problems. Less commonly, one or more jinns may perturb a human because of love for the person or one of their attributes, such as their voice. Sometimes, in addition, fear motivates jinns to act against humans. Uncontrolled emotion in one form or another is shown, through its reflection in the projected world of creation beyond our ken, to be a cause of deleterious consequences. Faith in Allah is the source of surety and emotional stability, and thus its lack may be seen as a sign of insanity.

Perturbation from or tenacious possession by jinns is commonly thought to be a cause of many chronic and acute illnesses. Epileptic or other seizures are almost assuredly thought to be caused by possession by jinns. Sudden death of infants and such chronic symptoms as weak eyesight, joint pain, and lameness are frequently attributed to them also.

Other non-human sources for physical and social problems include evil eye and evil magic. Evil eye, or *bad nazar*, is generally agreed to be a force that acts independently of the will of the perpetrator in response to the person's envy or praise of another. Unkempt children and black flags on trucks are typical deterrents. The often mild problems that result may be treated by fumigation with smoke of juniper and other high-altitude plants mixed together, at least in the northern mountains. Evil magic, *jadu*, is so reprehensible that people are very reluctant to speak about it at all. It is associated with filth and perceived to be the inverse of religion. Grave illnesses and serious or fatal accidents may be attributed to *jadu* that has been perpetrated by some evil person at the behest of one's enemies. Most agree that it can only be identified by a *mullah* or other religious leader, and can only be counteracted by such a religious person or by one who can perform counter magic, possibly only by the person who initiated the evil activity.

Presuming that people make logical choices in seeking treatment based on their assessment of the nature and/or probable cause of a health (or psycho-social) problem, it is easy to imagine that there is a considerable demand for measures designed to counteract troubles caused by beings and forces of the unseen domain. Popular religious treatments, and also preventive measures, generally involve channeling of the power of a verse or chapter, *sura*, of the Quran to a person. Techniques for doing this range, like all forms of medicine, from that considered relatively pure to that requiring considerable involvement with mundane materiality. First is recitation of the relevant passage followed by exhalation of the blessing onto the victim. Very commonly, amulets, or *tawiz*, containing coded representations (generally in the form of magic squares)[6] of the appropriate passage are prepared and worn, usually on a special string around the neck, for either protection or healing. Some religious conservatives condemn the use of amulets because they entail the use of paper and ink and thus constitute a form of denigration of the pure meaning behind the words of the Quran akin to idolatry. Less frequently various methods for the ingestion of blessing represented this way are encountered. The magic squares may be written on a plate in saffron ink, washed off with water and then drunk; or a *tawiz* may be burned, the ashes mixed with water, and then also drunk by the victim of some misfortune.

Exorcism of some jinns who are possessing a person often requires the concerted effort of a highly initiated healer. An *amal*, or practitioner of *amaliyyat*, the active as opposed to the contemplative aspect of religion, may refer to someone who has repeated a specific passage of the Quran one thousand times in order to obtain the power to write effective *tawiz*. More appropriately, it refers to an individual who has successfully undertaken a forty-day meditation upon a *sura* or passage of the Quran, usually accompanied by fasting from sunup to sundown, while remaining in a pure state throughout. Upon successful completion of the meditation, the *amal* generally has obtained power over one or more jinns upon whom he can call for assistance in explaining some phenomenon involving activities in the hidden domain beyond the limits of human sight. To resolve an intractable health situation -- often one involving unexpressed or normally illegitimate emotional conflict -- the assistance of a person who can facilitate articulation of distress through manipulation of the idiom of jinns and their possession of the victim is generally sought and may be very effective.

The daily press regularly contains numerous examples of popular religious healing and related advice. The authors of spiritual advice columns respond to questions from readers in the manner of Ann Landers. Diagnoses of health problems may be made by the writer, purportedly a qualified religious functionary, by opening the Quran randomly and noting the first letter (or the first letter of the first word) on which his eye comes to rest. Complicated remedies are commonly preferred, ranging from repeated recitation of specific *suras* or verses of the Quran each day for weeks to come in apparent cases of anxiety or depression, to nightly rituals of candle lighting and mirrors covered with blue green or yellow paper seemingly intended for adolescent boys distressed by their uncontrollable, emerging sexuality.

Undoubtedly, exploitation of the gullible and generally hopeless by charlatans who present themselves as adepts, and who demand high payments for miraculous cures, occurs regularly in Pakistan. But this is not sufficient reason to dismiss all popular religious healing practice as "superstitious," "pre-literate," or somehow temperamentally appropriate for women (whose lack of mobility in this *purdah* society restricts their access to many other forms of care) as do many Pakistanis. In relaxed, relatively private conversations very highly educated and urbane Pakistanis have shared stories of surprising cures that they attribute to occult power enabled by *tawiz*, visits to shrines (now condemned by ideologues), or other essentially religious means. Also, only the most radical young man would dare contemplate the non-reality of jinns, for they are amply described in the Quran, the uncreated word of Allah as revealed to Muhammad through the Angel Gabriel.

If a discussion concerns religion, examples of healing (humans, animals, and even automobiles that stall on the highway at night) and the religio-moral power of passages of the Quran upon which it is predicated may be readily elicited from the vast majority of Pakistani men and women of all educational and socio-economic levels. Those more highly trained at conservative religious institutions will inveigh against the legitimacy of saints, and possibly complain about the use of Quranic blessing in material form, as in amulets, rather than simply prayer or blessing. When the conversation concerns medicine, however, the speech tone of the self-consciously Westernized Pakistani elite hardens. The surety of scientific rationality combined with national pride and class identification overwhelm the inner understanding of the importance of religious belief in medicine.

Yunani Tibb

Yunani- or *Islami-Tibb*, based on ancient Greek formulations, primarily of Galen, is generally categorized as yet another form of religious medicine. Soon after the inception and spread of Islam, the medical system was translated into Arabic by scholars at the *Bayt-al-Hikmat* in Baghdad and subsequently resystematized and developed by a number of prominent Muslim scholar-physicians, notably Ibn Sina (Avicenna). Initially the entire medical system was suspected of contradicting Islam, for life is said to depend upon a vital force (*rooh*) which operates independently of the physical body. Ironically, it is precisely this feature that is stressed by those who now promote the medical system in Pakistan: that something other than the strictly material ground of life as postulated by rational science is recognized as the basis for life.

Based on an analogy with the separation of blood into four types of substances when heated in a crucible, four humors (blood, phlegm, yellow bile, and black bile) consisting of four primary substances (earth, air, fire, and water) and characterized by four basic qualities (hot, cold, wet, and dry) are said to constitute the body. In physiology the pattern of quadraplicities persists: food is heated (or matured or cocted) four times, in the stomach, liver, veins, and tissues, and utilized as directed by four essential organs in accordance with primary and secondary faculties, including nutrition (absorption, assimilation, and integration), growth, reproduction, and elimination that are in turn associated with four types of fibers that constitute the tissues.

Each individual has a unique point of balance among the qualities and the humors they represent, and thus a temperament, or *mizaj*, that is relatively sanguine (relating to blood, hot, and wet), phlegmatic (pertaining to phlegm, cold, and wet), choleric (relating to bile, hot, and dry) or melancholic (pertaining to black bile, cold, and dry). This notion has been extended by advocates of *Yunani Tibb* to apply to the nation as a whole as in the argument that it is an indigenous, Islamic medicine and therefore the best "suited to the temperament [sic] of people of"[7] Pakistan. Similar arguments have been proferred both following the establishment of the nation and during the period of Islamization under Zia when this research was conducted.

Yunani Tibb has long been practiced in Pakistan by older, respected men in their communities through the countryside. Less aggressive in professionalizing than *Ayurveda* in colonial India,[8] two distinct schools of practice, based in Lucknow and Delhi, nonetheless emerged before the creation of Pakistan. The conservative Lucknow practitioners advocated strict adherence to traditional herbal prescriptions and other remedies while those based in Delhi and their followers advocated use of biomedicines to supplement the traditional medications. Discussion of the best of these strategies continues today, crosscutting competing groups of indigenous Pakistani *hakims* and those who migrated from India in 1947.

Unlike the clinics and hospitals of biomedical practitioners, a typical *hakim*'s office has a warm, even homey atmosphere. The crowded clinic of a widely famed *hakim* in Lahore is only roughly segregated between men and women. Examination of patients is carried on in front of others, with some curtaining and deflection of attention when women consult with the *hakim*. The *hakim* does not charge for his services, though he does (possibly on a sliding scale based on judgment of a patient's ability to pay), charge for prescriptions that are filled in his pharmacy. In this manner the perception that his practice is morally grounded in a religiously conceived desire to help others is maintained. Additional qualities of the *hakim* and his practice that may be noted by his patients or admirers include his reputation for piety, and the fact that he may have descended from a long line of respected healers. He may be carrying on a practice in the same building or neighborhood as his father and grandfather and thus be thought to have the best possible knowledge of the areal conditions and lifestyle of its residents (which is valued as an element for diagnosis).

Biomedicine

There are many Pakistanis who rapidly avail themselves of biomedical treatment when it is available. They may seek treatment from private physicians, but access to them is very limited in rural areas and few can afford this. Most rely upon publicly sponsored services such as that provided by village dispensers who have a year or two of training beyond high school (tenth grade) matriculation, or hospital clinics of various sizes in large towns and small to large cities.[9] They may also seek care from private pharmacies in small towns and cities (many of which are run by former dispensers who do a brisk business), and clinics and hospitals sponsored in part by international donor agencies, including Christian missions. Outside of cities where "lady doctors" are posted, services for women are comparatively rare and limited to trained midwives. People in fact seek assistance from anyone they consider to be a doctor, meaning anyone from a "travelling salesman" with a small supply of vitamin and iron tablets, to a former army medic, or even an anthropologist who expresses an interest in medical care.

The physician who holds the MBBS degree[10] has high status within Pakistani society. Admission to medical school is known to depend largely upon connections or recommendations (*safarish*) and/or cash. A graduate is expected to return or pass on favors and introductions, and thus perpetuate networks of social debt and obligation that constitute the fabric of the society. Being assigned to a remote area frustrates a physician because he is isolated from family, friends, and those with whom he should be maintaining connections. His salary is low, his accomodations uncomfortable (and probably unsafe for women), and the equipment with which he is expected to work rudimentary. The permanent staff at the hospital may be irksome and manipulative as well. Often he does not speak the same language or dialect as his patients and they seldom seek his help before their illnesses have progressed to a very difficult stage to treat, especially for a novice practitioner. He is thrown back upon status as the basis for exercising the authority that is required for management of the hospital or clinic.

The physician's office is generally characterized by a formality that indicates status and a type of organization that seem distinctly unfamiliar to the average Pakistani. His clothing is of fine quality and carefully cared for. Rather than using a rough table, he may have a heavy desk covered with a white sheet overlain with a heavy glass plate. Pens and assorted office paraphernalia in onyx holders, basic tools for biomedical examination, and perhaps a few reference books, all symbolic of the authority and power of literacy and biomedicine, are arrayed on and around the desk in a somewhat orderly fashion. Practitioners of biomedicine are therefore stereotypically thought to be greedy, self-seeking, and snobbish. Many are in fact impressed with their own status; one physician explained that "many people can practice medicine, but very few can *be* a doctor." Status differentiation marks the rather formal and distant relations they maintain with the hospital or clinic workers that they must supervise. With the absence of familial, or even linguistic connections between a doctor and the staff, the unaccustomed bureaucratic structure is difficult for all, including patients who may feel alienated by the environment, rather than trust and support. Admission to, and each subsequent treatment in hospitals are widely believed to depend upon introduction by a private physician and bribery of the hospital personnel.[11]

Physicians are popularly said to withhold the more powerful medicines in their formulary[12] from the poor because they (MBBSs) do not consider them worth troubling over, or because the poor are unable to offer the requisite payment for good treatment. Many seem to be saying, in essence, that could they only establish a personal connection with the clinic physician, through money if by no other means, they would get better treatment.

The power of various treatments are graded by their form, with tablets lowest or least powerful, followed by capsules, injections, X-rays, glucose drips, and operations. Patients generally desire prescriptions that include a variety of medicines, including one or more injections, plus dietary recommendations to balance the (*Yunani*) *mizaj* of the treatment. They usually leave a clinic with an assortment of tablets and capsules, some of which may be intended to control side effects of the others, the timing and dosages of which they are rarely able to explain. Frequently these are stowed on a ceiling beam or in a simple wall closet of a humid, mud house, protected only by the paper in which they were handed to the patient. Their potency often dissipated, they serve primarily as icons of contact with the powerful healer.

Patients feel more comfortable in the homier environment of a private pharmacy where, rather than bureaucratic organization and authority, a traditional or family based model prevails, characterized by a network of interpersonal dependencies focused on the owner-healer. He will know the local language(s) and may be a distant relative or be introduced by a friend, so the patient arrives at his shop with a sense of connectedness. The sick may make several costly visits to a succession of pharmacists who prescribe an assortment of (potentially incompatible) medications before being seen by a fully trained practitioner of biomedicine.

Such "shopping around" is partially a reflection of the expectation that an immediate and permanent cure may be obtained through biomedical treatment. It should be noted that the cure expected of biomedicine is the one promised through the mystical (or "magical") dimension of Prophetic healing: obtaining the blessing of the Prophet, in which he said: "...the cure that leaves no disease." Whether relying upon pharmacists or physicians (or seeking treatment from many types of practitioners including *Yunani Tibb*, religious healing, and biomedicine at the same time or sequentially), there is a marked tendency to move from local to "bigger and bigger" healers, or increasingly prestigious sources of care in larger and more distant cities. This is analogous to pilgrimages to increasingly powerful shrines in search of healing power before other forms of therapy became readily accessible, and before conservative religious voices condemning the legitimacy of saints and their shrines within Islam gained strength.

In a number of ways traditional norms can be seen to function within biomedical treatment and its evaluation too. Physicians have told me that some patients have expressed a desire to be treated by those they have observed praying regularly at the hospital, stating that their injections or other treatments are less painful because they have (religious) healing power in their hands.[13]

Thus, ultimately, the divisions among the plural forms of therapy blur. Most patients seek in treatment from physicians efficacy that is ultimately conceptualized in holistic, religio-moral symbolic terms, and empower as a healer a person with whom they most easily establish a sense of connection based on traditional, familiar models of social status and authority. The bureaucratic organization and scientific rationale of biomedical care, coupled with hierarchy as reproduced within biomedicine and the society generally contribute to the suspicion felt by many that this form of therapy, though it may offer potent remedies for some, is both amoral and prejudicial.

Conclusion: Medicine and Society

The medical system of Pakistan, while plural in character, is also unified by deep symbolic and experiential constructs. Religion, always at the roots of thought about life and death and health and illness, provides the relevant moral explanatory context. Hierarchy, a dominant feature of social organization, is reflected in conceptions of the domain beyond human sight and replicated in the evaluation of various forms of therapy, individual healers, their clinics, and the specific treatments they recommend. Trust, and thus empowerment of healers, is facilitated by patients' responses to familiar forms of social connectedness with healers and may contribute to successful outcomes of treatment. Efficacy, in turn, is ultimately attributed to the functioning of divine will mediated by some devotional act or ingested substance, as counseled by a person believed to possess -- and thus empowered to have -- special competence. More successful healers are believed to better channel blessing or healing power to their patients and are given greater status and may fare better economically as a result.

The separation between religion and medicine and social position, involving active participation in a network of exchange relations, becomes less and less distinct as one focuses more and more closely on the lived and perceived experience of Pakistanis. Social position and economic well-being are in part perceived to be a consequence of blessedness, partly predestined and partly earned or reinforced through piety and generous, moral behavior, including, perhaps, healing. Bad luck is not expected to plague an outstanding member of society, rather good fortune is often accepted as a mark of Divine Will that a person is capable of, and deserves to, exercise leadership in society. Thus, both a landlord and an individual whose reputation for exorcising jinns led to his social prominence were each strong candidates for election to political office in the community where I conducted extensive field research.[14]

It is into this web of connections among people in which social position, economic and political influence, healing, and religiosity blend that a national politician may bestow an allocation for development of a medical institution. Choosing to promote a form of medical care that is perceived to be grounded in the moral and practiced in a manner that is recognized as familiar and comfortable by ordinary citizens enhances the probability that affected citizens will respond favorably. In further rounds of on-going social exchange, practitioners of *Yunani Tibb* and local, religiously oriented men of influence may both garner additional support from those living near them and rise in prominence within their particular set of exchange networks as a consequence. Ultimately, a national *Tibbi* organization like the Hamdard Foundation gains greater influence with the government in this manner, not just as a response to public statements of support for *Yunani Tibb* initiated at high levels.

Zia ul-Haq's policy of support for and expansion of *Tibbi* hospitals, dispensaries, and colleges, which tapped into his grassroots political support mediated by numerous levels of social exchanges -- in contrast with Zulfikar Ali Bhutto's establishment of additional biomedical teaching hospitals that serve and are appreciated by the elite -- was thus a very effective way of obtaining widespread popular support for his government and its broader policies of Islamization. What appears to have been a simple shift in policy from support of Western biomedicine to support of indigenous, Islamic medicine is in fact far more complicated. Failure to examine the nature of the religio-moral notion of healing power on which medical practice is constructed and the pluralistic medical system is united, and the complex relations of this notion with social hierarchy and political influence in Pakistani society, results in failure to truly apprehend the basis for the ability of an astute politician to mobilize support through manipulation of health policy initiatives.

Notes

1. National Council for Tibb, "F. No.5-2/80-NCT," paragraph 2.

2. According to Hakim Abdul Hafeez Malik, Registrar of the National Council for Tibb in 1981, there were ten *Tibbia* colleges open at that time. Faisalabad and Hyderabad each had two, while Rawalpindi, Lahore, Karachi, Bahawalpur, Multan, and Sargodha each had one. Earlier, an additional college had been closed due to unrest related to the National Assembly's 1974 declaration that Ahmadi were non-Muslims. Data for 1992 was supplied by Hakeem Nazeer Ahmad Asad, Assistant Director (Unani) Health Division, Government of Pakistan.

3. *Hadiths* are the compiled sayings of the Prophet as remembered and recounted by close associates.

4. Burgel notes that this identification (black nigella as black cumin) came only in later commentaries. J. Christoph Burgel, "Secular and Religious Factors of Medieval Arabic Medicine," in Charles Lester, ed., *Asian Medical Systems* (Berkeley: University of California Press, 1976), pp. 44-62; 58.

5. This healing verse or blessing often appears in the *hadiths*. The last word is sometimes translated "ailment," sometimes "disease." Maulana Fazlul Karim, *Al-Hadis* (Lahore: Book House, n.d.). Volume I, p. 284; Volume II., p. 80.

6. Ja'far Sharif, *Islam in India or the Qanun-i-Islam* (Oxford: Oxford University Press, 1972), pp. 247-263.

7. National Council for Tibb, "F. No. 5-2/80-NCT," paragraph 3.

8. Charles Leslie, "The Ambiguities of Medical Revivalism in Modern India," in Leslie, ed. *Asian Medical Systems* (1976), pp. 356-367.

9. The government maintains a network of rural hospitals plus hospitals in sub-district, district, and divisional cities. In addition the military has a system of highly regarded hospitals.

10. Essentially a British medical degree, the MBBS is a combined B.S. and medical degree requiring five years of training beyond the FSc.

11. Anne T. Sweetser, "A Force to be Reckoned With: Counteracting Illness Via the Pakistani Press," paper presented at the annual South Asian Conference, University of Wisconsin, 1987.

12. The complex British formulary, not generic drugs, was in use in Pakistan at least through the early 1980s.

13. "*Hath men shifa hai.*"

14. Anne T. Sweetser, "The Power to Heal: Medicine and Society in the Pakistani Himalaya," PhD. dissertation (Harvard University, forthcoming).

7

Pakistan and the Resolution of the Afghan Conflict

Marvin G. Weinbaum

Throughout the Afghan war, Pakistan was indispensable to any efforts, political or military, to bring the conflict to a close. The Afghan resistance's capacity to pursue a military victory as well as its interest in a compromise diplomatic settlement was largely determined by how the government in Islamabad defined its own interests and the lengths it was prepared to go to pursue its objectives. Much as there could have been no sustained armed resistance without Pakistan, neither could negotiations leading to the Soviet withdrawal have occurred without the Islamabad government's persistence and, in the end, willingness to agree to the terms of a Geneva accord. Pakistan continued to play an influential role in events leading to the fall of the Kabul regime and in efforts to install an interim government of Afghan mujahidin. Throughout the conflict, the decisions reached in Islamabad reflected domestic factional and partisan struggles together with the weight of international pressures and sense of threat. Many of the same factors are also expected to govern Pakistan's policies in the post-war era.

Pakistan never had anything approaching a national consensus on how to bring the war to an end most quickly and favorably to the country's interests. Moreover, neither in aiding the Afghan resistance nor in pursuing a settlement did officials in Islamabad ever manage to square Pakistan's covert and overt policies. What the Islamabad government professed publicly was often at considerable variance with its behind-the-scenes role. While often part of an effort to avoid criticism and responsibility for its acts, the inconsistencies were also a product of disagreements among governmental actors -- the prime minister, the foreign office, military intelligence, and the president -- over what constituted a desirable and feasible course. The differences were sometimes highly personal, though more often they reflected long-standing institutional rivalries.

On some issues of Afghan policy there existed, to be sure, a convergence of views among policy makers, shared by a wider public: that Pakistan should not be solely saddled with the burden of the war and care of its Afghan refugees; and, however the fighting ends, it should not lead to an Afghan government unfriendly to Pakistan. These assumptions were also believed compatible with the view that no solutions could be forced on the Afghan people, who were ultimately expected to decide on their own future. There was less agreement on who could speak for the Afghan people, what degree of cooperation between the two countries was necessary, and how much external pressure on the Afghans was constructive and legitimate.

Pakistan's role in bringing about an Afghan peace had been much of the time affected by a number of miscalculations and misperceptions. For many Pakistanis there existed a tendency to simplify the Afghan conflict. Originally it was often viewed as merely an artifact of the cold war and later it was interpreted all too readily as merely a continuation of tribal rivalries. Officials had trouble believing that the Pushtunistan issue, the tribal and ethnic threat to Pakistan's territorial integrity, was not prone to an early revival, or that every decision had to be weighed by its meaning for the adversarial relationship with India. Policy makers had badly underestimated the staying power of the Kabul government and overrated the possibilities of coordination among the mujahidin. There had been slowness to appreciate in Islamabad what had changed with the Soviet military withdrawal and how the priorities of the U.S. administration and the commitment of the international community might alter with the end of the cold war. By contrast, in discerning more recently how a continuing conflict in Afghanistan impedes opportunities in Central Asia following the Soviet Union's demise, Pakistan has shown early sensitivity along with concern.

The Two-Track Policy

Pakistan's two-track approach aimed at ending the war in Afghanistan, so apparent during the years of Zia ul-Haq's presidency, remained the controlling policy after his death in August 1988. Governments in Islamabad proclaimed their desire to end the conflict peacefully but continued their support for the mujahidin's armed efforts. The latter point of view in Pakistan's policy-making circles focused on the necessity of a military defeat of Kabul's communist regime, both to bring the right kind of government into power in Afghanistan and to assure its survival against rivals. The military route would also best assure that India could be stymied in its anticipated future attempts to exercise influence in Afghanistan. Through better coordination among the mujahidin and more effective use of the arms available, Pakistan military intelligence personnel, together with their CIA partners, remained committed to seeing things through to a decisive victory.

An opposing view held that a military victory was probably impossible and that, in any case, in view of the diversity of political forces, a negotiated settlement in advance of a change in power in Kabul was required if there were to be long-term stability in Afghanistan. There had always existed the danger that the pursuit of a military solution would increase the chances that a more radical Islamist group or groups would assume power in Kabul. It also increased the possibility of a rise in Islamic sectarianism, pitting Iran and its minions against the Saudis and their favorites. Further, a delayed solution could help fuel ethnic rivalries among the Afghans. There was a better chance of a national consensus allowing for a stable regime if a peace resulted from a political agreement that preceded a transfer of power from the communists. A minority of resistance leaders, the so-called moderates or traditionalists, accepted this point of view, including its corollary that power would have to be shared with at least some officials of the previous communist regime.

The two approaches toward a conclusion to the war were not necessarily mutually exclusive, and advocates of a military solution included many who expected that the right kind of political solution could only follow the route of military victories. Tangible gains on the battlefield were needed to obtain the best terms or accelerate a settlement, specifically, to gain major concessions from the communists. In general, it was not unusual for the authorities in Islamabad and their U.S. intelligence contacts to urge the mujahidin to mount more attacks while working toward improving conditions for negotiations with the Soviets and Kabul government.

The expectation of a quick fall of the Afghan communist government after the February 1989 Soviet pullout, had renewed attention to the possible role of an interim government. Without central authority in Kabul, drawn from many elements, a civil war loomed as a distinct possibility. Moscow anticipated, along with many in the region and the West, that the Najibullah regime would have at best only a decent interval before succumbing to the mujahidin. The Soviets were believed to be prepared to settle for an orderly transfer of power, leaving elements of the regime, if not its top leaders, to join a broad, mujahidin-dominated government.

With the Soviet departure imminent, the Islamabad government had, however, lost interest in diplomacy for the time being. There appeared no reason to compromise on any points when most Pakistani officials believed that the communists would soon be ousted militarily. The mujahidin's failed military campaign at Jalalabad in the spring of 1989 might have pushed Pakistan back toward the political track. However, Pakistan's military leadership, which had orchestrated much of the attack on the far eastern city, felt the need to redeem itself.

Reasoning that the Afghan resistance was politically and militarily weak, Pakistan's generals opposed early negotiations. According to this view, the Peshawar party alliance, constituted as the Afghan Interim Government (AIG), needed, most of all, to bring into the fold the more independent commanders and the Shia parties based in Iran. The Pakistani military also called periodically for direct talks between the mujahidin and the communists together with their Soviet supporters. Yet the military coupled its statements with insistence that its backing for the Afghan resistance would continue until the mujahidin were satisfied that they had attained their aim, thus precluding real policy changes.

The military as well as civilian leadership also had reasons to be concerned about bringing on strong resentments and security problems for Pakistan if it pushed the resistance parties in Peshawar too far. Not surprisingly, the Afghan resistance was convinced that, despite occasional signs of more independent policies, it had no reason to fear a break with the Islamabad government or the need to concede anything politically. In practice, Pakistan's call for a just and equitable settlement, acceptable to all parties, meant for much of the war that it would be willing to give the hard-line Afghan groups a virtual veto on policies affecting a settlement.

The coup attempt in Kabul by Afghan General Shahnawaz Tanai in March 1990, supported by Islamabad, demonstrated the preference by Pakistan's civilian and military leadership for a short cut in bringing the war to a conclusion through a quick military solution. However, with the failure of the leftist cum Islamist coup to topple Najibullah, and the resistance's inability, principally the forces of Gulbuddin Hekmatyar, to capitalize on the challenge in the countryside, Pakistan once more reasserted its commitment to a two-track strategy. Public statements stressing diplomacy were revived and the military returned to the blueprint that called for the kind of patience that would produce a string of smaller military victories leading to the desired results. This strategy was best demonstrated by the attack on Khost, a strategic garrison city close to the Pakistan border, at the end of March 1991.

Interestingly, instead of the success at Khost strengthening the hand of those seeking a military solution, it helped to make a case for those in the leadership anxious to prevent further bloodshed.[1] Khost's fall, after a difficult campaign, brought home the extent to which Pakistan would be obliged to get directly involved in the conflict if there were to be further mujahidin victories. Based on the experience of taking and occupying the city, it was obvious that the resistance parties were not sufficiently unified to win a series of similar victories. Pakistan, which had provided weapons to several mujahidin groups (probably more to Hezbi-i-Islami than its presence warranted at Khost), was clearly embarrassed by the behavior of the mujahidin in Khost. The resistance had been unable to control its militias in their looting of the city and battling among themselves for arms and ammunition, and other spoils of war.

The defeat of the Kabul regime at Khost, although not in itself significant in altering the political or military balance of power, was nevertheless thought to be valuable for improving Pakistan's position in future negotiations.[2] Yet, as had occurred before, when the Kabul government appeared ready for a political settlement, the mujahidin, sensing a military breakthrough, pulled back from political discussions. Indeed, the Khost victory confirmed the worst fears of some over what a mujahidin military success would bring: an ungovernable society given the country's political diversity and ethnic heterogeneity. And, for whatever reason, a larger planned offensive by the mujahidin on the Khost model never materialized.[3]

Pakistan's civilian and military elites both agreed that either a military victory or a negotiated settlement would require a broader based, legitimate, more representative Afghan resistance leadership. To bring the Afghan leaders together and in the process take from them some of their perquisites and powers could, however, only be accomplished with popular backing created by the national appeal for a consensus. Greater public support would also have been required if any government hoped to discourage Saudi Arabia and others from encouraging its hard-line proteges in the resistance.[4] Popular agreement over the proposition that the refugees leave sooner rather than later had always been present. Otherwise, Afghan policy did not enjoy a national political consensus within Pakistan. Indeed, none had ever been built, in large part because so much of the Afghan operation had remained secret.

At the core of Pakistan's difficulties with the Afghan issue was the lack of a coherent set of policies externally and domestically. The centers of decision in the country, namely the prime minister, the president, the military (especially its Inter-Service Intelligence [ISI] division), the Punjab-based parties in the National Assembly, and the Foreign Ministry were often sharply at odds on the Afghan issue. The resulting paralysis prevented a clear, consistent course aimed at ending the conflict and prescribing a post-war role for Pakistan. Pakistan had to be more certain about what it sought and how to best attain its objectives in a "clear and unambiguous approach."[5] This might involve some critical and painful choices, forcing Pakistan's government to deal with the domestic political ramifications of its tough decisions.

It was plain that while Benazir Bhutto was in power, a clearer direction to policy was unlikely; policy drift was evident. She was concerned about how a continuing and possibly intensified war could raise the danger to Pakistan's integrity and security. Moreover, Benazir was less supportive than Zia of certain groups of mujahidin, rejecting what she believed was Zia's attempt to impose a government on the Afghan people.[6] But beyond her preference for a political outcome to the war, Benazir had at best vague goals and was unable to articulate policies to implement them.

Modalities for a Settlement

Throughout 1990 and until May 1991, rounds of intense international diplomatic activity took place, although very little of it became public. Above all, the negotiators preferred quiet diplomacy both because they felt that more could be accomplished with none being blamed for failure, but also in an effort to keep it from appearing that they would be imposing a solution on the Afghans. At times the talks took on some urgency as a result of the belief, wrong as it turned out, that the Soviets were ready to drop their $300 million-a-month support of arms, food, and fuel to the Kabul regime.

Negotiations had to take into consideration that, with the Soviet Army out of Afghanistan, intrinsic differences in goals among the mujahidin were more visible than ever, while the Najibullah government had shifted to more conciliatory policies toward its opposition. Also, a settlement had realistically to reflect the transformations inside Afghanistan after years of war, namely the uneven survival of the traditional power structure, the emergence of strong local militias and commanders, the experiences and aspirations of the long-exiled Afghans, and the strengthened hand of the Islamists and their foreign backers. There was also the reality that years of communist rule had so altered the country's urban population as to put constraints on the type of post-war regime that would be acceptable and viable. This included evidence that, however unpopular Najibullah might be in his country, large numbers of Afghans in the capital and elsewhere, fearing an Islamic dictatorship, preferred the social freedoms of an essentially secular regime.

The superpowers reached agreement by mid-1990 on the broad outline of U.N.-supervised voting for a *shura* (assembly) inside Afghanistan and within the camps. Both Washington and Moscow could agree that stability required that the Afghans be allowed to choose their own leaders, and that the choice be an open one. The key was in Najibullah's resignation, which could open negotiations and would presumably bring the resistance leadership to the table. The Afghan president was unwilling, however, to relinquish power, at least in advance of the U.N.-supervised election. He demanded to be allowed to remain in office during the transition, sharing power during the election period.

The several Peshawar resistance-party leaders differed on the degree of participation they could foresee for Najibullah's followers in a future vote and after. The more hard-line ruled out those individuals associated with repressive acts by the communists, a definition open to wide differences in interpretation and application. At most, if any good Muslims could be found, they might play a role in a future regime. Some in the resistance spoke openly of the need to subject Najibullah and others to trials for their crimes. But on the proposition that communist leader Najibullah should step down in advance of any election, the views of the mujahidin leaders largely coincided.

Moscow continued to hold out for a transitional government to be installed with a role for former government officials and party members. Pro-Soviet elements in the country, it was felt, could not be protected if Najibullah were deposed prior to the holding of an election. Yet Najibullah was not, in fact, the major stumbling block. For the Soviets had signaled their readiness to dump the Afghan leader, were a reasonable alternative found. However, nothing the Soviets saw convinced them that a government in Islamabad could guarantee an Afghan regime of moderate Muslims willing to co-exist with former communists who would stay on.

The preferred political solution for Pakistan remained what it had been for some time: a broad-based government in Kabul, acceptable to the mujahidin. But many Pakistanis, most vocally the intelligentsia, were increasingly of the view that the Afghans had to be pushed to a settlement. Pakistan was "morally bound" to interfere, in their opinion, to override Afghan group interests and, in effect, save them from "ideological interests alien to Afghan society."[7] Above all, it would be necessary to neutralize the Peshawar-based resistance parties. One way would be to nominate people to stand for elections in districts within Afghanistan as well as in the party-dominated camps inside Pakistan. The repeated declaration that the Afghan people should decide their future raised the question of whether this merely meant a majority or whether there had to be some consensus among all major elements. The Afghan ethnic minorities were concerned that their interests would be overridden by the Pushtun majority. Anyway, it was difficult to determine where the majority stood without elections.

Pakistani authorities revived efforts in early 1990 to form a new coalition among the squabbling resistance factions in Peshawar. To salvage the reputation of the Afghan parties and legitimize mujahidin authority, officials pressed for elections to a representative assembly that could ratify a negotiated agreement and serve as the basis for an interim government. The civilian leadership hoped that a *shura*, by opening the path to a full political solution, would help to isolate the more radical Afghan elements. It was reasoned that even if the Kabul government were overthrown through military means, a civil war might be avoided with an effective interim arrangement. The key role performed by Army Chief of Staff General Aslam Beg in these efforts to galvanize the resistance parties was both a token of the military's continued key role in Pakistan's decision-making structure and recognition of its close ties with the mujahidin.[8]

The former king, Zahir Shah, provided the answer to those seeking a leader who could attract support and enhance the legitimacy of an interim government. To many U.S. and Soviet officials, and at least two of the more moderate, traditionalist resistance parties, Zahir Shah offered the key to a peaceful transition. His role was envisioned to be a temporary one, with no return to the monarchy contemplated. Ideally, the former monarch, acting as the symbol of unity for the nation, would help establish a new system, particularly one that tolerated political differences. Najibullah dropped hints that he might be willing to step aside in favor of Zahir Shah. Many suspected Najibullah of using the prospect of the former king's return as a means to split the Afghan mujahidin leadership and to separate it from the rank and file refugees, among whom Zahir Shah had a strong popular following.

Prior to the Soviet withdrawal, high-level discussions took place between the Pakistani foreign minister and those close to the former king. Meetings continued into September 1989 between senior Pakistani officials in the Benazir government and aides to Zahir Shah. While the diplomats were willing to talk to the representatives of the former king, the military intelligence branch and the IJI were adamantly opposed. The more radical Afghan Islamists contended that Zahir Shah had long ago forfeited his right to play any role in Afghanistan's future. To many, including the Shia parties in Tehran, he had been a puppet of the Soviets. Even among officials in Benazir's government there was considerable suspicion of the former king who was considered to have been partial to India while he was in power. Reports of contacts between Zahir Shah and Indian envoys made it more difficult for Pakistan's government to consider the king seriously in a political solution.

It was a widely held belief that Pakistani and U.S. intelligence held the key to the resistance's intransigence. A threat to withdraw arms and other forms of aid, especially when combined with material incentives was thought sufficient to force the mujahidin into serious negotiations and major concessions. Whatever their stockpiles of weapons, it was doubtful whether the mujahidin could sustain their military effort from within Pakistan at anywhere near the same level without the approval of the Islamabad government. Yet, notwithstanding that Islamabad had so well managed and manipulated Afghan politics within its borders, most doubted that Pakistan could force terms on the resistance. Anything resembling an imposed peace would probably not work with the resistance, and threats to withhold resources would only stiffen opposition to new policies. Hard-line resistance elements already interpreted doubts about a military victory as proof that the superpowers and others, maybe even some Pakistanis, were conspiring against self-determination for the Afghan nation.

It was a mistake to underestimate the determination of the resistance leadership. Most party leaders and commanders held a clear vision of their country's future -- be it an Islamic state or the restoration of traditional authority -- on which they were loathe to compromise. The resistance leaders were fond of pointing out that at the war's beginning they had managed to carry the fight without the West and with minimal help from Islamic countries, and that they could, if forced to, carry on alone in the future. Additionally, the leverage of Pakistan's ISI over the Peshawar parties did not extend appreciably to commanders inside Afghanistan should they independently decide to continue with plans to fight. Not unimportantly, the composition of a post-communist regime would also have to be acceptable to the Saudis and Iranians who, like Pakistan's military, remained determined that their favorite resistance factions prevail.

International Context

Through its aid for the mujahidin, overt and covert, the international community had always been in a position to influence the course of negotiations. Military and humanitarian aid to the resistance, including promised programs for the reconstruction of the country, provided incentives able to influence the timing and shape of a settlement. Particular parties and mujahidin groups had their foreign benefactors, governmental or private, whose preferences could not be ignored. There was also a very real threat that intransigence and in-fighting among the resistance elements could prompt their international supporters to walk away from involvement in the ongoing conflict as well as from the subsequent rehabilitation of Afghanistan. Officials in Islamabad worried about the possibility that Pakistan might be deserted by allies tired of backing the Afghan resistance.

At the same time, a growing international consensus on the need for an early political settlement served the interests of those in the Pakistani leadership wishing to revise policies. The Islamabad government found it easier to accept compromises -- criticized by domestic groups and resistance parties -- by blaming irresistible international pressures. Accusations by mujahidin leaders of foreign collusion with the Kabul government and Moscow, reflected their concern that an international consensus could accelerate if not force a political settlement opposed by them.

Pakistan had demonstrated throughout the 1980s the ability to talk to all the major players -- Iran, Saudi Arabia, China, the Soviet Union, and the United States. Only with India was it difficult to hold a dialogue over Afghanistan. Pakistan importantly provided a possible bridge between the United States and Iran and could mediate differences between Iran and Saudi Arabia. The extent to which Pakistan was able to retain good relations with countries that were themselves so adversarial is indeed remarkable. In part this was possible because Pakistan's contacts with these countries were compartmentalized: different sectors of the government were close to different countries with which Pakistan had to deal; and individuals in positions of high authority in Islamabad often served as the "point men" for relations. In the case of Iran, for example, General Aslam Beg was known to have long played that role.

Throughout most of the war, the national interests of Pakistan, the goals of most of Pakistan's allies, and the aims of the resistance were essentially compatible; at times identical. Only with the changes in the wider international environment did the strategic equation alter and the underlying strains among former partners in the anti-communist, anti-Soviet struggle become manifest. The decision in Moscow to withdraw from the Afghan battlefield was no doubt the most important of these changes, widely altering priorities and leading to a reassessment of threats by resistance supporters. On a wider scale, the end of superpower military confrontation and, specifically, the intent of both the United States and Soviet Union to disengage from regional conflicts had a major, if somewhat delayed, impact on the Afghan conflict and efforts to bring it to a conclusion. In a post-cold war era, neither the Afghan resistance nor the Pakistan government could take for granted continued military and economic assistance or assume that others would accept their visions of a future Afghanistan. The Gulf war and responses to it within Pakistan and among the mujahidin leadership cast further doubt on the continuity of policies, including those of Saudi Arabia and Iran. The failed August 1991 putsch in Moscow left Soviet policies even more uncertain. What remaining interest the Soviet Union (later the individual republics) had in the war was their mutual concern that Afghanistan not become the bastion of a fundamentalist regime, conceivably linking up with similar ideological regimes in Iran and possibly Pakistan.

The divergence of Washington and Islamabad over Afghan policy is most clearly marked as beginning with the Soviet military withdrawal in February 1989. The subsequent Jalalabad debacle underscored the need for a new approach. To be sure, in the immediate aftermath of Jalalabad, Washington continued to support the view that the mujahidin had to be strengthened through continued arms supplies before any serious renewal of negotiations. U.S. officials, observing the Soviet buildup of weapons for the Kabul regime, saw no reason to cut off arms supplies precipitously. But even many long-time supporters of the Afghan cause in Washington had become convinced that a military solution anytime soon was unlikely and that a political compromise with Kabul was unavoidable. With the abortive March 1990 coup in Kabul, Washington became increasingly committed to an approach to negotiations that bypassed the Peshawar-based parties altogether. The United States sought an early conclusion to the conflict, preferring that moderate elements prevail if possible but prepared to accept almost any kind of leadership in Kabul. The official position in Pakistan remained insistent, however, on an Afghan solution that gave strong promise of close and amicable ties with future governments in Kabul.

Domestic critics of Islamabad's policies had long claimed that Pakistan had no Afghan policy independent of U.S. interests and objectives. These elements had always believed that their country was fighting an American war and argued that a settlement was blocked by Pakistan's dependence on the United States as well as Zia ul-Haq's reliance on the conflict in order to remain in power. In fact, Washington had largely deferred to Pakistan on the pivotal decisions involving who should receive military assistance and how it should be used.[9] Pakistan also shaped the diplomatic agenda, such as it was. Even with the more active, post-Geneva role of the United States in efforts to find a solution, Washington was ready to follow gladly Pakistan's lead regards negotiations. Consequently, much of the U.S. diplomatic initiative was a result of still largely reactive -- at least until mid-1991 -- Pakistan government policies.

Leftist opposition elements in Pakistan had always contended that a peace settlement could be accelerated with a full Pakistani-Soviet rapprochement. While the Soviets held sway in Afghanistan, the idea was to plan for a new bilateralism in the establishment of relations with the Soviet Union that better reflected Pakistan's unfavorable geopolitical circumstances and its economic interests. It was not clear how much incentive the Soviets would have felt in risking their relations with India if that were the price of a more cooperative Pakistan. For, in economic terms, Pakistan could never compete with India in its value to Moscow as a trading partner. The idea of playing a Soviet card was revived after the cutoff in U.S. economic assistance in late 1990. Not only was this thinking short-lived as the Soviet empire crumbled, in the post-cold war circumstances, the threat of warming relations with Moscow could not be a very useful lever to pry loose American aid. At best, through 1991, Islamabad could do little more than remain hopeful that with better relations with the Soviets, Moscow would halt arms shipments to the Kabul regime and, in its new demands for hard currency payments for food and other supplies, further weaken Najibullah's regime.

The Islamic government in Tehran had always insisted that it would support the legitimate demands of the Muslim people of Afghanistan, including the establishment of a non-aligned Islamic government. With its large Afghan refugee population, Iran could hardly ignore the war on its eastern border. Yet Pakistan's ability to involve Iran directly in a negotiated peace in Afghanistan was understandably influenced by Tehran's long preoccupation with its conflict with Iraq. Suspicion of the United States among the Islamic Republic's leaders and their unwillingness to put much faith in the AIG, especially after its failure to accommodate Shia resistance parties in the Sunni-dominated Peshawar-based alliance, also restrained their active participation in a solution.

The Islamic Republic kept close tabs on their client Afghan Shia groups based in Tehran and, in 1990, encouraged eight of the factions to form a single Islamic Unity (*Vahdat-i-Islami*) party. Iran's leaders also kept up a dialogue with several moderate Afghan parties as well as Burhanuddin Rabbani's (ethnically diverse) Jamaat-i-Islami. In their desire first to normalize relations with the Soviet Union and then to follow the international community, Iranian leaders left no doubt that they favored political means over a military solution. In mid-1989, Iran let it be known that it preferred an intra-Afghan dialogue to decide the modalities of an international peace conference. The increased flexibility of the Tehran government was notable in the position it took late in 1990, dropping its earlier insistence that the Kabul government step aside and a transitional government be in place prior to the holding of elections. The Islamic Republic's leaders at one point seemed to be arguing that communists could remain in power during elections with control of security forces still in the hands of Najibullah, a position they urged on the mujahidin.[10] Tangible signs of improving relations between Iran and the Kabul regime were evident in food aid for floods in Afghanistan and landing facilities for the Afghan national airline in Iran. Besides sectarian differences, Tehran's policies alienated several of the more radical Afghan resistance parties, most notably Hezb-i-Islami, which accused the Iranian authorities of terrorism and interfering in Afghan affairs.[11]

Differences remained with Islamabad: Tehran had reservations about a Pakistan-supported mechanism for an intra-Afghan dialogue and, for some time, opposed a convening of a *loya jirga* (assembly of tribal notables), the traditional means of installing a new government -- since this promised to favor the Sunni Pushtuns. But differences did not stand in the way of an evolving close cooperation with Pakistan, based on their common belief in the importance of an Afghan settlement for regional security.[12] Like Pakistan, the Tehran government came to desire a regime in Kabul sufficiently stable to cooperate economically and able to withstand extra-regional political and economic dependencies. Eventually the patience of both would wear thin, and Iran's leaders, along with those in Islamabad, would focus on the Afghan fighting as an obstacle to economic and cultural openings with Central Asia's former Soviet Muslim republics.

Diminishing concerns in Beijing about Soviet military intentions meant that China, long Pakistan's most reliable ally, had less reason to lend material and political backing to the mujahidin. Yet close political ties with China, even though only marginally useful in times of real crisis, were certain to continue, given both countries' lasting suspicions of India. And, with a cooling of relations between Islamabad and Washington, relations with the Chinese took on added meaning. It was of some importance, then, that by mid-1991, the Chinese had gone over to a policy of encouraging Pakistan to seek a political solution to the Afghan problem.

Close relations with Saudi Arabia had for many years acted as a constraint on those Pakistani policy makers willing to press the mujahidin toward a diplomatic settlement. The Saudis firmly supported a decisive military victory, and particularly the ascendance of Wahabi-Sunni groups. Direct and indirect financial assistance that was provided by the Saudis during the Zia years and that continued during his successors' regimes gained them a sympathetic hearing in Islamabad. During Benazir's tenure in office, there was, moreover, always the fear that, if offended, the Saudi leadership would side with the domestic religious opposition who were chronically on the verge of seeking a ruling that a woman could not head an Islamic government. The Gulf crisis and war offered the clearest sign that any government in Islamabad was obliged to remain sensitive to the Saudi royal family. Notwithstanding highly vocal domestic critics, the Islamabad government sent 11,000 volunteers to Saudi Arabia for the declared purpose of defending Islamic holy places -- not to liberate Kuwait.

Yet the war also prompted considerable revision by the Saudi regime in its attitudes toward the Afghan resistance and the diplomatic process. Three mujahidin factions, including two that had received generous assistance from Saudi Arabia, had sided with Iraq in the crisis. In the war's aftermath, not surprisingly, then, Saudi Arabia withdrew some of its financial backing for these Peshawar-based parties. Even so, Saudi shipments of Soviet-built Iraqi arms, including tanks and other heavy equipment captured in the Persian Gulf war, reached mujahidin forces in the late spring and summer 1991. With the ISI handling the distribution and private Arab funding available, the supposedly-punished Hekmatyar and Rasul Sayyaf groups continued as recipients.[13] Privately donated, large sums of money also continued to flow to mujahidin for the financing of thousands of Muslim volunteers, mostly Arabs, who trained and fought alongside the resistance parties.

While continuing to insist that the Afghan people be allowed to make their own decisions, most concerned states were ready to conclude that the resistance elements, left to their own devices, were incapable of agreeing on a peaceful solution. To have a political settlement, however, the international community would, first, have to reach a consensus among themselves. This was largely accomplished within the broad framework of a U.N. plan offered in May 1991 by Secretary-General Javier Perez de Cuellar. Second, the involved states had to be prepared to use both the carrot and stick: promises of post-war assistance; and threats to withdraw all material, especially military support. As in the political settlements in Angola and Nicaragua, progress, above all, required the coordinated efforts of peacemakers in Moscow and Washington, specifically their willingness to halt all military supplies to the combatants.

The participation of the Saudis and Iranians was especially critical. They each could now be counted on to throw their considerable weight behind a political settlement. With the strained relations between Iranians and Saudis somewhat eased, Saudi Arabia, after prodding from Washington, joined the call in late 1991 for a peaceful solution through the United Nations. In cooperation with Islamabad, the Saudis pressed the mujahidin to halt their bickering. Renewed diplomatic relations with the Soviet Union (later Russia) also created an improved international climate, which prompted Saudi support for direct talks between the mujahidin and Moscow.[14] Importantly, the willingness of Saudi Arabia and Iran to seek an accommodation made it politically safer for Pakistan to pursue the same policy.

New Priorities

It was under Muhammad Nawaz Sharif -- who assumed the post of prime minister in October 1990 -- that serious indications first appeared that Pakistan was about to give the Afghan issue new priority. The Islamabad government's energized diplomatic activities in pursuit of a political settlement occurred, ironically, as already noted, in the wake of the mujahidin's success at Khost. Pakistani policy did not turn its back on a military approach; the supply channels to the resistance forces were kept open. The Islamabad government had, however, breathed new life into the two-track strategy by trying to fashion a solution and find cover from expected critics in an international consensus. Contacts aimed toward a peaceful resolution of the conflict were stepped up with Iran, Saudi Arabia, the Soviet Union, and the United States, as well as the U.N.

Those officials in Islamabad who had argued for the need to bypass the Peshawar-based Afghan parties were now given a better hearing. Under the circumstances, Pakistan's leaders came increasingly to recognize that they could not be supportive of the ISI's creature, the AIG, and also be in favor of a solution calling for a broadly based government that included the field commanders inside Afghanistan and Iran-based Afghan parties, much less former Afghan communists. Some in Islamabad were privately ready for direct, face-to-face talks between high ranking Pakistani and Kabul government officials -- against the wishes of the AIG leadership. Informal but secret contacts were undertaken in mid-April 1991 in Geneva between the then ISI head, General Asad Durrani, and a close advisor to Najibullah, Afghan General Tukhi.[15] By some accounts, Durrani also met with General Ghulam Yaqubi, head of the Afghan intelligence agency, WAD.[16] A decision had been reached in a January 25th meeting of the government's Afghan policy cell composed of the country's top military and civilian leaders that a political settlement now be pursued seriously and that lines of communications with the Soviets be opened.[17]

Clearly, there remained some in positions of authority in Islamabad holding out for installing an Islamist-dominated government and resisting any effort to throw Pakistan's weight behind a negotiated agreement. These elements remained committed to Hezb-i-Islami as future partners, even if not necessarily the preeminent force in Kabul. The inclusion of a high-level representative and son-in-law of Hekmatyar in the April 1991 Geneva meeting seemed to confirm this fact.[18] About the same time, Hekmatyar's ally of convenience, former Afghan General Tanai, was believed to have traveled to Moscow, also for the purpose of exploring the chances of a deal involving Hezb-i-Islami that would bring a new regime to Kabul. Moscow's probable motive was to assure itself of some influence with more radical elements in the event of Najibullah's fall.

Meanwhile, renewed contacts -- probably without the full endorsement of the ISI -- between the officials of Pakistan's foreign ministry and representatives of the former King Zahir Shah took place in June 1991.[19] Importantly, these representatives were welcomed publicly and allowed to make their case in meetings with Nawaz Sharif and Afghan resistance leaders.[20] Their discussions were followed up with a meeting in Rome between new Army Chief of Staff Lieutenant General Asif Nawaz Janjua and the former king's son-in-law, Abdul Wali, in early January 1992. For the first time, a Pakistan government was prepared to seriously consider the former monarch's active participation in a political settlement, though only in a transitional government. It also seemed to presage a willingness in Islamabad to include a fuller spectrum of acceptable Afghans, including personalities and parties with some considerable following among exiled Afghans, in shaping the country's future.

There was good reason for the shift in thinking in Islamabad. In terms of Prime Minister Nawaz Sharif's domestic aims, Afghanistan had clearly become an obstacle. On balance, whatever its earlier value, continuation of the war did not seem to be in Pakistan's interests.

Opinion in Pakistan appeared to be coming closer to the view of the war's long-time critics that the country's "national interests were rendered hostage to the needs and interests of particular mujahidin leaders or groups."[21] Resentment in Pakistan also grew against the perception that the government was prolonging the war. To serve its own interests, Pakistan would have to stake out a policy free of any intimidation by the mujahidin. Despite this and the popular consensus in Pakistan that time was ripe for a political settlement, every effort was to be made to avoid forcing distasteful terms on the resistance.

More than ever, with international assistance dwindling, conditions for the early, safe return of the refugees was imperative. Nawaz Sharif's desire for sweeping economic and social changes in Pakistan was believed hampered by the continued involvement in the Afghan war. Pakistan would continue to see a drain on its resources as a result of the conflict, with the probability that the demands on its treasury would increase with the decline in international support. The domestic violence, notably in the Sindh, showed signs of foreign involvement, allegedly Indian but possibly with an Afghan connection. Sought-after investment from abroad was considered unlikely until a more peaceful Pakistan was realized. Without Afghanistan, popular and elite pressures for an accelerated nuclear program could diminish. As a result, new U.S. and Western aid might be facilitated.

Defections from Nawaz Sharif's ruling coalition and the rapidly deteriorating law-and-order situation across the country beginning in mid-summer 1991 weakened the prime minister's government. Notwithstanding this, the prime minister was in a far stronger position to stand up to Pakistan's military than his predecessor, Benazir Bhutto, had been. The possibility increased that Afghan policy might be taken from the generals, specifically out from under the direction of the military intelligence. The reduced role of the military as the conduit for U.S. and other foreign arms to the resistance no doubt promoted a greater willingness to allow the civilians to take political command on the Afghan issue.

In any case, the civilian leadership had assumed the forefront in a streamlined Afghan policy.[22] The apparent willingness of President Ghulam Ishaq Khan to seek a peaceful resolution of the Afghan issue was especially significant in view of his influence with a military that had so recently opted for jihad against Kabul and had helped to undermine domestic, secular forces in Pakistan. Yet not until the retirement of the outspoken General Aslam Beg could Prime Minister Nawaz Sharif feel reasonably secure in his authority. During the Gulf war, Beg had led political attacks that castigated the Nawaz Sharif government for its "anti-Muslim" stance.[23] To some extent, Beg's line of policy had been discredited by Iraq's defeat. Still, rumors of a Beg-led coup were widespread throughout June and July 1991. When Beg stepped down on schedule in August and was replaced as Army Chief of Staff by Asif Nawaz, a man with no obvious political ambitions and a close friend of the prime minister, it augured well for civilian rule.[24] The military stood far closer to a consensus with the elected civilian government than it had for some time.

Under General Asif Nawaz, a series of power plays leading to personnel changes in the command structure gave indication of a military more reconciled toward ending the conflict in Afghanistan quickly. The modification in thinking appeared to go beyond mere strategic calculation. Key figures in the army were now ready to see a reduction in the influence of Pakistan's Islamist parties and their militant, radical agenda. A telltale sign of change was the demotion and premature retirement from the Pakistan Army of Lieutenant General Hamid Gul, former head of the ISI and a continuing voice opposing a shift of policy on Afghanistan. ISI chief and Beg loyalist, General Durrani, was also replaced, although the change in Afghan policy was effected before his departure in March 1992.

If the Afghan war was proving politically destabilizing and economically detrimental for Pakistan, the continuing conflict also seemed to militate against the country's larger security requirements. The suspension of U.S. economic and military aid over the country's nuclear program in fall 1990 had left Pakistan largely alone to confront its regional problems. Plainly, if it were necessary to choose, the country's limited resources would be used to defend against India. The possibility of Pakistan taking on fuller responsibility for the Afghan war was increased with Washington's formal arms cut off to the mujahidin on January 1, 1992. In fact, officially-approved U.S. supplies of weapons to the resistance had ended the previous October, and for some groups long before that date. The chances of Indian economic and political involvement filling the vacuum left by Soviet disengagement had increased. A new, more vigorous effort to find a diplomatic solution became imperative if Pakistan hoped to avoid having to sustain simultaneously both continuing conflict on the Afghan frontier and heightened danger of armed confrontation with India with the revival of the Kashmir issue.

Compromises and the Collapse

A critical juncture in the Afghan war appeared to have been reached by March 1992. Either the framework for realizing a political compromise was at hand or the conflict would rapidly de-internationalize, and likely to settle into a protracted civil war. International and regional events appeared to be conspiring to force as well as entice the Afghans toward a compromise solution. If the endgame were finally in sight, the untiring mediation by U.N. representatives could take most of the credit. Fresh from its brokering and monitoring of peace in several former regional conflicts and carrying some momentum from its association with successes in the Gulf war, the world organization seemed well positioned to break the impasse. Pakistan's approval of the U.N. initiative and determination to close off other options for the resistance gave promise that even the more recalcitrant mujahidin could be brought along. As it happened, the U.N.'s timetable and design for a compromise settlement were overtaken by events in mid-April.

Until then, the Nawaz Sharif cabinet had looked particularly to the U.N. Secretary-General to play an active role in facilitating a peaceful solution. The May 1991 U.N. initiative, no doubt encouraged by the shifting attitudes in Islamabad, was designed to bring a settlement through an Afghan dialogue. The five-point plan -- more a collection of principles than a detailed plan or specific mechanism for a settlement -- envisaged a halt to the supply of weapons to both sides and elections to establish a broad-based government in Kabul. Through Perez de Cuellar's personal envoy, Benon Savon, the U.N. pressed the search for a group of more independent Afghan personalities to assume interim government roles. Savon's consultations involved Saudi Arabia, Iran, the United States and Soviet Union, as well as Pakistan.

A notable effort to win backing for the U.N. initiative was a late July 1991 quadrilateral meeting of officials from Iran and Pakistan together with leaders of the mujahidin from Peshawar and Tehran. The purpose of the conclave as conceived by Pakistani officials was to find positive elements in the May plan. In the end, the conference held in Islamabad offered little more than an opportunity for the dissidents to air their feelings. Only the more pro-Western Sunni mujahidin organizations, those led by Ahmed Galani, Sibghatullah Mojaddedi, and Mawlawi Mohammadi, were in large measure in agreement with the U.N. plan. A follow-up meeting took place in late August in Tehran, importantly, with the ISI formally part of the Pakistan team.[25] A surprising degree of accommodation and understanding marked relations between the Tehran-supported and Peshawar-based groups. On this occasion, however, three of the mujahidin's Sunni parties refused to send representatives.

The major sticking point in any early progress in negotiations was the continued insistence among the more radical Islamists that all members of the communist hierarchy be excluded from participation in a coalition government or have a political future in Afghanistan. They were particularly insistent that Najibullah not participate. In calling for an intra-Afghan dialogue, the U.N. plan appeared to leave a role for Najibullah's Watan (Nationhood) Party, renamed from the People's Democratic Party of Afghanistan (PDPA), and perhaps Najibullah himself. Rather than debate the merits of the U.N. plan or its possible modification, the more radical Islamists indicated a fresh resolve to force a military solution and interpreted the talk of a political solution as deliberately intended to divert their attention from the jihad.[26] The AIG's prime minister and Islamist leader Rasul Sayyaf publicly rejected any political solution that would include negotiations with the communists and vowed to fight on until final victory of the mujahidin and until a true Islamic government in Afghanistan was formed. Any dialogue was considered traitorous, and the U.N. representative was labeled a "devoted servant of Zionists and international colonialism."[27] Hekmatyar, the Hezb-i-Islami leader, threatened any mujahidin leaders who might agree to cooperate in trying to forge an interim regime.

In April 1991, Nawaz Sharif had reopened dialogue with the Soviet government. However, a high-level Soviet delegation that was supposed to visit Islamabad in May 1991 canceled its trip. Even so, Pakistan's Secretary-General for Foreign Affairs, Riaz Mohammad Khan, traveled to Moscow at the end of May in order to keep the exchanges going. On August 11, a Soviet foreign ministry delegation arrived in Islamabad to renew talks, with particular focus on the U.N. Secretary-General's plan. Yet negotiations had become more complicated with the apparent increased influence of the military in Moscow in the spring and summer. The Soviet Union appeared less flexible in finding a solution for Afghanistan. Hard-liners were determined not to desert entirely their former allies in arms. The lobby in the Soviet parliament calling for a continuation of international aid to Afghanistan appeared strongly entrenched, intent on blocking an agreement on negative symmetry.[28] According to one source, 500 to 600 Soviet military advisers were still assigned to Afghanistan, with an additional 1,500 Soviet civilians.[29] Progress on talks between Soviet and U.S. representatives were clearly stalled, mainly over differences in the powers to be enjoyed by Najibullah during the transition. The Soviets were disturbed by the Khost offensive and by reliable evidence, despite claims of innocence made to Moscow and others, of direct Pakistani involvement in the military operations.

The failed Soviet coup of mid-August 1991 removed the remaining obstacles to direct superpower cooperation. With the ascent of the reformers and the rapid decline of military and KGB influence in political circles in the coup's wake, the very elements that saw continued support as a moral obligation to the Soviet soldiers who fought in Afghanistan as well as to a brotherly communist party had been pushed aside. In view of the deteriorating budgetary conditions and transport difficulties inside the Soviet Union, continued economic aid to the Najibullah government was certain to be curtailed as well. Russian President Boris Yeltsin was on record as asking for a reexamination of Soviet military and economic aid to the Kabul regime. It came as little surprise, then, when in September 1991, the Soviet Union and United States announced a mutual, complete halt in arms to the warring sides beginning in January 1992. The joint communique also announced support for the U.N.'s attempts to mediate a settlement, although without specifying the need for a formal caretaker government in the transitional period. Inadvertently, however, the developments of August and September 1991 worked against a peaceful resolution.

Until this time, a consensus had formed among most observers in Pakistan that a mujahidin military victory over Kabul was out of reach. Pakistan had sought to put together a caretaker government, composed of figures who would not be candidates for leadership in a future, elected government. However, the failed coup in Moscow and joint U.S.-Soviet declaration on arms, which Pakistani officials welcomed publicly, brought new concerns and opportunities, and reactivated the military track for ending the war. Once again, with the Najibullah regime seemingly having its back to the wall, there was renewed interest in Islamabad as well as among key resistance leaders in pushing a military solution. Although the Kabul government was thought to have up to a two-year supply of weapons and ammunition, continued supply of food and fuel was in doubt, especially with Moscow's newly imposed hard-currency purchase requirements. The ability of the Kabul government to sustain morale in the cities and loyalty among its army officers was also problematic.

On the diplomatic front, the Islamabad government argued for some time for a package settlement along with negative symmetry, one that would include a ceasefire, an interim government, and arrangements for the return of refugees. For without these provisions, once Washington and Moscow had finally abandoned the conflict, the fighting was believed likely to go on for some time, especially given the ability of the warring sides to finance their operations with drug money. As leverage, the Islamabad government refused for months following the U.S.-Russian declaration to commit Pakistan to following their lead to halt arms shipments to the combatants. Islamabad's diplomatic efforts to mobilize regional backing for a comprehensive settlement was meant to give added content to the U.N.'s five-point plan and to go beyond the concept of negative symmetry.

By the end of 1991, renewed military offensives on Jalalabad and Gardez had stalled, owing largely to differences among the mujahidin field commanders and the superior firepower of the Kabul regime forces. Even more, the mujahidin, despite the continued presence of Pakistani army officers providing logistical and tactical advice, appeared unable to gear up for a sustained fight. The reassertion of the military option against the Kabul regime, approved in Islamabad, had only delayed, not derailed the political process. Increasingly, the ISI had become resigned to finding a political way out, though the extent of the military intelligence's willingness to fully implement decisions in Islamabad was still to be tested.

Even the appointment of a known religious ideologue as new ISI chief, General Javed Nasir, did not so much signify second thoughts as an apparent "balancing act," intended to coopt the intelligence community, thereby assuring greater stability to the civilian government.[30]

Events moved more quickly. The Sunni mujahidin alliance, the AIG, in effect dissolved at the end of 1991. The most auspicious of the changes was the beginning of a dialogue with the Soviets, later the Russians, in Moscow and subsequently in Pakistan. Prodded by Pakistan to open talks, only the most radical Islamist groups boycotted the mid-November Moscow meeting. The endorsement by both Iran and Saudi Arabia of the mujahidin-Soviet meetings was apparent with the participation of the Tehran-based Shia resistance parties and the stopover in Saudi Arabia of the Peshawar delegation before proceeding to Moscow. From these direct negotiations the leaders of the then disintegrating Soviet state had indicated their acceptance of the proposition that the interim government should be an essentially Islamic one.

While trying to remain true to the promise that the Afghan people would be permitted to determine their own future, Pakistan's civilian leadership was finally committed to a process that seemed to leave the mujahidin few good alternatives to a negotiated settlement. During January 1992, Islamabad finally went along with "negative symmetry," declaring its intention to end military support for the mujahidin. The Nawaz Sharif government pressed openly for acceptance of the U.N. program, warning that peace would not be "held hostage" to the opposition of a few resistance groups and that they would be "left behind" if they posed obstacles.[31] Defying objections from radical Islamist parties and Pakistan's own religious right, the government endorsed the idea of a U.N.-sponsored assembly of 150 representatives from the various Afghan groups to be convened in Europe, leading to the formation of an interim Afghan government in advance of national elections.

Just when it appeared that the necessary groundwork for the U.N. plan was in place, the Kabul government's hold on power rapidly dissolved. Najibullah's efforts to assert his authority over the northern command (located around the ethnically Uzbek city of Mazar-i-Sharif) by putting Pushtuns in key military posts encouraged dissident non-Pushtun army officers led by General Abdul Rashid Doestam to forge an alliance with mujahidin groups. The defections occurred against a background of dwindling supplies of food and fuel in the cities, a crisis sufficiently acute that Pakistan, the United States, and others had begun shipping wheat to Kabul, intended both to stave off hunger and maintain the regime long enough for it to administer an orderly transition of power. When the majahidin closed in on Kabul and Najibullah was observed trying to flee, government forces across the country gave up the fight.

It was left to the contentious mujahidin to determine how and when peace would finally come to Afghanistan. If the various Afghan factions insisted on taking retribution against their ideological enemies, the communists and their sympathizers, there was little that outsiders could or would try to do. Former patron-client relationships would also not easily constrain the mujahidin if they acted to settle old personal grudges or if ethnic fears and ambitions led to full-scale fighting among former allies. In the end, the Afghans would decide for themselves who would emerge to lead the country -- if anyone.

Yet Pakistan's influence on internal Afghan affairs, even if limited over the long run, was far from negligible in the short run. The personal mediating and cajoling of Prime Minister Nawaz Sharif was necessary to meld the Peshawar party leaders into an interim 50-member ruling council (agreed to on April 25), with the approval, to be sure, of the leading field commanders, most notably Ahmed Shah Masoud. When the convoy of autos transferred the council's leaders into Afghanistan, their security was assured by an armed Pakistani escort.[32] Both Nawaz Sharif and Saudi Prince Turki-al-Faisal endeavored to get Hekmatyar to accept a cease fire and join the temporary political structure headed by Sibghatullah Mojaddedi. Nawaz Sharif also flew to Kabul briefly together with his army and ISI chiefs to demonstrate Pakistan's full backing for the shaky interim arrangement.

Pakistan had good reason to try to stay engaged. The idea that Afghanistan might carry on a protracted civil war had become a highly unattractive prospect. Failure of the resistance leaders to put together a broad-based Islamic government might well lead to the ethnic fragmentation of Afghanistan. A Pushtun political entity, almost certain to emerge with the country's disintegration, could be expected to revive ethnic nationalism likely to covet Pakistani territory. Even more, Afghanistan was now critical to Pakistan's plans to serve as an economic corridor and cultural bridge to the newly emergent Muslim republics of the defunct Soviet state. At least while these republics continued to be led by their formerly communist leaders, a radical regime in Kabul, liable to export revolutionary Islam, would be an impediment to close ties. A stable, peaceful, and largely moderate Afghanistan thus seemed imperative if Pakistan hoped to compete with Iran, Turkey, China, and India for the markets and loyalties of the peoples of Muslim Central Asia.

Notes

1. BBC Foreign Service in *Afghan Jehad* (Islamabad), Vol. 4 (July-September, 1991), p. 224.

2. Oliver Roy, "The Lessons of the Soviet-Afghan War, *Adelphi Papers* no. 259 (Summer 1991), p. 25.

3. Barnett R. Rubin, "Political Elites in Afghanistan: Rentier State Building, Rentier State Wrecking," *International Journal of Middle East Studies* Vol. 24 (1992), p. 95.

4. See Ahmed Rashid, "View From the Bunker," *The Herald* (March, 1990), p. 18.

5. M. Lodhi, *Muslim* (September 13, 1989).

6. Interview with Benazir Bhutto, *Pakistan Times* (July 20, 1989).

7. Nasim Zehra, *Nation* (January 28, 1990).

8. Mushahid Hussein, *Nation* (February 18, 1990).

9. Marvin G. Weinbaum, "War and Peace in Afghanistan; The Pakistani Role," *The Middle East Journal*, Vol. 45, no. 1 (Winter 1991).

10. *Foreign Broadcast Information Service (FBIS)*, South Asia (December 7, 1990), p. 43.

11. *FBIS*, South Asia (September 11, 1991), p. 39.

12. Nasim Zehra, "A Common Cause for Pakistan and Iran," in the *News* (August 3, 1991).

13. *Frontier Post* (September 19, 1991); *The Economist* (June 15, 1991), p. 33; and *Afghan Jehad* Vol. 4, no. 4 (July-September, 1991), p. 293. With Bush administration approval, 7,000 tons of captured Iraqi weapons were destined to go to the mujahidin, this despite the mounting disillusionment in Washington with the Afghan resistance. *Los Angles Times* (May 19, 1991).

14. *FBIS* (October 29, 1991), p. 58.

15. *Nation* (May 5, 1991), pp. 1; 12. Reported in *FBIS* (May 9, 1991), p. 44.

16. Ahmed Rashid *Far Eastern Economic Review* (October, 17, 1991), p. 21.

17. Khawar Malik, *Frontier Post* (February 7, 1992).

18. Roy, "Lessons," p. 42.

19. Afghan Information Centre, *Monthly Bulletin*, Nos. 123-124 (June-July 1991), p. 13.

20. *Afghan Jehad*, Vol. 4, no. 2 (April-June 1991), p. 173.

21. Eqbal Ahmad,"The Spoils of War," *The Herald* (December 1989), p. 93.

22. Salamat Ali, *Far East Economic Review* (June 27, 1991), p. 18.

23. Beg in retirement accepted the view that Pakistan did not have sufficient military resources to help the Afghans reach a military victory over the Kabul government. *Afghan Jehad* Vol. 4, no. 4. (July-September), p. 319.

24. *The Herald* (February 1991), pp. 22-33.

25. *The Muslim* (August 27, 1991).

26. *FBIS* (July 25, 1991), p. 41.

27. *Pakistan Times*, (April 4, 1991); *FBIS* (July 5, 1991), p. 36.

28. Rusian Budrin, "The Endless War", *Far Eastern Economic Review* (August 1, 1991), p. 21.

29. *Jane's Intelligence Review* (June 1991), p. 245, from comments by U.S. Senator Gordon Humphrey, March 12, 1990.

30. Najam Sethi, *The Friday Times* (March 12-18, 1992), p. 3. Significantly, General Nasir was associated with a religious party opposed to Pakistan's Jamaat-i-Islami.

31. *Frontier Post* (February 7, 1992); *The New York Times* (February 18, 1992).

32. *The New York Times* (April 30, 1992).

8

Kashmir Conflict: The New Phase

Robert G. Wirsing

India-Pakistan relations have suffered a serious decline in the four years that have passed since the death in an aircrash in August 1988 of Pakistan's President Muhammad Zia ul-Haq.[1] The decline stems in considerable measure from the massive violent unrest that erupted during those years among Kashmiri Muslims in the Indian state of Jammu and Kashmir. The decline has been particularly evident along the Line of Control (LOC) that separates the Indian-held sector of the state from the somewhat smaller sector, including the territories designated by Pakistan as Azad (Free) Jammu and Kashmir and the Northern Areas, that is in Pakistani hands. India has routinely alleged that the Pakistan Army was masterminding heavy infiltration of Kashmiri "terrorists" across the LOC into Indian Kashmir. Pakistan, in turn, has charged India with brutal repression of Kashmiri "freedom fighters" and with gross violation of human rights in Kashmir. Since spring 1991, serious armed clashes, including heavy artillery shellings across the LOC, have taken place with worrisome frequency between the huge forces both sides have concentrated in Kashmir. The danger exists that these hostilities could escalate out of control and plunge India and Pakistan into their fourth war since independence was gained in 1947.

Reversing the decline in the India-Pakistan relationship, or even arresting it, promises to be difficult. There is little trust to be found in this relationship even in ordinary circumstances, and the current intensification of the Kashmir dispute inevitably arouses even greater suspicion. This dispute concerns the political fate of a Muslim-majority province, with a population today of about 7 million, lodged uncomfortably between Hindu-dominated India and Muslim-dominated

Pakistan. Originating in the calamitous communal-based post-World War II partition of the Subcontinent, this dispute triggers intense emotions and fuels powerful political crosscurrents on both sides of the border.[2] It places India's commitment to secularism, and Pakistan's to Islamic statehood, equally under strain. It also deepens apprehension over the future material wellbeing and security of these two countries. For one thing, Pakistan's largely agrarian economy is enormously dependent for irrigation water on the Indus, Jhelum, and Chenab rivers, all of which flow into Pakistan from Kashmir. For another, Kashmir borders on India's adversary, China, in the north and on the politically restive and secession-threatened Indian state of Punjab in the south, investing it with exceptional political and strategic importance. The dispute over Kashmir provoked the first two wars between India and Pakistan (1947-1949, 1965). It has already defeated numerous, strenuous, and prolonged attempts at mediation by the international community. Furthermore, political circumstances within India and Pakistan of late have seemed anything but congenial for renewed serious discussions in regard to it. For both countries, the political stakes in Kashmir -- and the reluctance to compromise in regard to them -- are still very great.

While the Kashmir dispute thus seems far from ripe for resolution, dampening the current crisis and making at least modest progress toward a future settlement are by no means entirely out of reach. There are some indications, in fact, that even major progress along these lines may no longer be absurdly utopian. For one thing, there has been a profound transformation in the last few years in the *external* or global context of the Kashmir dispute. It was this dispute's misfortune, one should recall, to have been born of the Subcontinent's partition in the same year that the Cold War was born from the global community's division into two implacably opposed ideological blocs. The Cold War appears irretrievably over; and there can be little doubt now that this fact alone enlarges at least somewhat the grounds for optimism over Kashmir. With the collapse of the Soviet Union, no more is the "danger in Kashmir" likely to be colored by the ideological fallout of the East-West struggle.[3] On the contrary, with their swords drawn over Kashmir, India and Pakistan now appear oddly out of step with a global order swiftly shedding its Cold War rationales and impatient for an end to chronic regional conflicts -- those until recently permissively labeled "conflicts unending."[4] The international community has suddenly been braced with new agendas for regional peacemaking, with unprecedented political leverage gained from the sudden amity between the superpowers, and with surprising consensus in regard to the potential uses of this leverage. Insofar as the global community is concerned, therefore, coming to agreement on the steps required to put India and Pakistan on the path of accommodation over Kashmir faces no recognizably insurmountable obstacles.

Less obvious, perhaps, but no less important is the fact that changes in the external environment of the Kashmir dispute have been accompanied, especially in recent years, by fundamental changes in its regional or *internal* context. The Kashmir dispute that confronts the world in 1992 is not the same dispute that confronted the world in January 1948, when India's request for U.N. intervention in the dispute launched global efforts to restore peace in Kashmir. It is not even the same dispute that existed 40 years later at the time of Zia's death in 1988. The marshalling since then of a mass-based Kashmiri Muslim separatist movement has obviously altered the dispute's *dramatis personae*. This is, however, only the most recent and spectacular change in the dispute's internal context. Earlier developments, including Pakistan's defeat in the 1971 war and India's success in staking its claim to the Siachen Glacier in northern Kashmir in early 1984, had already begun the process of transformation. All together, these developments have drastically reshaped the Kashmir dispute and dispatched it, probably irreversibly, upon a new phase in its history. This new phase may or may not prove more congenial to settlement than earlier phases. The grounds for optimism, at least in so far as the internal context of the Kashmir dispute is concerned, are clearly not particularly weighty; but neither, for that matter, are the grounds for pessimism as granite-like as they once appeared. Discussion of this dispute, in particular of appropriate ways to encourage India and Pakistan to move toward a settlement, has to take this fact into account. The Kashmir dispute requires new thinking to match this new phase in its development.

Precisely what is the character of the Kashmir dispute in this new phase? What are now the main areas of contention in this dispute? And how do they differ from earlier phases? In particular, how has the current Kashmiri separatist uprising, and the steps India and Pakistan have taken either to support or suppress it, contributed to the shape and content of this new phase? Finally, what does this new phase in the dispute spell in regard both to the quest for settlement and the level or desirability of international involvement in that quest? These questions are the focus of this chapter.

Dimensions of the Conflict

Three fundamental and distinct problems underlie the Kashmir conflict: (1) the problem of boundary delimitation, (2) the problem of Kashmiri self-determination, and (3) the problem of cross-border interference. All three have been present from the outset of the Kashmir conflict in 1947. All three have undergone significant changes since then. Combined, the changes in them represent a very fundamental transformation of the Kashmir conflict as a whole. The earliest of them to change substantially was the problem of boundary delimitation.

Boundary Delimitation

The boundary problem in Kashmir is a leftover of the undeclared war between India and Pakistan that broke out almost immediately after the partitioning of British India into two separate states. The war, which was modest in scale and never spread beyond Kashmir, was finally brought to an end on January 1, 1949, upon implementation of a truce agreement mediated by the Security Council-appointed U.N. Commission for India and Pakistan (UNCIP). The truce was soon followed by a bilateral accord between India and Pakistan (the Karachi Agreement) authorizing establishment of a Cease-Fire Line (CFL) in Kashmir. By November 1, 1949, this line had been delimited in detail and one of the United Nations' earliest peacekeeping operations -- the U.N. Military Observer Group in India and Pakistan (UNMOGIP) -- had been posted in Kashmir to monitor the ceasefire.

The original CFL in Kashmir was drawn between the positions of the Indian and Pakistani armies held at the time hostilities ended in 1949. It extended from a point near Chhamb in Jammu in a rough arc running a bit under 500 miles (497.12 miles) north and then northeastward to a point (map coordinate NJ 9842) about twelve miles north of the Shyok River in the Saltoro Range of the Karakoram Mountains. Its southern terminus near Chhamb fell on the traditional provincial border between the pre-independence state of Jammu and Kashmir and what is now Pakistan's Punjab province. From there to the recognized international border between India and Pakistan beginning near Kathua on the Ravi River was a distance of about 120 miles. That stretch of boundary, included neither within the CFL nor within the international border dividing East from West Punjab that resulted from the partition award of 1947, retained an anomalous status. Pakistanis have always resisted any reference to it as "the border between India and Pakistan," insisting that it is simply the border dividing Indian-occupied *Jammu* from Pakistan.[5] At the northern end of the CFL lay an even more anomalous situation, for there no clear traditional boundary existed and none had been delimited in 1949. The UNCIP-supervised Indian and Pakistani military teams that had undertaken the delimitation exercise at that time had stopped their work about 40 miles short of the present Chinese border. From that point on lay heavily glaciated and seemingly inaccessible mountainous terrain in which neither side's troops had ever been deployed.

From the beginning, the Indians and Pakistanis thus had between them three distinct types of boundary situation to contend with in Kashmir: no boundary at all for about 40 miles in the far north; about 500 miles of delimited (but formally undemarcated) Cease-Fire Line cutting through most of the state; and about 120 miles of traditional, quasi-recognized provincial border at the southern end. Conversion of the CFL to the LOC in the 1972 Simla Agreement, following Pakistan's defeat in the Bangladesh war, involved some minor territorial exchanges along the line and a full redelimitation exercise as well, this time around without benefit of any U.N. supervision. But since there were again no troops in contact in the area north of map coordinate NJ 9842, the new line was not extended beyond it. Neither was there any change made to what had been the CFL's southern terminal point. Thus Kashmir entered the post-Simla period with the trinary boundary system erected in 1949 essentially intact and with no part of it yet qualifying as international border.

There were two potentially troublesome legal loopholes inherent in this boundary system.[6] First, of course, was the obvious incompleteness of the LOC, its abrupt termination about 40 miles short of Kashmir's northern border with China's Xinjiang province. This stretch encompasses some of the highest, most rugged, glaciated, remote and unpopulated portions of the Karakoram Mountains. It is perfectly understandable, therefore, why the LOC's designers, like the designers of the CFL before them, failed to foresee any compelling military justification for extending the line through such territory all the way to the China border. Their decision to leave the northern terminal point untouched was, nevertheless, unfortunate. India's unresolved border dispute with China over the Aksai Chin region already assured a high level of strategic tension in northern Kashmir; and the signing of the Sino-Pakistan Border Treaty in March 1963, within four months of the disastrous rout of India's forces by China in the 1962 border conflict, had long since made plain that serious differences in regard to the location of China's border with Kashmir also existed between India and Pakistan. In effect, that treaty scrapped India's territorial claims reaching as far north into China as the Yarkand River, replacing them with an international boundary running immediately north of the Siachen Glacier eastward to the Karakoram Pass.[7] Obviously, the status of Indian, Pakistani, and Chinese territorial claims in the eastern Karakorams had materially changed between the drawing up of the CFL and the LOC. This seems to have been ignored in the 1972 delimitation exercise, however, which was guided by the same rule of thumb as in 1949 -- that the LOC was a temporary arrangement, a marking off of forces-in-place on a stilled battlefield, not a permanent international boundary.[8]

The potential for trouble inherent in the boundary's incompleteness was dramatically exposed in 1984. In that year, special units of the Indian Army were airlifted to pre-selected mountain outposts in the undelimited sector of Jammu and Kashmir state immediately north of map coordinate NJ 9842. The daring maneuver, codenamed Operation Meghdoot, planted the Indians astride three key passes (Sia La, Bilafond La, Gyong La) in the Saltoro Range dominating traditional approaches onto the massive Siachen Glacier. For a few years, the Pakistan Army made strenuous efforts to dislodge the Indians; but these efforts, faced with extraordinary hazards of altitude and climate, ultimately proved futile. Both countries committed substantial military assets to the struggle. Costs mounted, but neither side seemed willing or able to break the resulting stalemate. Lengthy negotiations aimed at curbing the Siachen hostilities finally foundered in 1989.[9] Progress in India-Pakistan relations was undermined; and, in the meantime, the whole issue of boundary delimitation in Kashmir was given a new, and particularly violent, dimension.[10]

The second legal loophole inherent in the boundary system erected in 1949 exists as a result of ambiguities in the definition of the boundary itself. These ambiguities derive from the LOC's treaty origins.

In regard to its treaty origins, there is, of course, no question that the LOC, technically speaking, was the direct offspring of the Simla Agreement -- a strictly bilateral accord, without international participation or guarantees of any kind, signed by the prime ministers of India and Pakistan on July 2, 1972. This agreement called for a new ceasefire line, specifically for a "line of control" to be drawn based on the positions held by the armed forces of the two sides at the time of the ceasefire of December 17, 1971. Physical modifications to the original CFL were kept to a minimum; but in its name and formal design, and certainly in the minds of its Indian makers, it obviously replaced the CFL constructed in the 1949 agreement under U.N. auspices. In sharp contrast to that earlier agreement, which was also a direct bilateral accord, the Simla Agreement was devoid of any explicit reference to the U.N.'s mediation and peacekeeping roles in Kashmir. Nothing was said in it of the U.N. resolutions that had enabled the original ceasefire; and there was no mention of the role that UNMOGIP (by that time, more than 20 years in existence) might play in policing the new ceasefire.

The 1972-crafted LOC did not fully replace the CFL, however, since at least part of the legal and institutional apparatus of the earlier line remained more or less intact. The Simla Agreement did not disestablish UNMOGIP, and neither did it constitute a formal repudiation of the U.N. resolutions that had brought UNMOGIP into being. On the contrary, Indira Gandhi's apparent reluctance at the time of the Simla negotiations to force Pakistani Prime Minister Zulfikar Ali Bhutto's hand in regard to Kashmir left the Kashmir issue practically as beclouded as ever. In the final hours of the talks, Bhutto managed to obtain Indira Gandhi's consent to wording that substantially diluted the agreement's bilateralism as well as its intended break with the past. The new LOC, said the final draft, was to be respected by both sides but "without prejudice to the recognised position of either side." This formulation left Pakistan's right to invoke the U.N. resolutions in defense of its territorial claims in Kashmir -- and, more than that, the legality of continuing multilateral involvement in regard to the LOC -- reasonably well-protected.[11]

Nevertheless, the Simla Agreement's omissions clearly cut away some of the legal ground from under Pakistan's territorial claim to Kashmir as well as from under the military observer teams operating in Kashmir under UNMOGIP auspices. For almost two decades, in fact, UNMOGIP has been operating essentially -- and dishearteningly -- on one leg in Kashmir.

UNMOGIP's Simla-induced limitations are multiple. First, on the Indian side, the military observers are totally barred from access to the LOC except at three crossing points.[12] Second, the Indians no longer bring complaints of ceasefire violations to the attention of the U.N. observers; hence, UNMOGIP's "awards" of responsibility for ceasefire violations, which now unavoidably favor Pakistan, are entirely lopsided and of even less value than before.[13] And third, the definition of what constituted a "violation" of the ceasefire has been significantly abbreviated. A six-part definition of a breach of the ceasefire had been agreed to by the two sides in 1949. Prohibited were (1) crossing of the CFL; (2) firing and use of explosives within five miles of the CFL without advance warning to the U.N. observers; (3) new wiring or mining of positions; (4) reinforcing of existing defensive positions with men or war-like stores; (5) forward movement from outside into the state of Jammu and Kashmir of any warlike stores, equipment, and personnel other than reliefs and maintenance; and (6) flying of aircraft over the other side's territory.[14] The fifth element of the definition had never been even remotely enforceable; and since 1972, the fourth element of the definition -- reinforcement of existing defensive positions with men or materiel -- has been essentially dropped. The Karachi Agreement had specifically barred strengthening of fortifications in the ceasefire zone, that is, a 500-yard-wide strip on either side of the line. Prior to 1972, the U.N. observers customarily visited both Pakistani and Indian forward pickets to confirm visually that no alterations in defenses had been made in this zone. With the CFL's conversion to the LOC in 1972, this zone effectively disappeared. The whole basis of the Karachi Agreement, a senior UNMOGIP officer commented in 1991, was simply "not there."[15] At the end of the 1971 conflict, troops were not withdrawn to their old positions. As a result, the U.N. observers had no choice but to fall back on the new ceasefire line of December 17, 1971. This line had no ceasefire zone; hence, the ban on reinforcement of positions in it could not be applied.

After 1971, the Pakistanis insisted that UNMOGIP carry on according to the Karachi Agreement. The United Nations apparently continues to view that agreement as valid; and UNMOGIP does continue to monitor fortifications *but strictly on the Pakistani side*. On the Indian side, it maintains a presence, but little more than that. Said an UNMOGIP observer: "We regularly visit Pakistani headquarters units and pickets along the Line of Control [to monitor fortifications]." Hence, "we know a great deal about Pakistani troop deployments; we know *nothing* about Indian deployments because we are not allowed to move about in their forward areas."[16]

The cumulative impact of all these limitations has been apparent for some years. It has become glaringly apparent, however, only in the last two years. Blatant breaches by both sides of the original ceasefire agreement have become routine all along the entire LOC. On the Indian side, however, UNMOGIP is unable to fill any peacekeeping role whatsoever; and on the Pakistani side, its role is extremely circumscribed. With an observer team numbering about 40 officers -- far and away the smallest U.N. peacekeeping mission in existence today -- its resources are wholly incommensurate with the scale of violations now occurring.[17]

In regard to the problem of boundary delimitation, then, the last two decades have witnessed two clearly negative developments: one, the severe functional decline of UNMOGIP, the multilateral peacekeeping force originally sent to Kashmir to monitor the ceasefire; and two, the resort to armed force at Siachen to settle the matter of the boundary's incompleteness. By the time of the Kashmiri uprising in more recent years, in other words, the principles upon which the boundary had originally been founded were already facing a severe military test; and they were doing so in an environment of greatly diminished international peacekeeping. As we shall see, yet more severe tests of these principles lay ahead.

Kashmiri Self-Determination

Kashmiri Muslim separatism has a tradition of militancy in the present century stretching back over sixty years. Its first noticeable appearance came in July 1931 in a mass agitation that swept the Valley of Kashmir in protest against the rule of Maharaja Hari Singh. It was the first ever open public demonstration against the Dogra Hindu Rajput dynasty that had ruled the princely state of Jammu and Kashmir under British tutelage since 1846. It marked the founding of the Muslim, later on, National Conference party, and launched the public political career of the renowned Kashmiri nationalist leader, Sheikh Muhammad Abdullah. It was put down with relative ease; but it is generally acknowledged to have sparked the modern political awakening of the Kashmiri Muslim people.[18]

While separatism has thus long held some appeal for Muslim Kashmiris, this appeal was largely kept in check during the Indian independence struggle against Britain by the close friendship and political understanding that existed between the Indian leader Jawaharlal Nehru and Sheikh Abdullah. Nehru allied the Congress party with Sheikh Abdullah's

National Conference during the early 1940s. In 1947, a few weeks before Kashmir's accession to India, Nehru obtained Abdullah's release from jail in Srinigar, and then, after the state's accession to India was secure, his appointment as prime minister of the state. Nehru, however, obviously patronized Abdullah and encouraged his Muslim-based political movement against the Hindu Maharaja in recognition of Abdullah's espousal of a united and secular India, not out of any intention to promote Kashmiri separatism.

Neither India nor Pakistan, in fact, championed Kashmiri Muslim separatism at independence in 1947. Indeed, at that time it was ignored by just about everyone. Maharaja Hari Singh flatly overrode the arguably democratic principle underlying partition, that giving primacy to majority community (and thus to an assumed "popular will"), and instead, on the lapse of British paramountcy, inserted his own autocratic will (to join neither India nor Pakistan) in its place. For his part, Nehru conceded a condition of accession -- that is, a future reference to the will of the people -- that the British Governor-General of India, Lord Louis Mountbatten, had included in his formal acceptance of the Instrument of Accession on October 27; but not then or ever thereafter did Nehru allow, publicly at least, that the people's will might choose other than either India or Pakistan.[19] The Pakistani leader, Muhammad Ali Jinnah, having assumed that the partition would go as expected on the basis of communal majority, initially showed no interest at all in providing Kashmiris with the opportunity to decide the popular will for themselves; and when events proved his assumption unwarranted, he took the same constricted view of self-determination -- a choice limited to accession to either India or Pakistan -- as had Nehru.[20] Britain and the new United Nations raised no objections to the restriction on Kashmiri choice. Whatever there was in 1947 of *Kashmiri Muslim* independence-mindedness, in other words, was simply swept aside in the rush to complete Indian and Pakistani statehood.

What awaited Kashmiri Muslim separatism in the post-independence period was even greater restriction on its expression. Pakistan had promptly declared Kashmir's accession to India a fraud and refused to recognize it. That stance led to war with India, whose leadership formally referred the matter to the Security Council of the United Nations on January 1, 1948. U.N. mediation efforts succeeded by August 1948 in winning both sides' consent to a cease-fire. A truce was implemented on January 1, 1949; and in July of that year agreement was reached on a Cease-Fire Line in Kashmir. The result of all this was that Kashmir was split in two, occupied by the armed forces of the two rivals, with a U.N. peacekeeping team deployed to monitor the ceasefire between them. The U.N. resolutions authorizing these steps also called for conduct of a U.N.-supervised plebiscite to determine the political will of the Kashmiri people.[21] Pakistan quickly took up the demand for Kashmiri self-determination and the conduct of a plebiscite; but its definition of self-determination -- like that contained in the U.N. resolutions -- remained restricted to a choice between India and itself. India, which with considerable irony had not only acquiesced in Mountbatten's stipulation of a plebiscite in his reply to the Maharaja's accession letter but had then been the first to invite U.N. intervention in the dispute, rapidly lost its enthusiasm for both the plebiscite and the U.N.'s presence. By 1953, Sheikh Abdullah, around whose person Kashmiri separatist feelings had never ceased to gather, was in prison, where he would spend most of the rest of his life. And early the following year, with ratification of the accession of Jammu and Kashmir to India by the Kashmiri Constituent Assembly, India moved closer to the position -- which it soon adopted formally -- that the accession to India was irrevocable and that there would be no plebiscite. Subsequent U.N. efforts to resolve the stalemate ended in failure in 1958. There was to be no reference to the people, not one under neutral international auspices in any case, and certainly not one with an enlarged notion of the possible alternative political futures from which Kashmiri self-determination might be fashioned. On the contrary, for the next several decades the will of the Kashmiri people was hardly to be heard at all.

When the will of the Kashmiri people finally began forcefully reexpressing itself, towards the end of the 1980s, it did so in a fashion for which neither Pakistan nor India was especially well prepared, either psychologically or politically. Common in India up until then was the belief that Kashmiris were an especially gentle, submissive, and genial folk. That stereotype was rudely shattered by the outbreak of terrorist bombings, strikes, attacks on public buildings and officials, mob violence, and demonstrations that marked the onset of the present uprising in July 1988. Some efforts were made in India at the time to pin responsibility for these developments on a carefully laid plan hatched by Pakistani intelligence.[22] While most Indian observers agreed that a "foreign hand" (meaning Pakistan's) was involved, the great majority of them freely conceded that the breakdown in relations between the central government and the people of Kashmir was due also to New Delhi's gross political mismanagement of the state, in particular its almost unbroken record of interference in and debasing of the state's electoral process.[23]

Pakistanis naturally welcomed the new rebellious spirit of Kashmiris. The depth of their alienation from New Delhi deflated the Indian claim to having achieved a successfully secular, democratic, and federal state; and, at the same time, it retrieved for Pakistan some of the virtue of the "two-nation theory" lost in the Bangladesh war of 1971.[24] It gave a much-needed boost to Pakistan's claim to international support for the Kashmiri cause; and it restored to the demand for plebiscite, which had over the years seemed increasingly fanciful and ritualistic, a degree of respectability.

At the same time, however, it also gave a new and essentially *Kashmiri* content to the "self" in self-determination, a development that could obviously detract from Pakistan's traditional "elder brother" posture in regard to Kashmiri separatism. Even more worrisome, perhaps, was its exposure of a serious weakness in the way Pakistan described its political relationship to the state of Jammu and Kashmir -- a weakness that India did not share and that rendered Pakistan's relentless espousal of Kashmiri self-determination potentially self-defeating.

The weakness referred to derives from the fact that India and Pakistan differ fundamentally in the way they define the nature of the Kashmir dispute. For one thing, they do not agree on the territorial limits of the "disputed territory" which the LOC divides. The spatial scale of the territory that is in dispute, in other words, is itself in dispute. Kashmir as India defines it is far larger than Kashmir as defined by Pakistan. Included in the Indian definition is all of the state presently held by India (the Valley of Kashmir, Jammu and part of Ladakh), the Aksai Chin region of Ladakh presently under Chinese control, those territories to the immediate north and west of the LOC presently under Pakistan's control (Azad Kashmir and the Northern Areas, including both Baltistan and Gilgit), those territories north of the present Sino-Pakistani border that India claims were illegally ceded to China in 1963, and -- in some formulations -- even Chitral district in Pakistan's present Northwest Frontier Province.[25] Included in the standard Pakistani definition, on the other hand, are only those parts of the state presently in Indian hands, Azad (Free) Jammu and Kashmir, and Baltistan district in the Northern Areas. A variety of political and strategic motivations may be cited to explain these differences.[26] Of importance about them in regard to the present discussion, however, is that Pakistan's licensing of Kashmiri self-determination might at some point turn the tables of territorial liberation against Pakistan. There is evidence, in fact, that the government of Pakistan, recognizing the danger, moved some years ago to shrink the scale of the territory marked "disputed" on its own maps.[27]

To complicate Pakistan's position even further, there is no agreement between India and Pakistan, in fact, that the territory of Kashmir is even in dispute. India, for its part, has argued from a very early point in the Kashmir conflict that Kashmir is not disputed territory, that India exercises sovereignty over it by virtue of the act of accession to India, that the CFL was thus drawn through *Indian* territory, and that the problem in Kashmir is one therefore simply of Pakistani aggression against a neighboring country. This problem required Pakistan's military withdrawal from Kashmir, its "vacation of aggression," not a territorial redivision. As we have already observed, New Delhi did officially and unequivocally concede, not only at the time of Maharaja Hari Singh's accession to India in late October 1947 but repeatedly for some years thereafter, that the matter of accession should ultimately be settled by popular plebiscite. It maintain almost from the start, however, that its relationship with Kashmir, ev if in some limited sense provisional, was still fundamentally proprieta and, ever since discarding in 1954 any concession at all to Kashmi provisional status, it has maintained that India's sovereignty was comple That part of Kashmir yet under Pakistan's control was dubbed Pakist Occupied Kashmir (POK), underscoring what India insisted was t illegality of Pakistan's claim -- in other words, of the non-existence of *legitimate* territorial dispute. When the Simla Agreement gave summo to the signatories to continue the search for durable peace in the regio its Indian-inspired phrases referred only to "a final settlement of Jamn and Kashmir" -- not of the Jammu and Kashmir *dispute*.

Pakistan, in contrast, has argued with considerable consistency virtua from the outset of the conflict that Kashmir is disputed territory, that belongs to neither India nor Pakistan, and that the question of permane possession of the territory could only be resolved by reference to t Kashmiri people, that is, by allowing them to exercise the right of politic self-determination through plebiscite. This right, as seen from Pakista was formally guaranteed by U.N. resolutions passed in the early stages the conflict and repeatedly acknowledged by both India and Pakistan the years thereafter. As we have seen, it was never expressed as unfettered right: Kashmiris were to be held to a choice of accession either India or Pakistan. Neither, however, was Pakistan's own claim Kashmir held to be unfettered: Pakistan did not then nor has it ev claimed Kashmir outright. It named the territory under its control Az (Free) Jammu and Kashmir and described its relationship with th territory as temporary and custodial. It has gone to considerable lengt over the years, in fact, to invest Azad Kashmir with the formal (albeit n the substantive) attributes of independent statehood, including its ov constitution, flag, president, prime minister, and supreme court. In theo it is the extension of this "independence" to the rest of Kashmir, not t arbitrary joining of Kashmir to Pakistan, which Pakistan seeks pendi conduct of a U.N.-supervised plebiscite. Its generosity aside, this provisi is obviously double-edged: once granted, independence might not be easily taken back.

At the moment, these weaknesses in Pakistan's territorial claim Kashmir place Pakistan at a disadvantage relative to India only in t abstract. Kashmiris have few places to turn for aid in the struggle agair India except to Pakistan; and ever since the uprising began India h supplied plenty of reasons for them to turn there. In fact, Indi response to the uprising so far has done nothing to reassure Kashmi about their future in the Indian union or to neutralize t uncompromisingly secessionist elements within the separatist movemen

The Indian military's attempts to crush the uprising by force have unquestionably been brutal. Numerous violations of the human rights of Kashmiris, including widespread extrajudicial executions and reprisal killings, torture, rape, assaults on civilians, arson, as well as arbitrary arrest and detention without trial, have now been credibly documented by respected international human rights groups.[28] The author's own inquiries in India and among Kashmiri refugees in Pakistan tend to confirm that these abuses have been fairly routinely practiced by the Indian armed forces, very likely including, at least in some instances, regular army troops. The most offensive behavior is generally attributed, no doubt deservedly, to the paramilitary forces, especially the poorly trained and poorly paid Central Reserve Police Force (CRPF) and the Border Security Force (BSF).

Understandably, the Indian military has reacted angrily to these charges, accusing its critics of exaggeration and bias. One of the highest ranking generals in the Indian Army declared flatly to the author, for example, that Indian troops in Kashmir were under terrible strain; they were being sniped at from all directions; and that, under the circumstances, the Indian Army was not going to make anything of charges against them. The foreign media, he said, was reporting only one side of the story. Human rights activists, he observed, were "nitwits." "I speak of them," he said, "as the uninformed speaking to the ignorant."[29] There were certainly ample grounds for his irritation. Much of the reporting was glaringly irresponsible. There was merit, too, in his complaint that foreign reporting tended to be one-sided, more often casting a spotlight on Indian human rights abuses in Kashmir than on Pakistan's not insignificant role in fanning the flames of discord there. Nevertheless, his language was intemperate and hardly fair. After all, it was nearly impossible for foreign or even Indian observers to report events accurately in the face of mammoth formal and informal restrictions on travel and information gathering. And the evidence was piling up that the reports of human rights abuses were not infrequently on the mark.

The Kashmiri separatists themselves, of course, have not escaped documented human rights abuses.[30] In fact, in this and in other respects their movement thus far is hardly above reproach. Practically all observers, whether favorably or unfavorably disposed towards Kashmiri separatism, agree that the separatist movement is chaotically organized and beset with innumerable cleavages; that its few capable leaders are either dead, incarcerated, or in exile; that it has been captured to some extent by criminal elements more concerned with extortion and racketeering than with Kashmiri liberation; that many of its followers are very poorly indoctrinated, barely aware of the movement's objectives, and motivated as often as not by the promise of material rewards; and that it is largely dependent for continued vitality on foreign (mainly Pakistani) support. In view of the militant organizations' various weaknesses and extreme vulnerability to Indian retaliation, even observers most friendly to the militants are apt to characterize their fighting capabilities as "meager," some of their reported exploits as a "joke," and the movement as a whole as "pathetic."[31]

The militant groups are increasingly well-armed with automatic weapons, light machine guns, grenades and rocket-launchers; but few, if any, observers believe them capable of driving India's sizeable, well-led, and far-better-equipped armed forces from the Valley. On the contrary, India's military forces appear wholly willing and able to contain the uprising, and in most respects seem to be taking it in stride. Kashmir Valley (the Jhelum River valley), the most heavily populated portion of the state and the center of the insurrection, is relatively small geographically, ringed by mountains, and not readily accessible from outside. The Indian Army lately (since January 1990) has maintained three heavily augmented divisions there along with large numbers of paramilitary formations (the CRPF and the BSF). According to a Pakistani estimate, the troop strength of the BSF alone in the Valley has grown from 13 to 30 battalions since January 1990, and may today number in the vicinity of 100,000.[32] Since there are very likely only about 1 million or so able-bodied Kashmiri Muslim males (in the 16-40 age cohort) in the entire Valley, the ratio of troops to militants is likely to remain overwhelmingly in India's favor.

The Kashmiri uprising, now approaching the end of its third year, thus seems utterly incapable of precipitating India's defeat on the battlefield. It has had, on the other hand, some fairly startling political successes. For one, it has stimulated profound soul-searching among fairly substantial elements of the Indian intelligentsia, many of whom interpret Kashmiri disenchantment with India as an indictment of the entire political system. Indeed, at least some Indians have been driven to propose quite radical and hitherto unmentionable solutions up to and including complete independence for Kashmir.[33] Second, the uprising has unquestionably mobilized vast numbers of the traditionally politically inert Kashmiri Muslim population, and equipped them with a cause for which many seem prepared to sacrifice and die. Third, it has created an environment in the Muslim-majority Kashmir Valley which forces India into the unfamiliar and awkward position of an alien (and oppressive) colonial power, and in which members of the Indian armed forces presumably defending Kashmir against foreign adversaries can scarcely emerge from their cantonments except under heavy guard.

True, the uprising has not attracted much attention from world media, nothing in any event even remotely comparable to media coverage of the Palestinian intifada. But its potential for embarrassing India over issues of human rights and self-determination is far from negligible. This was graphically underscored early in 1992 when the *ekta yatra* (march for unity) of the Hindu nationalist Bharatiya Janata Party, after crisscrossing much of India in a shower of national and international publicity for nearly seven weeks, finally ended in Kashmir's capital, Srinigar, with a humiliatingly brief flag-raising ceremony judged by most of the Indian press to have done more for the reputation of the Kashmiri militants than for the goal of Indian unity.[34] Indians seem as yet only dimly aware of it, but the Kashmiri militants' ability to exploit global sensitivity to human rights abuses has subtly curtailed New Delhi's options for coping with the uprising.[35]

Some Indian analysts claim to see "unmistakable signs that the [Kashmiri] insurgency is tending to peter out," providing New Delhi with mounting opportunities to seek a political solution mainly on India's terms.[36] More revealing, however, is the fact that the Kashmiris, even when faced with utter economic ruin, have somehow managed to sustain the uprising for nearly three years against overwhelming military odds. Kashmiri separatism may well be temporarily put down by sheer force of arms, one senses, but not permanently put out by it. That, it seems, would take implementation of political measures in Kashmir that India has avoided for over 40 years and, so far as one can judge, seems still disinclined to adopt today.

Cross-Border Interference[37]

The CFL/LOC has been violated from both sides and in countless ways on a continuing basis ever since its establishment in 1949. In only two cases, however, has violation of the boundary taken the form of largescale infiltration of irregular (guerrilla) forces.[38] The first such case was in July-August 1965, when Pakistan attempted to infiltrate several thousand armed men (most of them drawn from the regular Azad Kashmir armed forces) across the CFL into Indian Kashmir. Most of the would-be infiltrators were stopped at the border by Indian forces; and the effort (codenamed Operation Gibraltar) has generally been judged a failure. It led directly to full-scale war between India and Pakistan.

The second case of major cross-border infiltration developed only in the last three years. It has involved thousands of politically disaffected Kashmiri Muslim youths. It has been a significant factor in the development of widespread and violent secessionist activity in the Valley of Kashmir; and it has proven far more difficult to counter than Pakistan's ill-fated Operation Gibraltar. It led in early 1991 to a major escalation in cross-border mortar and artillery shellings and, thus, to further undermining of the ceasefire protocol in effect on the LOC. It helped to stimulate massive military redeployment, especially on the Indian side, vastly intensifying the existing heavy militarization of Kashmir. We consider two aspects of the issue: first, the character, motivation and scale of the infiltration itself, in which we focus on the question of Pakistan's involvement; and second, the character and consequences of India's counter-infiltration tactics, including the question of India's ability to curtail the flow of armed infiltrators from Pakistan.

Infiltration. Pakistan currently supplies substantial political, diplomatic and material support to the Kashmiri uprising. Officially, Pakistan denies that its support includes *military* assistance. The evidence is overwhelming, however, that its contributions to the training, indoctrination, arming, and cross-border movement of Kashmiri Muslim insurgents have been very substantial. The Indian press routinely exaggerates the number of infiltrators poised on the Pakistan side of the LOC, awaiting the opportunity to cross undetected. But an Indian Army tally of what the Army calls Anti-National Elements (ANES) supplied to the author at 15th Corps headquarters in Srinigar in June 1991 seemed, if anything, to have understated the facts. It was stated that the total number of ANES was 10,000 to 12,000, with 8,000 to 9,000 of those based in the valley of Kashmir.[39]

The Pakistan Army, in particular the Inter-Services Intelligence branch (ISI), is generally considered to be the key agency for planning and coordinating Pakistan's support, the same role it played until recently in the Afghanistan conflict. According to a 1991 Indian Army estimate, the ISI was then maintaining approximately 48 training camps in Azad Kashmir (POK in Indian parlance), in which training in light arms and guerrilla warfare tactics was imparted, generally by retired army NCOs, to Kashmiri Muslim recruits.[40] Exfiltration and infiltration of the recruits across the LOC, according to the Indians, was arranged at five ISI base camps located in Azad Kashmir. Presently, the ISI appears, moreover, to be the principal vehicle for the supply of weapons and cash to the Kashmiri secessionists; and in the judgment of many Indian (and some Pakistani) observers the ISI is also the chief supplier to the Kashmiri uprising in the Valley of virtually its only effective leadership. Groups other than the Pakistan Army (the Jamaat-i-Islami party for example) have operated their own training camps for Kashmiri recruits (including at least a few inside Afghanistan); and funds have flowed to the militant organizations from a variety of foreign sources, including Gulf Arab states. But there is very little likelihood that many infiltrators have made their way across the LOC, in either direction, without the knowledge and active cooperation of the Pakistan Army and, indeed, of key elements in the civil bureaucracy of Azad Kashmir. The LOC is heavily fortified and patrolling is heavy on both sides. Topographic perils, including, for example, the swift-flowing, freezing, and extremely turbulent Kishanganga (also called Neelam) river that abuts one lengthy stretch of the LOC, are many; safe crossing points are limited; and extraordinary precautions are essential to secure passage through the thicket of Indian checkpoints. For the most part, the infiltration has been a Pakistan-directed operation. It has not been, as some Pakistanis aver, a largely spontaneous affair; and it most certainly has not been an ISI rogue operation.

Pakistan has had several objectives in supporting the Kashmiri uprising. Promoting the secession from India of Kashmir has clearly been among them. Even a few years ago, this objective did not have much of a following in policy-making circles in Pakistan, least of all among those most familiar with the discrepancy between Indian and Pakistani military capabilities. To them, India's power to protect its claim to Kashmir seemed insuperable, and Pakistan's eventual capitulation to the LOC's conversion to a permanent border, even if not publicly admissible, seemed inevitable. The emergence recently for the first time in modern history of a powerful Kashmiri Muslim separatist impulse has unquestionably altered perceptions. And these perceptions have obviously been reinforced by the collapse of the Soviet state and the almost overnight acquisition of independence by the Muslim republics of Central Asia. Articulated nowadays at all levels of the civil and military leadership, in fact, is the view that history is marching against the world's remaining multinational conglomerate or "imperial" states, like India, and that patience in regard to its Kashmir territorial claim will ultimately reward Pakistan. India, it is often claimed, is in the early throes of a process of disintegration that may require decades to materialize but that is virtually certain to result in its breakup into several separate states. Kashmir, the argument goes, is very likely to be one of these breakaway segments.

As frequently vocalized as this argument may be in some quarters of Pakistani society and government, unqualified commitment to it in Pakistan's policy-making community remains quite rare. Promoting Kashmiri liberation unquestionably has the ring of wishful thinking about it; few Pakistani policymakers believe that Pakistan can bring it off soon or singlehandedly; and for most of them, in any event, it simply is not the most important, certainly not the most practical or immediate of Pakistan's objectives. These, including the "bleeding" of Indian resources, the demoralization of its army, the undermining of India's reputation abroad, the acquisition of diplomatic leverage against India, and, not least, the disarming of the Pakistan government's domestic political opponents, surely dominate Pakistan's day-to-day strategy.

The truth is that Pakistan has done relatively little to lay the groundwork for an effective, longterm, and sustained insurgency in Indian Kashmir. Such evidence as we possess, for example, in regard to the management in Pakistan of Kashmiri recruits to the secessionist movement hardly supports the thesis that Islamabad has made an unequivocal commitment to Kashmiri liberation. Most Kashmiri recruits are given extremely limited training in Pakistan, often only a few weeks in duration, and are often infiltrated across the LOC improperly equipped and under conditions that virtually guarantee their failure, capture, or slaughter by Indian forces. The author's interviews in June 1991 with two groups of Kashmiri infiltrators recently apprehended by Indian forces revealed that many of them were very poorly motivated, barely conversant with the weapons supplied to them, and disillusioned with Pakistan.[41] Some described their training in Pakistan as a joke. Some confessed, with seeming sincerity, that they had been lured to Pakistan largely by promises of generous pay, others that they had been used by Pakistan simply to generate bad publicity for India. They told of colleagues who had been sexually or otherwise abused in the training camps, and of so-called "guides" who, once having led the recruits across the LOC, had stripped them of their weapons and fled, leaving the hapless infiltrators to fend for themselves.

Concealed in the torrent of pro-Kashmiri slogans pouring from the Pakistani propaganda machine is the ironic fact that the motives of the Kashmiri insurgents are viewed with nearly as much suspicion in Pakistan as they are in India. As a consequence, Pakistan's support of the uprising, in terms of militant organizations financed, trained, and equipped, showed unmistakable signs of increasing selectivity after the secessionist movement broke out in full fury in January 1990. A conscious policy decision appears to have been taken very quickly in Islamabad, in fact, to curb the *independence* sentiment that clearly lay at the foundation of the movement. A generally very well informed Kashmiri observer, resident in Pakistan, put it this way to the author:

> While the People's Party was yet in power, Pakistani leaders became aware of the need to assert more Pakistani control of the uprising. The movement was getting huge in size and the cry for *azadi* -- independence of *both* India and Pakistan -- was growing loud. In early February 1990, a meeting was held in Islamabad, with Prime Minister Benazir Bhutto in the chair, and with the Chief of Army Staff General Aslam Beg, and the President and Prime Minister of Azad Kashmir in attendance. They considered the possibility that the uprising could boomerang on Pakistan, and that Pakistan could lose not only Jammu and Kashmir but the Northern Areas as well. They decided they had to curb the *azadi* forces, meaning they would not equip them and not send them into the Valley. It was decided that the Pakistan Army should take over the training camps, and that the private camps that had sprung up be shut down. Benazir Bhutto addressed a press conference later that month, on returning from a visit to Muzaffarabad. She said at this conference that accession to Pakistan was the only option open to Kashmiris. That understanding of the issue then became the policy of Pakistan, which was then focused on restricting both access to the Valley and supply of arms to pro-accession forces.[42]

Having decided to curtail the mounting popularity of pro-independence groups in the Valley, the Jammu and Kashmir Liberation Front (JKLF) and Operation Balakot, for instance, the Pakistan government has swung its support largely to the decidedly less popular but pro-accession (meaning pro-Pakistan) groups such as the Hizb-ul Mujahideen and Muslim Janbaaz Force.[43] Funds and weapons have dried up substantially for the pro-independence groups, and the access of their Pakistan-based leaders (and followers) to the Valley has been made more difficult. Pakistan's support of the militants has not only grown in size, in other words, but has become more carefully focused to reflect Pakistan's own political interests.

Naturally, Pakistanis interpret these developments in a rather different way. They claim that national liberation takes both time and sacrifice; Kashmiri victims of the Indian military meatgrinder are the necessary price, they say, of eventual Kashmiri freedom. Unacknowledged, of course, is the strong possibility that Pakistan's interest in the Kashmiri uprising falls short of liberation, possibly even of Kashmir's union with Pakistan. Pakistani motives are certainly mixed. There is, however, an undeniable element of calculated, in some respects ruthless, self-interest underlying Pakistani support of the Kashmir uprising.

Pakistan's self-interest and fundamental pragmatism when it comes to Kashmir were made painfully apparent in February 1992, when Pakistani troops and riot police, according to press reports, opened fire on unarmed Kashmiri separatist protest marchers threatening to force their way across the LOC into the Indian-controlled portion of Kashmir. Amanullah Khan, a Pakistan-based leader of the JKLF, had jolted Islamabad weeks earlier with the announcement of his plan to lead thousands of his followers from Azad Kashmir to the Indian border, which he said he intended to storm in a demonstration of solidarity with the secessionists fighting to end Indian control of the state of Kashmir. In an increasingly tense atmosphere, which included threats by the Indian Army to shoot any marchers attempting to cross the LOC, negotiations between the Pakistan government and the protesters came to naught. The government resorted to extraordinary measures to stop the march, including the setting off of landslides and the dismantling of bridges; and when these efforts failed, they allegedly fired into the oncoming marchers, killing at least twelve and wounding many more.[44]

The February march was a repeat, on a much larger scale, of a less-publicized procession taken out near Muzzaffarabad a year earlier, on March 15, 1991, by the JKLF, Operation Balakot, and their allies. The motivation of these groups then was much the same as it was for this year's demonstration -- to pressure Pakistan into lifting curbs on the infiltration across the border into Indian Kashmir of independence-minded Kashmiri separatists. On that occasion, the Pakistan government succeeded in persuading the marchers to disband before reaching the border, and violence was avoided.[45]

Justifying its decision to halt the February march with whatever force necessary, the Pakistan government declared in the days preceding the event that the government had no choice in the matter: it did not want another war with India and it could not permit the marchers recklessly to provoke an incident at the border that might have explosive consequences. Though one could hardly argue with this reasoning, there was a strong possibility that the incident developed in the first place at least in part because of the considerable gap that had grown between Pakistan's public profession of unqualified support for the Kashmiri separatist movement as a whole and its private preferment of more narrowly focused support for a select group of pro-Pakistani parties within that movement. Widely believed to have the bulk of Kashmiri opinion in the Valley of Kashmir on their side, the JKLF naturally resented being shunted to the sidelines. For them, the traumatic events of February exposed a hollowness in the Pakistan government's claim that it backs the self-determination of Kashmiris. They were, in fact, a brutal reminder that Kashmir's political future could not be charted without due regard not only for the national interests of India but for those as well of Pakistan. When these interests hung in the balance, Pakistanis, like Indians, might not hold back from shooting independence-minded Kashmiri Muslims.

Counter-infiltration. India's counter-infiltration efforts have been seriously handicapped by a number of factors. Terrain, climate, and costs have thus far prohibited either full fencing or full mining of the 500-mile-long LOC. Patrolling of the LOC is extremely difficult at higher elevations, where deep snows hinder movement most of the year, and cannot by itself seal the border against scattered bands of determined infiltrators. Hazardous as is their mission, the infiltrators are at severe risk of detection only for a relatively short period of time following crossing of the LOC.

The problems in regard to counter-infiltration faced by India's 19th Infantry Division, responsible for protecting a lengthy stretch of the LOC to the north and east of Srinigar, are representative. As a senior officer of this division explained it, the distance between the LOC and the Indian-defended mountain ridges to the east varies anywhere from about 1.8 to 18 miles.[46] The infiltrators tend to make their crossing where the distance is least. Key objectives for them are the fairly numerous small passes, actually gullies or ravines, numbering about 15 in the nearly 168-mile-long sector of the LOC defended by the 19th Infantry Division, that cut through the ridgeline at elevations running between 11,000-12,000 feet. Ordinarily, the infiltrators require about six to eight hours -- one night, in other words -- to make it from the LOC, across the Indian-defended ridgeline, to the safety of the thickly pine-forested slopes on the other side. Even fairly large groups of infiltrators are apparently able to make it across from time to time. Discovery by an Indian Army patrol of an especially large group of infiltrators attempting to cross the Shamshabari ridge near Baramula on May 5, 1991, seems to have resulted in large part from the failure of the infiltrators to get past the ridgeline before daybreak.[47]

The LOC is by no means impenetrable. Indeed, natural geographic barriers form only parts of it. There are no mountains, for example, to obstruct passage for about 15 to 20 percent of the sector guarded by the 19th Infantry Division. Even where natural barriers exist, moreover, they are not uniformly formidable. One short stretch of the LOC, for example, follows the Poonch river, which is relatively shallow and fairly easily crossed, winter or summer.

Geography aside, the Indian Army, to tell the truth, is neither well-equipped nor well-trained for counter-infiltration duty. It has prepared itself for decades to face a potential onslaught by the regular forces of Pakistan, not to act as a screen against surreptitious border-crossers. The paramilitary forces that are, in principle, better designed for such duty are themselves, it seems, even less well suited for it. When asked whether the troops guarding the LOC were open to bribery, an Indian general in command of troops on the LOC replied: "It is absolutely impossible to bribe an Indian Army man." But a senior Indian government official with decades of experience in Kashmir insisted unequivocally that the movement of armed infiltrators across the LOC was the product in large measure of what he called the "massive corruption of Indian troops."[48] Even the general confessed, with a wink, that his statement did not necessarily blanket the paramilitary forces.[49]

The Indian Army has greatly amplified its efforts to seal the border in Kashmir over the last year or so. These efforts, including the laying of additional minefields; the passage of new emergency legislation governing disturbed areas to facilitate preventive arrest and detention by the armed forces; the establishment of an elaborate informant apparatus throughout the Valley; the clearance of civilians from a "dead zone" immediately adjacent to the LOC; the erection of a three- or four-tiered security belt stretching back about three miles from the LOC; as well as more aggressive air and ground patrolling, have almost certainly raised the risks of infiltration very substantially. Indians suggest that they discover and apprehend only about 25 percent of the infiltrators. Accurate or not, the figure seems very likely to grow.

Whatever may be the rate of apprehension, however, it is crystal clear that India's political and military leadership views Pakistan's direct material support of the uprising in the gravest conceivable terms and, moreover, that it is willing to adopt extraordinary measures -- going well beyond sealing of the border -- to curb it. Since spring 1991, these measures appear to have included unusually heavy and frequent mortar and artillery bombardments aimed at Pakistani civilian settlements across the LOC in Azad Kashmir. The great bulk of these bombardments have occurred along the stretch of the LOC that runs roughly parallel to and in some portions very close to the Neelam Valley road -- a road that follows the Kishanganga (Neelam) river about 100 miles from Muzaffarabad (the capital of Azad Kashmir) to Kail. At three points on this route, Indian forces occupy distinctly advantageous positions in the heights overlooking the road from which they can bombard the highway and civilian settlements, as well as delicately suspended footbridges across the raging Kishanganga. Since virtually all supplies to Pakistani forces and civilians in this sector must travel via this road, India is obviously in a position to inflict serious damage on Pakistan virtually at will. "To be difficult," said the Indian Army general whose forces man the artillery batteries in the mountains overlooking the Neelam Valley road, "the Indian Army can easily choke this key artery." "Beyond Kail," he said, "there are no all-weather, all-year roads."

In one widely reported episode of shelling on the Neelam Valley road, between May 2-8, 1991, Pakistanis claim that Indian guns (120mm mortar, 130mm and 155mm artillery pieces) fired as many as 10,000 rounds at one cluster of villages in Athmuqam subdistrict, flattening many homes and shops.[50] Pakistani forces focused their own heavy fire on the Indian gun batteries. Which side actually precipitated the firing is unclear. It was at exactly this same time, however, that massive infiltration efforts appear to have been launched from the Pakistan side (witness the encounter, mentioned above, between May 5-6), suggesting a possible link between the two. Indians typically argue that the Pakistanis initiate such exchanges as "cover" for infiltration operations. Pakistanis generally argue, in contrast, that Pakistan's vulnerability to Indian artillery along the Kishanganga river is an especially tempting point at which the Indians can apply pressure to Pakistan for any number of diplomatic or military purposes. According to a Pakistani officer in command of a mujahid force (paramilitary) battalion at Athmuqam, for instance, the Indians simply wanted to make the statement: "We can close this road whenever we want."[51] On this point, at least, the two sides seemed in perfect agreement.[52]

These increasingly routine artillery and mortar barrages are not without precedent. Small arms firing incidents have been common along the LOC for many years. In the Athmuqam area, for instance, such incidents appear to have been quite regular, occurring, on average, every few weeks or so. These usually involved initially small arms fire; but in every case, according to Pakistani Army men, the firing would escalate to heavy mortar and artillery exchanges lasting, normally, one or two days. What distinguishes the more recent exchanges, say the Pakistanis, is their extraordinary intensity and duration. And in this sense, at least, they unquestionably added an ominous wrinkle to the pattern of firing across the LOC. Among other things, the ferocity of these barrages suggests that whatever constraints on violation of the Kashmir boundary may once have existed are rapidly breaking down. On both sides of the LOC, civilian and military leaders seem prepared to vent their wrath against the other side through increasingly direct and sustained military assault.

Summary and Implications

To summarize the discussion thus far: This chapter has argued that there have been numerous changes in the character of the Kashmir dispute in the several decades since its inception in 1947, that these changes have been particularly marked in the last few years, and that the cumulative impact of all these changes has been to transform the dispute fundamentally. Three basic dimensions of the dispute were identified: (1) boundary delimitation, (2) Kashmiri self-determination, and (3) cross-border interference. Fundamental transformation over time was visible in all three.

In regard to delimitation, we observed that legal deficiencies in the boundary system dividing Jammu and Kashmir state -- namely incompleteness of the CFL/LOC and ambiguities in the definition of the boundary -- resulted, by 1972, in the severe functional crippling of the U.N. peacekeeping mission, UNMOGIP, and, by 1984, in the resort to major and sustained armed force by the armies of India and Pakistan to settle the matter of the boundary's incompleteness.

As for the problem of self-determination, there is now incontrovertibly a third actor on the scene -- the Kashmiri Muslims themselves. Their stunning political debut has confronted the Indian state with perhaps the severest mass disavowal yet of the presumptive benefits of its secular, democratic and federal charter. But while seeming to repudiate these, the recent Kashmiri uprising has also bluntly called into question the legitimacy of the territorial claims on Kashmir of *both* India and Pakistan. No longer could these two countries expect the world to accept without question the claim that "self-determination" was or could be served simply by the accession of Kashmir either to India or Pakistan. The possibility of a third alternative -- the complete independence of Kashmir -- now unmistakably offered itself.

Finally, in regard to the problem of cross-border interference, we have observed that massive infiltration of Kashmiri separatists from Pakistan into Indian-controlled Kashmir has triggered a major escalation in both the quantity and intensity of fighting along the LOC and that the protocol governing the two armies' conduct in the vicinity of the line was in constant danger of breaking down entirely.

The implications of these developments are far-reaching, both in regard to the Kashmir dispute's potential for settlement and in regard to the role that the international community might play in increasing that potential. We have space here to provide only a brief outline of some of these implications:[53]

(1) The Kashmir dispute's passage to its "new phase" has been marked by sharp and relatively synchronous upheaval in all major aspects of the dispute: boundary delimitation, Kashmiri self-determination, and cross-border interference. As a result, it is today, militarily and politically, more confused, turbulent and dangerously unpredictable than at any earlier moment in its history. Only a bold and imaginative effort to restabilize the boundary between India and Pakistan, one that takes fully into account the profound changes that have occurred in the character of the dispute, will hold much promise of eventual success. The oddly anachronous suggestion of one author that the crisis be met with a "formal acceptance of the status quo by both sides for the next twenty or so years, coupled with a "no-war pact," is a prescription for continued instability and potential catastrophe.[54]

(2) No proposal in regard to Kashmir that fails to take careful account of the interests of both India and Pakistan is likely to get very far. By the same token, however, no proposal that accommodates the interests of these two countries *to the exclusion of the interests of Kashmiris* is likely to get very far either. This is not because the interests of Kashmiris cannot be fairly readily trampled: the experience of recent years, let us be frank, is far from reassuring on that count. Rather, it is because the interests of these two countries in regard to Kashmir cannot readily be accommodated *except* via concessions to the Kashmiris themselves. For the foreseeable future, neither India nor Pakistan -- for reasons that include but go well beyond the existence of their incompatible territorial claims -- is at all likely to ratify the permanent absorption of Kashmir, in particular of the Muslim-inhabited Valley, by the other. At the same time, neither India nor Pakistan is any more likely to accept an interpretation of Kashmiri self-determination that unambiguously forecloses ultimate accession of the state, or at least parts of it, to itself. In between these two improbables, however, is considerable room for haggling over *some* form of revised jurisdictional status for Kashmir -- call it neutralization, demilitarization, or something else. The Kashmiri uprising creates the urgent need for some such agreed mutual adjustment. Ironically, it also creates the perfect excuse for it: glaring shortcomings in the traditional definitions of self-determination inherent in the territorial claims of India and Pakistan to Kashmir now stand equally and nakedly exposed to light.

The argument that "no government in India could possibly survive [making territorial concessions]" may still be sound;[55] but sounder yet, increasingly, is the argument that there will be no end to the Kashmir crisis until concessions, whether or not territorial in form, are made to the Kashmiri demand for self-determination. Pakistani arguments that seek to satisfy this demand by monotonous invocation of the U.N.'s original resolutions in regard to a plebiscite betray a failure to recognize the changes that have taken place in the Kashmir dispute, in particular the erosion that has taken place in Pakistan's case for a bifold definition of self-determination.[56] The same may be said, however, of Indian arguments that hold Kashmiri Muslims forever hostage to the allegedly precarious "welfare" of their 100 million Muslim co-religionists in India.[57] The frailties of Indian secularism in regard to its huge Muslim minority do not excuse the denial of basic human rights in Kashmir. Kashmiri welfare deserves to be reckoned with for its own sake.

(3) No proposal in regard to Kashmir that relies exclusively or very heavily on <u>bilateral</u> instruments of conflict management or resolution is going to make much of a dent in the present confrontation between India and Pakistan. Very little government-to-government security cooperation has been formally institutionalized between them in the past; and what little exists by way of confidence-building measures between them today is of very recent origin, largely untested and scarcely reliable.[58] The record of bilateral negotiations India and Pakistan have built up over the years in regard to Kashmir is not one to inspire confidence in their present capabilities; and, given the unstable political environments in which both governments now operate, these capabilities may be even weaker than usual. While it is often invoked, the commitment to bilateralism India wrung from Pakistan in the Simla Accord of 1972 today has little substantive meaning. Pakistanis view Simla as a codeword for defeat in war and submission to Indian regional hegemony, not as a model framework for subcontinental negotiations. The Simla formula may not be entirely dead, but it certainly does not measure up to the task of deescalating the conflict in Kashmir. While the international community has displayed no great eagerness of late to engage again seriously in the quest for settlement in Kashmir, international intervention -- in the form, for example, of U.N. or U.S. mediation -- is an obvious alternative. Indeed, it may well prove to be an inescapable alternative.[59]

(4) Even if the alternative of international mediation is adopted in regard to Kashmir, no one should expect much more than modest and incremental progress to be made. Properly organized and executed, however, intervention in the Kashmir dispute by the international community has better chance for success today than at almost any time since 1947. The external context has been largely cleansed of Cold War contaminants; higher priority can now be given to the amelioration of regional conflict;

and international pressure, hitherto constrained by the requirements of superpower rivalry, can now be applied more deliberately, consistently, and evenhandedly. The key word here is evenhandedly. This implies recognition that both India and Pakistan have a legitimate stake in Kashmir, furthermore that proposals for settlement of Kashmir cannot possibly move ahead if those making the proposals are thought to be more interested in forging new alliances (or in building up new regional hegemons) than in forging more peaceful regional relationships. Regional reconciliation, not the reconfiguration of regional power, should be the objective of international intervention. It is the only practical objective. Without it, no settlement of any kind in Kashmir is likely.

Notes

1. Research for this chapter was supported by grants from the United States Institute for Peace, the Office of Research of the U.S. Department of State, and the Department of Government and International Studies, University of South Carolina. The opinions, findings, and conclusions or recommendations expressed in this chapter are those of the author and do not necessarily reflect the views of the grantor agencies.

2. The best recent source for historical background on the origins and development of the Kashmir conflict is Alastair Lamb, *Kashmir: A Disputed Legacy, 1846-1990* (Hertingfordbury, UK: Roxford Books, 1991). Among earlier works, see Sisir Gupta, *Kashmir: A Study in India-Pakistan Relations* (New Delhi: Asia Publishing House, 1966); Michael Brecher, *The Struggle for Kashmir* (New York: Oxford University Press, 1953); and Josef Korbel, *Danger in Kashmir*, revised edition (Princeton: Princeton University Press, 1966).

3. The many references to the potential for communist subversion of Kashmir in Josef Korbel's 1954 study of the problem, *Danger in Kashmir*, today seem almost quaint. Korbel, a Czechoslovak diplomat appointed chairman of the United Nations Commission on India and Pakistan when it was first created in early 1948, was forced to resign his post soon after the communist takeover of Czechoslovakia later that year. Despite its ideological slant, Korbel's work was an impressive achievement and remains today one of the most penetrating studies of the Kashmir conflict.

4. This was the title of a recent book focusing on the management of U.S. policy in seemingly intractable regional conflicts. The India-Pakistan dispute over Kashmir was included among the disputes discussed. Curiously, some of the disputes considered in the book -- South Africa and the Palestine dispute, in particular -- seemed at least a bit less intractable in 1992 than they had when the book was published in 1990. Richard N. Haass, *Conflicts Unending: The United States and Regional Disputes* (New Haven: Yale University Press, 1990).

5. Rosalyn Higgins, *United Nations Peacekeeping, 1946-1967, Documents and Commentary, II: Asia* (London: Oxford University Press, 1970), p. 348.

6. For more detailed discussion of these deficiencies in the boundary system, see Robert Wirsing, *India, Pakistan, and the Kashmir Boundary Dispute: The Search for Settlement* (New York: St. Martin's Press, forthcoming).

7. The 1963 agreement fell well short of a definitive boundary settlement. It dealt only with a relatively small segment of China's southern boundary, leaving unaddressed the signatories' overlapping and vastly more complicated border disputes with India. Indeed, the joint declaration published at the time the Sino-Pakistan agreement was concluded conceded its provisional status pending Pakistan's final settlement of the Kashmir dispute with India. India declared the agreement wholly invalid. For background, see Yaacov Vertzberger, *The Enduring Entente: Sino-Pakistani Relations 1960-1980* (New York: Praeger, 1983), pp. 15-83.

8. The British historian Alastair Lamb speculates that India's ongoing dispute with China over the precise location of the northern Kashmir border may actually have been a key consideration in the decision to terminate the LOC short of an international boundary. *Kashmir: A Disputed Legacy 1846-1990*, pp. 325-6.

9. For a detailed analysis of these negotiations, see Robert Wirsing, "The Siachen Glacier Dispute: Can Diplomacy Untangle It?," *Indian Defence Review* (July 1991), pp. 95-107.

10. For a detailed discussion of the background and development of the Siachen Glacier dispute, see Robert Wirsing, *Pakistan's Security Under Zia, 1977-1988* (New York: St. Martin's Press, 1991), pp. 143-94.

11. See Kuldip Nayar, *Distant Neighbours* (New Delhi: Vikas, 1972), pp. 231-40; and Imtiaz H. Bokhari and Thomas Perry Thornton, *The 1972 Simla Agreement: An Asymmetrical Negotiation*, FPI Case Studies Number 11 (Washington, D.C.: Foreign Policy Institute, The Johns Hopkins University, 1988), pp. 19-21; 28-40.

12. One of these three crossing points, according to a member of the UNMOGIP team in India, has been closed for four years due to a jurisdictional dispute between India and Pakistan. Interview with the author, New Delhi, May 1991.

13. In 1985, for instance, Pakistan reported about 150 Indian violations of the LOC to UNMOGIP. All were investigated, and in nearly all cases (95 percent) awards were made -- that India had, indeed, committed the violation. Member of the U.N. observer team, interview with the author, Rawalpindi, January 1986.

14. Higgins, *United Nations Peacekeeping 1946-1967, Documents and Commentary, II: Asia*, p. 340.

15. Interview with the author, New Delhi, May 1991.

16. Interview with the author, Rawalpindi, January 1986. For related discussion, see Alan James, *Peacekeeping in International Politics* (New York: St. Martin's Press, 1990), pp. 158-63.

17. There have been 23 U.N. peacekeeping missions deployed since 1948. At the moment (February 1992), ten are deployed. Their designations and assigned personnel are as follows:

Angola Verification Mission	440
Truce Supervision Organization (Arab-Israeli conflict)	300
Peacekeeping Force in Cyprus	2,200

Observer Mission in El Salvador	1,000
Disengagement Observer Force (Golan Heights)	1,300
Military Observer Group (India-Pakistan)	40
Iraq-Kuwait Observation Mission	540
Interim Force in Lebanon	5,900
Mission for the Referendum in the Sahara	2,700
Advance Mission in Cambodia	1,380

Figures taken from Paul Lewis, "U.N. Votes to Send Force to Yugoslavia," *The New York Times* (22 February 1992), p. 3. The peacekeeping mission in Cyprus, with 2,200 members, patrols a no-man's-land extending 118 miles across the island between the quarrelling Turks and Greeks. This is about one-fifth the length of the LOC in Kashmir. A trend appears to be developing in favor of larger missions. A 14,000-member peacekeeping force was approved by the Security Council in February this year to monitor the ceasefire in Yugoslavia. The peacekeepers were to be deployed primarily in about 14 Serbian minority enclaves in the now independent republic of Croatia. In the same week, the Security Council authorized a peacekeeping mission for Cambodia that was to have between 22,000 and 26,000 members. Previously, the largest peacekeeping team ever authorized was the force of 20,000 sent by the United Nations to the former Belgian Congo in 1960.

18. For a recent study of the 1931 movement, see U. K. Zutshi, *Emergence of Political Awakening in Kashmir* (New Delhi: Manohar Publicatons, 1986).

19. Alastair Lamb suggests that at one point -- in the discussions on Kashmir held in Lahore between the Indian Prime Minister Jawaharlal Nehru and his Pakistani counterpart Mohammed Ali Bogra from August 17-20, 1953 -- Nehru may have given fleeting consideration to a plebiscite arrangement that would have allowed Kashmiri Muslims the option of complete independence. *Kashmir: A Disputed Legacy, 1846-1990*, pp. 225-7.

20. In the weeks immediately following Kashmir's accession to India, Pakistan's leaders apparently first rejected, then endorsed the proposal for a plebiscite carried out under U.N. auspices. Ever since then, however, Pakistan has never retreated from its formal support of plebiscite -- nor from its insistence that the plebiscite be limited to a choice between Pakistan and India. Lynn H. Miller, "The Kashmir Dispute," in Lawrence Scheinman and David Wilkinson, eds., *International Law and Political Crisis: An Analytic Casebook* (Boston: Little, Brown and Company, 1968), p. 49.

21. There were three major U.N. resolutions bearing on the plebiscite question: Security Council Resolution 726 of April 21, 1948, an enabling resolution spelling out the conditions for plebiscite in great detail; UNCIP Resolution 995 of August 13, 1948, which only briefly and vaguely endorsed the idea of Kashmiri self-determination; and UNCIP Resolution 1196 of January 5, 1949, which again spelled out the conditions for plebiscite in great detail. These conditions varied in important respects from one resolution to another. India and Pakistan both expressed strong reservations about some of these conditions. Both, however, formally accepted the proposal for a plebiscite made in the January 5, 1949 resolution.

22. See, for example, IDR Research Team, "Op Topac: The Kashmir Imbroglio," *Indian Defence Review* (July 1989), pp. 35-48. This extraordinary article, which appeared to reveal the shocking details of a high level meeting of military and intelligence officials allegedly called together by Pakistan's President Zia in April 1988 to chalk out a secret strategy for the liberation of Kashmir, was clearly identified in preambular remarks by its unnamed authors as a mix of fact and fiction. Numerous Indian and even some Pakistani writers appear to have overlooked that caveat and to have read the article as a revelation only of fact. Included among those who mistook fiction for fact were leading defense analysts. For one instance, see K. Subrahmanyam, "Kashmir," *Strategic Analysis* Vol. 13, no. 2 (May 1990), pp. 137-8.

23. Criticism of New Delhi's management of Kashmiri politics had been a staple of Indian politics for decades. It grew more intense than ever after 1984, when Sheikh Abdullah's son, Farooq Abdullah, was toppled from power in the state in an egregiously heavy-handed manner by Prime Minister Indira Gandhi. No state in India had a worse reputation when it came to the conduct of elections. A major New Delhi-based daily editorialized about the March 1987 state elections, for example, that "such is the State's murky record in this sphere [vote-rigging and other election malpractices] that barring the 1977 poll not a single election could be said to have reflected the people's will truly and faithfully." *The Hindustan Times* (April 15, 1987). For a lively account of New Delhi's political meddling in Kashmir in the 1980s, see M. J. Akbar, *Kashmir: Behind the Vale* (New Delhi: Penguin Books, 1991), esp. pp. 196-223.

24. According to the "two-nation theory," Muslims and Hindus are not merely two religions but two nations, each deserving of its own separate state.

25. Prime Minister Nehru himself stated in the Lok Sabha on May 26, 1956 that Chitral was a part of Jammu and Kashmir state and that Pakistan's sovereignty over that area would no longer be recognized. Sisir Gupta, *Kashmir: A Study in India-Pakistan Relations* (Bombay: Asia Publishing House, 1966), pp. 305-6. See also the White Paper, *Statement of Facts on Gilgit, Hunza, Nagar, Yasin, Ponial, Chitral and Skardu*, produced in Srinigar by the Government of Jammu and Kashmir state (1983?).

26. The British scholar Alastair Lamb speculates, for example, that in laying claim to Chitral Prime Minister Nehru may have been "hoping to make the plebiscite less attractive in Karachi. After all, if Chitral really was a part of Kashmir, and if Pakistan did lose the plebiscite as it was then envisaged by the United Nations, then the consequences would be even more disastrous. It is possible that here was another Indian argument for the recognition, at any rate tacitly, of the cease-fire line as the legal boundary." *The Kashmir Problem: A Historical Survey* (New York: Praeger, 1966), pp. 90-1.

27. Pakistan's definition of Kashmir's territorial spread was initially much larger than it is now. Gilgit Agency, which, along with Baltistan, constitutes Pakistan's Northern Areas, used to be pictured on Pakistani maps, as on Indian maps, as a part of the disputed territory of Kashmir. In the mid-1950s, Pakistan apparently began issuing maps depicting Gilgit as an integral part of Pakistan. This practice prevailed, and by the 1980s Pakistani-made maps generally excluded Gilgit from the area marked "disputed territory." The changeover, incidentally, has prompted a heated discussion *within* Pakistan over the spatial issue, with Azad Kashmiri elements holding out for a more expansive territorial definition than the central government

seems inclined to support. For details, see Wirsing, *Pakistan's Security Under Zia, 1977-1988*, pp. 145-59. See also Robert C. Mayfield, "A Geographic Study of the Kashmir Issue," *The Geographical Review* Vol. 45, no. 2 (April 1955), pp. 181-96.

28. See, for example, *Human Rights in India: Kashmir Under Siege, an Asia Watch Report* (New York: Human Rights Watch, May 1991). This report concedes that Kashmiri militant groups have also been guilty of crimes against civilians, but it maintains that these have been on a much lesser scale.

29. Interview at Indian Army Headquarters, New Delhi, June 1991.

30. See, for example, *Kashmir Under Siege*, pp. 129-53.

31. Interviews, New Delhi, May-June 1991.

32. Pakistani brigade commander, Muzzaffarabad, Azad Kashmir, June 1991.

33. At a private gathering in New Delhi in June 1991, the author was astounded to hear the chief editor of a leading national daily argue at great length for the complete independence of Kashmir. India's economy, he said, had been mortgaged to Kashmir for decades. So long as the confrontation over Kashmir with Pakistan continued, he claimed, economic growth would be stymied. His was certainly not the majority view. For a fair cross-section of current Indian views on the issue, see "Kashmir: Wages of Manipulation," a roundtable discussion of Kashmir in *India Today* (August 31, 1991), pp. 47-59.

34. See, for example, Prem Shankar Jha, "Irresponsible Brinkmanship," *The Hindu* (December 18, 1991); and Dilip Awasthi and Harinder Baweja, "Ekta Yatra: An Odyssey of Futility," *India Today* (February 15, 1992), pp. 16-19. Only 67 BJP leaders and workers made it all the way to Srinigar, flown there from Jammu in Indian Air Force helicopters. The ceremony in the center of Srinigar, witnessed solely by a large contingent from the press and thousands of Indian troops, but by no Kashmiris, lasted only twelve minutes. On the eve of the ceremony, Kashmiri separatists had managed to set off a bomb inside the police headquarters in Srinigar, injuring a number of senior police officers.

35. See the remarks in this vein by Dilip Mukerjee, one of India's most esteemed journalists, in "Talking to Pakistan: Validity of Two-Track Approach," *The Times of India* (August 16, 1991), and in his two-part article "Foreign Policy: Time for Reorientation?," *The Economic Times* (August 20-21, 1991).

36. Jha, "Irresponsible Brinkmanship."

37. This section relies heavily on interviews in India and Pakistan conducted by the author in May-June 1991.

38. Reference here is strictly to the period *since* establishment of the CFL in 1949. There was, of course, a third major instance of infiltration in the Kashmir conflict, but it occurred in the period *prior* to formation of the CFL. It was India's complaint to the U.N. Security Council on January 1, 1948 that Pakistan was giving aid to tribal invaders of the state of Jammu and Kashmir that precipitated international intervention in the Kashmir conflict in the first place.

39. Estimates given to the author of the total number of armed Kashmiri "militants" undergoing training on the Pakistani side of the LOC ranged as high as 8,000.

40. Indian Army officers briefing the author on the infiltration problem in June 1991 made no effort to conceal the fact that precise data, whether in regard to the number of Kashmiri trainees in Pakistan or the number, type or location of training camps, simply didn't exist. Many of the camps, they said, were quite small, very modestly outfitted, located in remote areas, and easily shifted.

41. The interviews were conducted at 15th Corps Headquarters in Srinigar. A total of 34 captives were included, in two separate groups, for a period of two hours. Indian Army officers were present and acted, when necessary, as translators. There is no question that the captives, whose future wellbeing was obviously at stake, "slanted" their testimony to suit their captors' interests. Most had little or no formal education, however, and none gave any evidence of having rehearsed his comments.

42. Interview, June 1991. The quotation is abbreviated and paraphrased, but faithfully reflects the speaker's statement.

43. Apparently, the changeover by the Government of Pakistan was quite swift. According to one report, by October 1990 "Pakistani intelligence was training as many as 4,000 JKHM [Hizb-ul Mujahideen] cadre against fewer than 1,500 of the JKLF." Jha, "Irresponsible Brinkmanship."

44. Edward A. Gargan, "12 Are Killed as Pakistani Police Fire on Kashmiris Marching Toward Border," *The New York Times* (February 13, 1992), p. A3. Confrontations between the marchers and police occurred over several days at a number of different points along the border. Estimates of the total number of marchers ranged from 5,000 to 20,000. Following the most violent clashes, Pakistan's Federal Minister for Kashmir Affairs, Sardar Mehtab Ahmad Khan Abbasi, was reported to have denied categorically in the National Assembly in Islamabad that the marchers had been fired upon by law enforcing agencies. Aroosa Alam, "Police Firing on Marchers Denied," *The Muslim* (February 14, 1992). See also Shekhar Gupta, "Pakistan: Raising the Stakes", *India Today* (February 29, 1992), pp. 14-15; and Shakil Shaikh and A. Q. Ishrat, "15,000 Marchers Reach Chinari," *The Muslim* (February 12, 1992).

45. A number of the captive infiltrators interviewed by the author in June 1991 at the Indian Army's 15th Corps Headquarters in Srinigar claimed to have participated in the March demonstration. One of them displayed what were obviously torture marks on his body, according to him inflicted by Pakistani police interrogators after the demonstration was broken up.

46. Briefing, 19th Infantry Division Headquarters, Baramula, June 1991.

47. As many as 150 infiltrators were discovered attempting to cross on this occasion. The Indians claim having killed 72 of the infiltrators in the encounter, called Operation Dudhi by the Indians, which lasted three days. The author was briefed on this encounter at battalion headquarters at Chokibal by Colonel D. Kumar, Commander, 7th Assam Rifles, in June 1991.

48. Interview, New Delhi, June 1991.

49. What the Indian Army calls its Forward Defended Area along the border consists of three or four tiers of defensive lines. According to an Indian Army general in command of troops on the LOC, the paramilitary forces (the Border Security Force, primarily) are ordinarily deployed no further forward than the third or fourth tier. Implied, perhaps, was that if the infiltrators could make it through

the initial -- regular army-defended -- tiers, then perhaps bribery might facilitate passage the rest of the way.

50. The battalion tactical headquarters of the Indian Army at Bulbir Outpost (what the Pakistanis call DAT Top) is only 2.5 to 3 miles from Athmuqam and enjoys a commanding view of that section of the Neelam Valley. Pakistanis claimed in a briefing at Athmuqam that the Indians, employing 54 guns, had fired anywhere from 10-15,000 rounds at 8-10 villages in the subdistrict in the period May 2-8. The author's visit to Athmuqam confirmed that damage from the shelling was extremely heavy.

51. Interview, Athmuqam, June 1991.

52. A member of the UNMOGIP observer team in India suggested in an intervew with the author (May 1991) that the shelling, which was not only heavy but extremely expensive, revealed India's anger and frustration over the infiltration problem. It could serve no other conceivable purpose, he observed, except to signal Indian displeasure to the Pakistanis. The area of heaviest shelling, he noted, was also the area of heaviest infiltration. The Indians, he said, shell Pakistani villages, and the Pakistanis retaliate by shelling Indian gun emplacements.

53. The problems of reaching a settlement are explored in detail in the author's forthcoming book, *India, Pakistan, and the Kashmir Boundary Dispute: The Search for Settlement.*

54. Sumit Ganguly, "Avoiding War in Kashmir," *Foreign Affairs* Vol. 69, no. 5 (Winter 1990/91) p. 71.

55. *Ibid.*, p. 71.

56. See, for example, Fahmida Ashraf, "The Kashmir Dispute: An Evaluation," *Strategic Studies* (Islamabad) Vol. 13, no. 4 (Summer 1990), pp. 61-77. For a more unconventional Pakistani view, see Pervaiz Iqbal Cheema, "A Solution for Kashmir Dispute?," *Regional Studies* (Islamabad) Vol. 4, no. 4 (Autumn 1986), pp. 3-15. Cheema envisages a territorially somewhat lopsided settlement in which Pakistan retains all the territories of the former state of Jammu and Kashmir currently in its possession (Northern Areas and Azad Kashmir), while India retains only Jammu and Ladakh. However, he suggests that Kashmir Valley be turned over to a U.N. trusteeship for ten years or so, that interval to be followed by a plebiscite to determine finally the Valley's future. The plebiscite, he points out, should allow a third choice -- that of complete independence.

57. Ashutosh Varshney, "India, Pakistan, and Kashmir: Antinomies of Nationalism," *Asian Survey* Vol. 31, no. 11 (November 1991), p. 1000. In a curious misrepresentation of the Hindu Maharaja's autocratic decision in 1947 to accede to India, Varshney writes that "the voluntary decision of Muslim-majority Kashmir to join India bolstered the secular argument." For Kashmir to leave India now, he says, would only reinforce the anti-secular view of Hindu nationalists that Indian Muslims "are essentially disloyal to the country."

58. In spring 1991, India and Pakistan reached two confidence-building agreements, one providing for advance warning to each other of troop movements, the other against violation of each other's air space.

59. This is true in spite of the fact that India has repeatedly declared itself deadset against any further outside mediation efforts in Kashmir. A fairly recent such instance was at a press conference on October 19, 1991, when Indian Prime

Minister Narasimha Rao, returning from a meeting of Commonwealth heads of government at Harare, Zimbabwe, was reported to have categorically ruled out mediation of India-Pakistan differences by any country. *The Muslim* (October 20, 1991).

Chronology of Events: September 1988–April 1992

Ata Khan

1988

September 4. The Press and Publications Ordinance, 1963, is repealed.

September 7. The Registration of Printing Press and Publications Ordinance, 1988 is promulgated.

September 27. The Lahore High Court declares the dissolution of the National and Provincial assemblies illegal, but rules against their restoration. The Court also directs that elections be held on November 16, as announced. This decision is affirmed by the Supreme Court on October 5.

September 30. Sporadic firing by unknown gunmen leaves over 150 dead in Hyderabad and Latifabad.

October 1. The Hyderabad violence spreads to Karachi where hooded gunmen kill 58 people through indiscriminate firing.

October 2. The Supreme Court rules that elections to be held on November 16 will be held on a party basis.

October 6. Eight political parties and religious groups join hands to form the Islami Jamhoori Ittehad (IJI - Islamic Democratic Alliance).

October 9. The life of speedy trial courts, instituted to provide timely justice in cases involving heinous and anti-state activities, is extended for another year.

October 13. Salman Rushdie's novel, *The Satanic Verses*, is banned in Pakistan.

October 16. A joint U.S.-Pakistani committee established to investigate General Zia ul-Haq's death concludes that the crash was caused by "a criminal act of sabotage perpetrated in the aircraft."

November 16. Elections for the National Assembly are held. 1,370 candidates from 30 parties contest the elections for 207 Muslim and 10 non-Muslim seats. The low 42 percent voter turnout is attributed to the requirement by the government that voters present identity cards before casting ballots.

November 16. The Pakistan People's Party (PPP) emerges as the leading party in the National Assembly with 93 out of a possible 207 seats. The IJI secures 54 seats and the Muhajir Quami Mahaz (MQM- Muhajir National Movement) 13 seats.

November 19. Elections for the Provincial assemblies are held. The IJI gains 108 seats in Punjab and 29 in the NWFP; the PPP secures 94 seats in Punjab, 67 in Sindh and 21 in the NWFP; the MQM gains 26 seats in Sindh; and independents secure 59 seats nationwide.

November 26. Nawaz Sharif, the caretaker chief minister of Punjab, is given the option of either sitting in the Punjab Provincial Assembly or leading the opposition in the National Assembly. He chooses the former.

November 30. Members of the newly elected National and Provincial assemblies take oath.

December 1. President Ghulam Ishaq Khan designates Benazir Bhutto as the new prime minister. The emergency council is dissolved and the emergency lifted.

December 2. Benazir Bhutto takes oath of office as the first female prime minister of a Muslim nation in modern times. She promises to eradicate illiteracy and poverty, restore student unions, liberate political prisoners, provide equal rights to women, and free the media.

December 2. The PPP and the MQM sign an historic accord termed the "Karachi Declaration." The accord is expected to restore peace in Sindh.

December 2. The Punjab Assembly elects Nawaz Sharif as its chief minister.

December 4. A 23-member Federal Cabinet is formed. On March 22, 1989, 26 additional ministers and Begum Nusrat Bhutto as Senior Minister without Portfolio also become members of the Cabinet.

December 12. Ghulam Ishaq Khan is elected president for five years by winning 348 votes compared with 91 votes won by his closest opponent.

December 12. Benazir wins the mandatory vote of confidence in the National Assembly.

December 15. The Balochistan Assembly is dissolved by General (ret'd.) Mohammad Musa, the Governor of Balochistan, on the recommendation of Mir Zafarullah Khan Jamali, the chief minister, as no parliamentary group enjoys a majority in the House. Justice Khuda Bakhsh Marri takes over as caretaker Chief Minister of Balochistan on December 22.

December 31. Pakistan and India sign several accords at the SAARC summit held in Islamabad, including agreements not to attack each others' nuclear facilities, to avoid double taxation and to enhance cultural cooperation.

1989

January 16. Oil and gas reserves are discovered in Hyderabad district.

January 23. The dissolved Balochistan Assembly is declared "restored" by the Balochistan High Court.

January 25. The Jamiat Ulema-i-Islam (JUI) and the Balochistan National Alliance (BNA) form a broad based government in Balochistan headed by Nawab Akbar Bugti.

February 5. It is announced that Pakistan has successfully tested two indigenously manufactured surface-to-surface missiles, one with a range of 80 kms.; the other with a range of 300 kms. The missiles can carry a payload of over 500 kgs.

February 8. The People's Programme with a budget of Rs. 2 billion is launched. The programme is expected to cover basic needs of the people such as health facilities, potable drinking water, education and communications networks. On April 13, Balochistan Chief Minister Nawab Akbar Bugti charges that the People's Programme infringes on provincial autonomy.

February 9. An armed man with a gun concealed inside his walking stick passes several security check-points before being stopped on the second floor of the National Assembly. Benazir was inside the Assembly at the time.

February 11-13. During her visit to China, Benazir Bhutto reportedly signs an agreement on the supply of 75 Chinese-made F-7 fighter aircraft worth $225 million for the Pakistan Air Force.

February 12. At least five people are killed by police firing during a march on the American Cultural Center by demonstrators protesting against Salman Rushdie's book, *The Satanic Verses*.

February 14. Indigenously developed shoulder-fired surface-to-air missiles with a range of 50 to 5,000 meters equipped with Laser Range Finders with a range of 150 to 15,000 meters are incorporated into the Pakistan Army.

February 14. The Soviet Union completes its troop withdrawal from Afghanistan twenty-four hours ahead of schedule.

February 23. Prof. Sibghatullah Mojaddedi is elected President and Prof. Abdur Rasul Sayyaf is elected Prime Minister of the interim government of Afghanistan by the Pakistan-based Afghan *Shura*.

March 9. Afghan mujahadin capture Jalalabad's old city.

March 13. Nawaz Sharif, the newly elected Chief Minister of Punjab, wins a vote of confidence. The PPP stages a walkout before the vote.

April 21. Ten countries and financial institutions comprising the Aid-to-Pakistan Consortium approve an aid package worth $3.1 billion for Pakistan.

April 30. Jam Sadiq Ali, a senior PPP politician, returns home to Sindh after twelve years of self-exile.

April 30. The Pakistan Narcotics Control Board arrests drug baron, Anwar Khattak.

May 1. Restrictions on trade unions and collective bargaining in key public-sector enterprises are lifted.

May 13. Hundreds of teachers of the *Nai Roshni* (new awakening) project schools protest against expected dismissals.

May 22. India successfully launches the *Agni* long-range ballistic missile, which has a range of 2,500 kms.

May 30. Rifts between the PPP and the MQM surface as MQM leader Altaf Hussain and IJI leader Nawaz Sharif hold highly publicized discussions in Karachi.

June 4. Ayatollah Ruhollah Khomeni, Iran's spiritual leader, dies.

June 4. A Combined Opposition Party (COP) consisting of almost all opposition groups is formed in the National Assembly. Ghulam Mustafa Jatoi will lead the opposition.

June 4-10. During her visit to the United States, Benazir Bhutto declines a proposal by President Bush that Pakistan unilaterally allow inspection of its nuclear facilities to determine whether they are being used for peaceful purposes. She further declares that Pakistan does not possess nuclear weapons and won't "provoke a nuclear arms race" in the Subcontinent.

June 7. The United States agrees to provide $465 million to Pakistan in economic assistance. The funds are to be used to increase literacy, particularly among women, improve the quality of higher educational institutions, and help Pakistan finance more of its needs through the private sector.

June 12. It is announced that Pakistan will acquire 60 F-16 fighter aircraft from the United States.

July 1. It is announced that Pakistan is to receive $581 million in economic and military aid from the United States during the 1989-90 fiscal year.

July 3. It is decided to liquidate the National Construction Company which incurred a loss of Rs. 5 billion during the previous year.

July 3. Three Afghan majors and one Afghan captain seek asylum in Pakistan after landing at Quetta in two helicopters.

July 6. The Center-Punjab tussle enters a new phase as Ghulam Ishaq contacts the IJI and PPP leadership to end the confrontation.

July 10. Ethnic clashes in Karachi leave nine dead.

July 26. Drug baron, Haji Mirza Mohammad Iqbal Baig, surrenders to the Pakistan Narcotics Control Board.

July 29. Former NWFP Governor, Lt. General (ret'd.) Fazle Haq is arrested and jailed on charges relating to the murder of TNFJ leader Allama Arif Hussain al-Husaini.

August 16. A five-year plan for the design and development of nuclear reactors is approved.

August 25. A PIA Fokker en route to Islamabad from Gilgit disappears. Extensive searches yield no results.

August 31. At least nine prisoners are killed and twenty-two injured in an operation to rescue nine wardens held as hostages by prisoners at the Sukkur jail.

September 4. Benazir's controversial Placement Bureau, which made political appointments to the civil bureacracy, is abolished.

September 5. A Pakistan Air Force (PAF) F-16 crashes while on a routine training mission. The pilot, squadron leader Zafar Ahsan, is killed in the crash.

September 10. Gas is discovered in Khairpur district in upper Sindh. The field has a potential of 28 million cubic feet of production.

September 19. Four Federal Investigation Agency (FIA) officials are jailed in Punjab after their bail request is denied by the local magistrate. After intense debate relating to the Punjab-Center tussle, the FIA officials are "reluctantly" released by the Punjab government on October 7.

September 23. Federal Minister for Labor and Manpower, Malik Mukhtar Ahmed Awan, is declared a proclaimed offender. He is allegedly involved in a murder case. He is granted interim bail on December 5.

October 1. It is announced that Pakistan will soon begin exporting the trainer aircraft, *Mashak*, to some friendly countries.

October 1. After seventeen years of absence, Pakistan once again becomes a member of the Commonwealth.

October 23. The COP moves a no-confidence motion against the PPP government in the National Assembly. The motion is admitted in the Assembly on October 26.

October 23. The MQM terminates the Karachi Accord with the PPP and is expected to vote with the COP in the no-confidence motion against Benazir's government.

November 1. Benazir survives the no-confidence motion moved by the COP in the National Assembly. The COP's support falls short of the required 119 votes by a margin of 12 votes. Allegations of bribing and kidnapping members are made by both sides.

November 6. The government allows the free import of gold. This action is expected to check the smuggling of gold into the country.

November 11. Three opposition members who had sided with Benazir during the no-confidence motion are inducted into the Federal Cabinet.

November 13. The entire cabinet resigns allowing Benazir to form a new broad-based government.

November 15. Nawaz Sharif inaugurates the Bank of Punjab, the first provincial bank in Pakistan.

November 28. It is announced that the Pakistan Atomic Energy Commision (PAEC) has attained limited capability to reprocess uranium and has set up a small facility for this purpose. A small 27 KW research and training reactor has also been established near Rawalpindi.

December 1. Pakistan's first Women's Bank is inaugurated by Begum Nusrat Bhutto.

December 4. Pakistan International Airlines (PIA) enters into an agreement with the European Airbus Industrie and General Electric for the manufacture of aircraft and engine components at its Precision Engineering Complex in Karachi.

December 9. *Zarb-i-Momin* (Sword of the Faithful), the Pakistan Army's largest-ever military exercise, commences in Punjab. The exercise ends on December 24.

December 11. Ghulam Ishaq inaugurates the Hamdard University Library (*Baitul Hikmat*) at Madinat al-Hikmat, 35 kms. outside Karachi.

December 13. Shooting by terrorists leaves six dead in Hyderabad. The violence spreads to Karachi and continues till the end of the year leaving dozens dead.

December 15. Shoot-on-sight orders are given to Indian forces in Occupied Kashmir to quell large-scale violence by the Jammu and Kashmir Liberation Front (JKLF) militants.

December 16. The U.N. adopts Pakistan's proposal for a nuclear-free zone in South Asia.

December 21. Prime Minister V.P. Singh's newly formed government in New Delhi wins a vote of confidence in Parliament.

December 31. Oil and gas are discovered near Islamabad. Exploitation potential of the field is estimated at 1000 barrels of oil per day.

1990

January 4. Pakistan's worst-ever train disaster claims 300 lives near Sukkur.

January 10. At a meeting between President Ghulam Ishaq Khan and COP leaders, the opposition accuses the PPP government of conducting a "regular witch-hunt" of people opposed to the PPP.

January 16. Pakistan Railways resumes delivery of iron scrap to Ittefaq Foundries. Nawaz Sharif's family owns Ittefaq Foundries, which has been embroiled in this dispute with Pakistan Railways for the past seven months contributing to the Center-Punjab confrontation.

January 19. Governor Raj Jagmohan replaces Chief Minister Farooq Abdullah as President's Rule is imposed on Indian occupied Kashmir.

January 25. Benazir gives birth to a son.

January 26. A huge public gathering, said to be the largest-ever in Karachi, comes out to hear opposition leaders attack the PPP government.

February 3. The first convocation of Karachi University in fifteen years is held.

February 4. At a meeting held by the PPP government, the leaders of all the major political parties reach a consensus on the Kashmir issue.

February 6. Disturbances in Karachi leave around 60 dead over three days. The disturbances follow a general strike called by the MQM to protest the alleged abduction of its supporters by PPP workers.

February 19. Francois Mitterrand becomes the first French Head of State to visit Pakistan. Over the course of his stay he offers to sell Pakistan a nuclear power plant. In January 1992, France reneges on its promise insisting that Pakistan adhere to the restrictions of the Nuclear Non-Proliferation Treaty (NPT).

March 3. More than 20,000 school teachers go on strike protesting numerous government policies, including the denationalization of schools. The boycott ends on March 25 after assurances by the government, but no written agreement is signed.

March 9. A coup attempt against Afghan President Najibullah ends in failure and the coup leader Shahnawaz Tanai flees Afghanistan.

March 19. The Pakistan Army unveils indigenously made tanks, armored recovery vehicles, and armored personnel carriers.

March 23. Citing inadequate practical measures to help the Kashmiris, Nawaz Sharif withdraws unconditional support to the government over the Kashmir issue.

March 28. It is announced that approximately 8,000 Kashmiris have poured into Pakistan during the past month following the attempt by Indian authorities to quell the rebellion in Indian-held Kashmir.

April 3. A public transport strike protesting the increase in petrol and diesel prices paralyzes Karachi.

April 4. It is reported that Pakistan has developed a portable ground-to-air missile, which has a range of six kms. The system is thought to cost much less than American Stinger missiles.

April 5. Significant gas reserves are found near Sukkur.

April 6. The student wing of the JKLF kidnaps three people and threatens to kill them unless three of their fellow militants are released by Indian authorities. The hostages are killed upon the expiration of the deadline.

April 6. Indiscriminate firing in Karachi leaves at least ten dead.

April 7. Killings continue in Karachi and spread to Hyderabad. The next day, MQM leader Altaf Hussain, starts a fast unto death demanding the arrest of the persons involved in the recent murders. He ends his fast on April 14 after being assured by the Sindh Governor that all efforts are being made for peace.

April 11. V.P. Singh warns Pakistan of swift retaliation for its interference in Kashmir.

April 12. Increased tensions and sporadic firing is reported between Pakistani and Indian troops in Kashmir.

April 20. Thirteen countries and twelve international organizations that comprise the Aid-to-Pakistan Consortium pledge $3 billion for Pakistan's development.

April 24. Australia agrees to sell 50 "mothballed" Mirage jets to Pakistan. The first batch of 32 aircraft is delivered on November 28.

April 25. Pakistani and Indian foreign ministers meet in New York and pledge to reduce tensions and keep channels of communication open on the Kashmir border.

May 6. A time bomb explodes on a train near Lahore, killing eleven.

May 9. Two days of sniper firing leaves fourteen dead in Karachi.

May 12. Armed with rockets and hand grenades, dacoits in the interior of Sindh raze the village of Haji Sawan Khan Gopang.

May 14. Protesting the growing lawlessness in Karachi, a business strike is observed in the city.

May 17. Disturbances resume in Karachi and Hyderabad and leave over 300 dead during the next three weeks. These include the infamous "Pucca Qilla" killings of civilians by the police and Eagle Squad in Hyderabad.

May 18. A bomb explosion kills ten in Lahore.

May 21. Maulvi Mohammad Farooq, Kashmir's senior Muslim cleric, is shot dead in Srinagar, fueling further unrest in the Valley.

June 1. India withdraws some of its troops from the border with Pakistan. Pakistan reciprocates the move the next day.

June 13. Begum Liaquat Ali Khan passes away and is buried alongside her husband at the Quaid-i-Azam Mazar in Karachi.

June 15. The Symington Amendment that can be used to ban U.S. aid to Pakistan is waived for another year.

June 18. A provisional government of the independent state of Jammu and Kashmir is formed in Azad Kashmir.

June 19. Kashmiri militants use rockets to destroy two hotels in Srinagar housing Indian security forces.

July 8. The Punjab and the Federal governments hold conciliation talks to reduce tension between them.

July 15. A number of explosions in Hyderabad leave 45 dead.

July 16. Pakistan's first experimental weather satellite, "Badr-I," is launched from China.

July 19. President's Rule is imposed again on Indian-held Kashmir.

July 23. The army's powers to deal with the law and order situation in Sindh are enhanced to include the right to book suspects and register First Information Reports (FIR).

July 28. A UNHCR plan for the voluntary movement of Afghan refugees back to Afghanistan is launched. It meets with a poor response from the refugees.

August 6. Ghulam Ishaq dissolves the National and Provincial assemblies and COP leader Ghulam Mustafa Jatoi replaces Benazir as the caretaker prime minister. Benazir's immediate family and members of her government are barred from leaving the country. Elections are scheduled for October 24. The new government begins rounding up supporters of the PPP government.

August 20. A highjacked Soviet airliner leaves Karachi after its hijackers surrender to Pakistani authorities.

August 21. Pakistani and Indian troops exchange fire in Kashmir.

August 22. Terrorist attacks leave 27 dead in Karachi.

August 25. The deposed PPP government, including the former prime minister, is charged with fourteen cases of nepotism and corruption.

August 27. Sardar Abdul Qayyum Khan is re-elected President of Azad Kashmir.

September 1. The first contingent of the 10,000 Pakistani troops that will become part of the multinational force formed to defend Saudi Arabia from possible Iraqi attack leaves for the Kingdom.

September 22. Pakistan thwarts an Indian Army attack in the Kel sector of Kashmir where intermittment firing between the two armies has been taking place for the past few weeks.

September 23. It is announced that China will provide $84 million in credit to Pakistan for the Saindak project in Balochistan.

September 26. A Peshawar High Court order restoring the dissolved NWFP Assembly is overruled by the Supreme Court.

October 1. In a move that curiously follows the change of government in Pakistan, President Bush suspends economic and military aid worth at least $564 million to Pakistan, allegedly after new information is received concerning Pakistan's nuclear program.

October 10. Asif Ali Zardari, Benazir Bhutto's husband, is arrested in connection with a case involving kidnapping and extortion.

October 18. The Supreme Court postpones hearings on the dissolution of the National and Provincial assemblies till after elections. The dissolution of the assemblies is upheld by the Lahore High Court on October 14 and by the Sindh High Court on October 19.

October 20. The area encompassing the Babri Mosque in Ayodya is taken over by the Indian government. Fundamentalist Hindus, who believe it to be the site of Lord Rama's birth, are attempting to tear down the mosque and replace it with a Hindu temple. Such actions have led to communal violence.

October 22. An amendment to the Political Parties Act is promulgated to check floor-crossing by members of the Provincial and National assemblies.

October 24. The IJI gains 105 seats, the Pakistan Democratic Alliance (PDA) comprising mainly the PPP wins 45 seats, and the MQM gains 15 seats in elections held for the National Assembly. Voter turnout is 45 percent.

October 28. In elections for the provincial assemblies, the IJI wins 216 out of 240 seats in Punjab; the PDA 46 and the MQM 28 out of 100 seats in Sindh; the IJI 29 out of 80 seats in the NWFP; and the Jamhoori Watan Party (JWP) 9 seats out of 32 in Balochistan. Benazir accuses the caretaker government of rigging the elections.

October 30. Hindu extremists attack the Babri Mosque in Ayodhya leading to communal violence which leaves 60 dead.

November 3. Newly elected members of the National Assembly take the oath of office.

November 4. Gohar Ayub, the son of former President Ayub Khan, is elected speaker of the National Assembly.

November 6. Mian Mohammad Nawaz Sharif is elected prime minister. The state of emergency is lifted.

November 7. V.P. Singh, India's Prime Minister, resigns after losing a vote of confidence in the Indian Parliament.

November 10. Chandra Shekhar is sworn in as Prime Minister of India.

November 10. An eighteen-member Federal Cabinet is inducted.

December 3. Kidnapping becomes punishable by death.

December 11. Nawaz Sharif announces a grant of over Rs. 11 million for Karachi's development.

December 12. Pakistan asks India to protect Muslims after communal violence leaves up to 200 dead in India.

December 15. The Federal Cabinet allows the creation of an airline in the private sector.

December 16. An ordinance is promulgated to allow commercial banks to be set up in the private sector.

1991

January 1. The first Pakistani expedition to Antarctica crosses the Antarctic Circle.

January 17. Rallies are held throughout the country to show support for Iraq against the U.S.-led coalition.

January 27. A treaty between India and Pakistan not to attack each other's nuclear facilities comes into effect. However, lists of nuclear installations, a condition of the treaty, are yet to be exchanged.

January 28. General Aslam Beg, the Chief of the Army Staff, criticizes the government's pro-U.N. Gulf War policies and terms the U.S.-led assault a part of "Zionist" strategy.

January 31. Ghulam Ishaq warns against army interference in politics.

February 1. An earthquake measuring 6.8 on the Richter scale kills more than 300 people in the NWFP.

February 5. "Solidarity with Kashmir Day" is observed throughout the country.

February 7. Prime Minister Nawaz Sharif liberalizes the economy by lifting all controls on foreign currency entering the country and announces new policies to encourage foreign investment in Pakistan.

February 9. Nawaz Sharif reiterates his government's pro-U.N. stance on the Gulf war. There have been numerous pro-Iraq demonstrations and widespread public opposition to Nawaz Sharif's Gulf war policies.

February 10. The NWFP government announces that No Objection Certificates (NOC) will not be required to set up industries in the province.

February 17. 25,000 workers of banks expected to be denationalized strike to protest the government's denationalization policies.

February 20. The U.S., U.K., Germany, Japan, and Austria impose an embargo on the export of defense-related equipment to Pakistan.

February 21. The 1991 population census is postponed due to the potentially disastrous impact of the expected results on urban-rural harmony in Sindh.

February 26. It is announced that Foreign Minister Yaqub Khan has resigned. He officially resigns on March 20. Akram Zaki, the Secretary-General of the Foreign Office, assumes his responsibilities.

March 6. *Qisas* and *Diyat* laws are passed by the Senate.

March 11. The Disqualification for Membership Bill is adopted by the National Assembly.

March 12. The Governor of Balochistan, General (ret'd.) Mohammad Musa dies in Quetta.

March 14. Elections for 42 seats in the Senate lead to a victory for the IJI, which secures 23 seats against 5 won by the PDA. Wasim Sajjad is elected Chairman of the Senate.

March 27. Four Pakistanis who highjacked a Singapore Airline Airbus from Kuala Lumpur to Singapore are killed by commandos in Singapore.

March 31. The Prime Minister of Azad Jammu and Kashmir (AJK), Mumtaz Hussain Rathore, dissolves the AJK Assembly.

March 31. The Afghan garrision at Khost falls to the mujahidin.

April 6. India and Pakistan sign agreements in New Delhi aimed at reducing tensions between the two countries.

April 9. The PDA ends its boycott of the National Assembly after an agreement is reached with the IJI government.

April 11. The Shariat Bill is introduced in the National Assembly.

April 25. All funding by the Pakistan Government to the AJK Government is withdrawn.

May 5. Indian forces ambush Muslim separatists in Kashmir, killing 66.

May 7. The Aid-to-Pakistan Consortium earmarks $2.3 billion for Pakistan for the fiscal year 1991-1992.

May 12. Asif Zardari is charged with the murder of political opponents soon after being acquitted on charges of fraudulently obtaining a bank loan. Benazir is accused of misusing secret service funds.

May 16. The Shariat Bill is adopted by the National Assembly. The Bill is approved by the Senate on May 28. Pleas by opposition parties to amend the bill are rejected.

May 20. Syeda Abida Hussain becomes the first woman in the Federal Cabinet when she is appointed adviser on population welfare.

May 21. Former Indian Prime Minister Rajiv Gandhi is assassinated near Madras while campaigning for elections.

May 27. The Agha Khan Foundation for Economic Development (AKFED) receives permission to operate a private airline and compete with PIA on domestic routes.

June 11. Lt-General Asif Nawaz Janjua is named as the next Chief of Army Staff, replacing Aslam Beg.

June 11-14. A high-level Pakistani delegation visits the U.S. and holds talks with State and Defense officials.

June 13. The U.S. House of Representatives votes to maintain restrictions on aid to Pakistan.

June 16. The 1991-1992 budget is passed by the National Assembly. Spending on defense and debt servicing is increased while social sector spending is cut in half.

June 18. Special court judge Nabi Sher Junejo, who was hearing a case against Asif Zardari, is gunned down in Karachi.

June 20. China admits to supplying Pakistan with short-range tactical missiles.

June 29. Six members of a family are murdered in Sheikhupura. This killing follows another gruesome murder of thirteen members of a family in Lahore.

June 30. Due to the increased lawlessness in Punjab, Nawaz Sharif postpones his visit to Japan.

July 5. The caretaker Prime Minister of Azad Kashmir, Mumtaz Rathore, is dismissed and arrested under the Maintenance of Public Order Ordinance after he orders fresh elections claiming that the previous elections held on June 29 were rigged. Rathore is released from detention on July 17.

July 5. The United Kingdom freezes the assets of the Bank of Credit and Commerce International (BCCI). As a result of similiar action by numerous countries, many Pakistanis lose their jobs and deposits in the bank. The State Bank of Pakistan also imposes certain restrictions on BCCI the next day.

July 11. Sardar Abdul Qayyum Khan is nominated as the new Prime Minister of Azad Kashmir.

July 11. Nawaz Sharif warns "any country whose soil is used to attack Pakistan's nuclear sites," after is it reported that Israelis in Indian-held Kashmir are planning to attack the nuclear facility at Kahuta.

July 12. Sardar Gul Mohammad Khan Jogezai is appointed Governor of Balochistan by the president.

July 16. Opposition members as well as some members of the ruling IJI coaliton call upon the president to dismiss the IJI government because of the deteriorating law and order situation.

July 18. The 12th Constitutional Amendment is adopted by the National Assembly granting the government increased powers to control the growing lawlessness in the country.

July 27. *The Economist* reports that more than 1,000 alleged terrorists, mostly PPP supporters, have been arrested in Sindh.

July 29. Sardar Abdul Qayyum Khan takes oath as Prime Minister of Azad Kashmir.

July 30. The final date for surrendering illicit firearms is extended from July 15 to August 2. Later on, the date is extended even further.

August 4. The PDA stages a 12-hour hunger strike against the special powers granted to the government by the 12th Constitutional Amendment.

August 11. Sardar Sikander Hayat Khan is elected unopposed as President of Azad Kashmir.

August 16. Lt. General Asif Nawaz Janjua is promoted to the rank of General and takes over as the new Chief of the Army Staff.

August 17. Benazir's Pajero jeep is stoned and her party workers manhandled in Orangi, Karachi.

August 18. A report by a non-government group alleges that thousands of children are being forced into bonded labor, especially in the carpet-weaving and brick-making industries.

August 24. Several Punjab-based cooperative financial institutions collapse. Twelve high-ranking officials of seven cooperatives that went bankrupt are taken into custody by police in Lahore.

August 25. The government reverses the changes made by the Bhutto government in the *Zakat* and *Ushr* Ordinances and restores the power of provincial governments over the distribution of *zakat*.

August 28. The Foreign Office admits that skirmishes have taken place between Pakistani and Indian troops at the Line of Control.

August 31. Benazir is quoted as saying that "Pakistan has the information and capability to build a nuclear bomb in the event of a threat from India."

September 1. Indian troops attack a Pakistani post in Nezarpur on the Line of Control, killing three Pakistani soldiers.

September 1. The government sets up a commission to investigate charges of misappropriation of public funds by the Punjab-based credit cooperative societies. A government official confirms that up to Rs. 20 billion were lost in the cooperatives scandal. There is speculation that Nawaz Sharif and his government could be linked to the scandal.

September 4. Maulana Fazlur Rehman withdraws his party's (JUI) support from the IJI government.

September 4. Oil is discovered near Hyderabad.

September 10. The Federal Cabinet is expanded by 30 members to accomodate the wishes of certain members of the IJI coalition who want more say in the affairs of the govenment.

September 20. Firing by Indian forces leaves seven dead in the Neelam Valley of Kashmir.

September 25. Two American Muslim brothers are convicted of dacoity and sentenced to amputation of one hand and one foot each by a special court in Peshawar. The Supreme Court reverses the decision and acquits the brothers on October 14.

September 26. An Army investigation team busts a gang involved in theft and murders.

September 30. The Hizb-i-Jehad is expelled from the IJI for associating with opposition parties.

October 1. An 880 MW thermal power station is inaugurated at Jamshoro by Nawaz Sharif.

October 3. Former Governor of NWFP, General (ret'd.) Fazle Haq is shot dead in Peshawar. Allegations of Iranian involvement in the general's death leads to an attack on the Iranian consulate in Peshawar on October 7.

October 15. An agreement is reached between the government and workers of state institutions assuring workers of denationalized institutions that no retrenchment will take place in the first year after privatization; that workers will be allowed to buy up to ten percent ownership in their factories; and that special payments and aid in finding new jobs will be provided to those workers who volunteer to quit.

October 17. The 235 bids received for 89 state enterprises put up for sale are opened.

October 17. Vice Admiral Saeed Mohammed Khan is appointed as the new Chief of the Navy.

October 21. The Punjab Government freezes the assets of the 113 directors and sponsors of the cooperative financial institutions that have gone bankrupt.

October 23. Pakistan's top nuclear scientist, Dr. Abdul Qadeer Khan, is quoted as saying that Pakistan is manufacturing nuclear weapons. The Pakistan government later denies any such assertions and explains that Dr. Qadeer Khan was quoted incorrectly.

October 31. The modified and improved Pakistan Atomic Research Reactor, with its enrichment capacity enlarged from 5 to 10 MW, becomes operational.

November 4. Nine kidnappers are sentenced to death by a special court in Sargodha.

November 13. Religious leader, Senator, and IJI Vice President Maulana Sami-ul-Haq, resigns after allegations of his involvement in a sex scandal.

November 14. The Federal Shariat Court finds twenty economic laws related to interest (*riba*) "repugnant to Islam." It accordingly orders their revision.

November 19. The 50-share index of the Karachi Stock Exchange reaches a record high level of 2,822 points.

November 27. Six hundred people are arrested in Sindh in a government crackdown against PPP activists.

November 30. A strike called by the PPP to protest a crackdown against its workers fails to draw widespread support.

December 7. Veena Hayat, daughter of Sardar Shaukat Hayat, is allegedly gang-raped by masked men at her home in Karachi. It is alleged that the Sindh government is behind the attack as Ms. Hayat is a member of the PPP and a close friend of Benazir. A high-level probe on the incident begins on December 11. The probe finds no evidence of the alleged sexual assualt.

December 9. Agreements on space technology and technical cooperation are signed with China.

December 17. An anti-adulteration drive launched by the government is suspended after protests by vendors lead to strikes and scarcity of foodstuffs.

December 18. Seven Kashmiri political parties demand complete independence for Jammu and Kashmir.

December 31. A nuclear cooperation treaty intended for "peaceful purposes" is signed with China. The agreement includes the supply of a 300 MW nuclear power plant by China to be set up at Chasma, near Islamabad.

1992

January 1. Pakistan and India exchange lists of nuclear installations.

January 12. Top government officials cancel meetings with U.S. Senator Larry Pressler, the author of the so-called Pressler Amendment. During his visit to India, he had accused Pakistan of supporting terrorists in Kashmir and Punjab.

January 14-19. During a visit by Nawaz Sharif to France, an agreement is signed on the sale of 40 Mirage-2000 fighter aircraft and three minesweepers to Pakistan. The dispute on the nuclear plant that France never delivered to Pakistan is also settled.

January 15. General Asif Nawaz reportedly succeeds in winning support for the continued supply of spare parts from the U.S. for the Pakistani armed forces.

January 22. Lt. General Hamid Gul, former head of the Inter-Services Intelligence (ISI) is retired prematurely.

January 23. Reports that the Pakistan Air Force's fleet of F-16's have been grounded due to a lack of spare parts are denied by government officials.

January 25. In a complete turnaround of its Afghan policy, Pakistan decides to back the U.N. peace plan of convening an Afghan assembly to decide on an interim government in Kabul.

February 7. Shahryar Khan, Pakistani Foreign Affairs Secretary, is quoted as admitting that Pakistan has the ability and materials to assemble at least one nuclear explosive device.

February 7. It is reported that an agreement signed with a consortium of Western countries in June 1991 for the construction of a $1.3 billion power station near Karachi is in doubt after the international consortium expresses reservations on the Federal Shariat Court decision in November 1991 related to interest. Several domestic banks earlier had filed appeals to the Supreme Court against the ruling.

February 12. At least eighteen people are killed and over 350 injured as Pakistani security forces fire on Kashmiris trying to cross the Line of Control to "reunify" their homeland. Repeated warnings of firm measures to prevent the march had earlier been given by the Pakistan government to leaders of the JKLF because of concerns that the crossing could lead to a war between India and Pakistan.

February 13. Protest rallies are held in Muzaffarabad condemning the killing by Pakistani security forces of Kashmiris trying to cross the Line of Control into Indian-held Kashmir. Kashmiris pledge to gain independence from both India and Pakistan.

March 5. Jam Sadiq Ali, the highly controversial Chief Minister of Sindh, dies. He is replaced by Syed Muzzafar Hussain.

March 17. Advertisements appear in major U.S. newspapers for the sale of high-interest, five-year bonds by the Pakistan government that can be purchased without any disclosures regarding the identity of the purchaser or the source of the funds. The offer is soon withdrawn after U.S. agents tell Pakistani banking officials to stop the proposed sale as it violates U.S. banking laws.

March 18. President Najibullah of Afghanistan announces that he will resign once an interim government is in place.

March 23. JKLF leader Amanullah Khan is arrested in Rawalpindi.

March 25. After a dismal start in the tournament, Pakistan defeats England by twenty-two runs in the final to win the World Cup Cricket Tournament for the first time.

March 30. Kashmiris dodge attempts by Pakistani security forces to prevent another march into India and are finally stopped at Chinari close to the Line of Control. Pakistani security forces and JKLF militants clash in Muzzafarabad.

April 18. Najibullah takes refuge in a U.N. building in Kabul.

April 25. Ahmad Shah Masoud's forces take over key buildings in Afghanistan. Masoud's forces fight Hekmatyar's guerrillas for control of Kabul.

April 25. A 50-member Afghan interim ruling council is formed.

April 26. Meetings between rival mujahidin groups break down after Gulbuddin Hekmatyar insists that the Kabul Government surrender to him.

April 27. Afghan Interim Government President Mojaddedi arrives in Kabul and takes over as the new President of Afghanistan.

Source: The above chronology is intended to continue the chronology written by Shahid Javed Burki in Shahid Javed Burki and Craig Baxter, *Pakistan Under the Military: Eleven Years of Zia ul-Haq* (Boulder, Colo.: Westview Press, 1991).

The entries in this chronology are based on close readings of the following publications between August 1988 and April 1992: *Dawn*; *Herald*; *Keesings Record of World Events*; *Morning News*; *New York Times Index*; *Newsline*; and the *Wall Street Journal Index*.

Glossary

Allama. Title used to denote religious scholars, both Shia and Sunni. It does not indicate a specific level of "formal education."

Alim (pl. ulema). Literally, learned person. The term is used generically for all religious scholars.

Athna-Ashari. Literally, belonging to twelve; connotatively refers to the largest Shia school of jurisprudence believing in the twelve *Imams.*

Azadari. Literally, mourning. The term refers to the mourning by Muslims in general and the Shias in particular of the massacre in Kerbala in 61 A.H. of Husain, the second grandson of the Prophet Muhammad. *Azadari* consists of meetings called *majlis* in Pakistan where *zakirs* recite events of the Kerbala tragedy to mourners.

Azan. The call to prayers in Islam.

Benazir Bhutto. Prime Minister of Pakistan (1988-1990) and currently the leader of the opposition PPP in the National Assembly. She is the daughter of the late Zulfikar Ali Bhutto and the wife of Asif Ali Zardari.

Fatwa (pl. fatawa). An edict issued by a religious scholar (*alim; mujtahid*) competent to issue such orders. The *fatwa* may be based upon precedent or more rarely on the scholar's *ijtehad.*

Fiqh. School of jurisprudence.

Hadd (pl. hudood). Literally the term means limit or obstruction. In Islamic jurisprudence it means punishment specifically prescribed by the Quran or the Sunnah for certain crimes proven according to specific conditions. In 1979, Zia ul-Haq promulgated the *Hudood* Ordinances in Pakistan.

Hadiths. The sayings of the Prophet Muhammad as remembered and recounted by close associates.

Hanafi fiqh. In Pakistan, the majority school of Islamic jurisprudence. The other major Sunni schools of jurisprudence are: Hambali, Shafaee, and Maliki. The predominant Shia school of jurisprudence is the Jafari *fiqh*.

Ijtehad. Literally creation of a new path; the term means the discovery of law, or the judgment by an *alim* repealing or modifying an existing law or establishing a new law. Sometimes the term is used to denote independent reasoning.

Imam. Literally leader; among the Shias it refers to one of the infallible (*masoom*) "deputies" of the Prophet.

Ghulam Ishaq Khan. President of Pakistan (1988 -). He assumed the post in August 1988 following the death of Zia ul-Haq and was elected in October 1988 to a five-year term of office. Ghulam Ishaq is a former career civil servant. He dismissed the government of Benazir Bhutto in August 1990.

Islami Jamhoori Ittehad (Islamic Democratic Alliance - IJI). The dominant party in the National Assembly, Senate, and four provincial assemblies of Pakistan since the 1990 elections. The IJI was originally formed in order to contest the 1988 elections. The IJI's founder and current leader is Nawaz Sharif.

Jamaat-i-Islami. The largest, best-organized, and most influential activist Islamic party in South Asia. Its founder was Maulana Maududi.

Jammu and Kashmir Liberation Front (JKLF). Militant organization that advocates the secession of Jammu of Kashmir from India and the formation of an independent nation-state of Kashmir. Its leader is Amanullah Khan.

Kashmir. Originally a princely state nestled between present-day Pakistan, India, and China. Western portions of Kashmir, Azad (Free) Kashmir, were "liberated" by Pakistan from Indian control following Partition. The remainder, Jammu and Kashmir, acceded to India and became one of India's states.

Majlis-i-Shura. Literally Council of Advisors. In 1982, Zia ul-Haq established the Majlis-i-Shura and personally appointed its members.

In 1985, members of the reconstituted Majlis-i-Shura were elected on a non-partisan basis. Following the adoption of the 1985 Constitution ("restored" 1973 Constitution) members of the National Assembly and the Senate (the constituent components of the Majlis-i-Shura) have been elected on a party basis.

Masoom. Infallible. The Shias believe that all prophets and the twelve *Imams* (and Fatima, daughter of the Prophet Muhammad) never committed a mistake.

Mazhab (pl. mazahib). School of Islamic jurisprudence.

Muhajir Qaumi Mahaz (Muhajir National Movement - MQM). A political party organized in order to represent the interests of the Muhajir community (Urdu-speaking refugees from India and their descendents) in Pakistan. Support for the party is found predominantly in Sindh province, particularly in Karachi and Hyderabad. In the 1988 and 1990 general elections the MQM gained the third most votes behind only the IJI and PPP. The MQM's founder and current leader is Altaf Hussain.

Mujahidin. Just warrior; "freedom fighter." The term most often refers to the Afghan resistance to Soviet occupation. The term has more recently been applied to the armed resistance to "Indian-occupied Jammu and Kashmir."

Mujtahid. Literally a person who struggles to find a new path. In Shia jurisprudence it refers to a scholar who has acquired the scholarly status to issue *fatawa*. This status is usually only achieved after several years of formal education in Islamic jurisprudence and related subjects.

Asif Nawaz Janjua. Chief of Staff of the Pakistan Army (1991 -). The Office of Chief of Staff carries great political authority in Pakistan. Former Chiefs of Staff include: Aslam Beg (1988-1991), Zia ul-Haq (1976-1988), Yahya Khan (1966-1971), and Ayub Khan (1951-1958).

Pakistan People's Party (PPP). Political party that was formed by Zulfikar Ali Bhutto. The PPP formed the federal government during 1971-1977; and 1988-1990. Currently, the party is the main opposition to the IJI in the Majlis-i-Shura. The current leader of the party is Benazir Bhutto.

Riba. Literally increase. The term refers to financial interest, which is prohibited by the Quran. Some argue that the term should be interpreted as "usury."

Mian Nawaz Sharif. Prime Minister of Pakistan (1990 -). He is the former chief minister of Punjab. Nawaz Sharif is an industrialist and entrepreneur. He is the founder and leader of the IJI.

Shia. Literally, friend; connotatively a follower of Ali. Shias constitute the second largest *mazhab* in Islamdom and Pakistan.

Simla Agreement. Treaty signed in 1972 between India and Pakistan ending the 1971 war. It affirmed the Cease-Fire Line by establishing the Line of Control between India and Pakistan in Kashmir.

South Asian Association for Regional Cooperation (SAARC). Organization formed in 1985 in order to enhance regional cooperation in social, economic, and cultural affairs. SAARC's members are: India, Pakistan, Bangladesh, Nepal, Sri Lanka, Bhutan, and the Maldives.

Sunni. The largest *mazhab* in Islamdom and Pakistan. In Pakistan Sunnis comprise between 80-85 percent of the population.

Tazir. In Islamic jurisprudence all crimes and punishments which are not specifically defined in the Quran and Sunnah (i.e., that are not *hadd*) are *tazir*.

Vilayat-e-faqeeh. According to Muslim belief the prophets, culminating in the Prophet Muhammad, acted as Allah's representatives on earth. After Prophet Muhammad, the Shias believe, the *Imams* assumed the responsibility of being His viceregents. During the occultation of the twelfth *Imam,* learned religious scholars act as the *Imam's* deputies. The most learned of these scholars is designated as the *faqeeh*: the scholar in *fiqh*. He supervises the operation of the society in all spheres of human activity. The resultant social and political order will be designated as the *vilayat-e-faqeeh*.

Wahabis. Muhammad ibn Wahab (ca. 1703-1792) was a religious scholar of the Hambali *fiqh*. He advocated a "strict constructionist" interpretation of the Quran and Sunnah. Those who follow his interpretation are known as "Wahabis" in Pakistan.

Yunani-Tibb (also unani). The medical system originally developed by the Greek philosopher Galen and revised by Muslim scholar-physicians.

Zia ul-Haq. Former President and Chief of Staff of the Pakistan Army. He assumed power following a military coup as Chief Martial Law Administrator in 1977, and became president following a referendum in 1985. He is perhaps best-known for his promulgation of the 1985 Constitution, his unwavering support for the cause of the Afghan mujahidin, and for his introduction of policies of Islamization. He was killed (allegedly assassinated) in a plane crash in August 1988.

About the Contributors

Shahid Javed Burki. (M.Phil. Oxford). Director, China Department World Bank. He is a former economic advisor to Pakistan's Ministry of Commerce. His books on Pakistan include: *Pakistan: A Nation in the Making* (Westview, 1986; 1991); *Pakistan Under the Military* (Westview, 1992); *Pakistan's Development Priorities* (Oxford, 1986); and *Pakistan Under Bhutto* (St. Martin's, 1980).

Afak Haydar. (PhD. Southern Illinois). Professor of Political Science and Public Administration, and Director of International Education, Arkansas State University. He is the Treasurer of the American Institute of Pakistan Studies. His research interests include Pakistan and Islam.

Charles H. Kennedy. (PhD. Duke). Associate Professor, Department of Politics, Wake Forest University and Director, American Institute of Pakistan Studies. He is the author or editor of several books including: *Government and Politics in South Asia* (Westview 1987; 1991); *Civil Military Interaction in Asia and Africa* (EJ Brill, 1991); *Bureaucracy in Pakistan* (Oxford, 1987); and *Ethnic Preference and Public Policy in Developing States* (Rienner, 1986). He is currently working on a book-length manuscript on Islamization in Pakistan.

Ata Khan. Administrative Assistant, American Institute of Pakistan Studies. He is a student at Wake Forest University and permanently resides in Karachi.

William L. Richter. (PhD. Chicago). Professor and Head of the Department of Political Science, Kansas State University. His involvement with South Asia over the past twenty-five years -- primarily with Pakistan during the past fifteen -- has included research and writing, Fulbright teaching, lecture tours, and development consulting. In October 1990 he was a member of the National Democratic Institute's International Observer Team for Pakistan's national and provincial elections.

Anne T. Sweetser. (ABD. Harvard). Assistant Professor, Department of Anthropology, Connecticut College. She did field research for her dissertation, "The Power to Heal: Medicine and Society in the Pakistani Himalaya," in Lahore and the Kaghan Valley for over two years in the early 1980s. She also has conducted field research in Afghanistan.

Marvin G. Weinbaum. (PhD. Columbia). Professor of Political Science and Director of the Program in South and West Asian Studies, University of Illinois. He has written extensively on development politics in South Asia and the Middle East. His most recent publications have focused on the regional and strategic implications of the Afghan conflict. Professor Weinbaum is the Secretary of the American Institute of Pakistan Studies. Among his books are: *Egypt and the Politics of US Economic Aid* (Westview, 1986); and *Food, Development, and Politics in the Middle East* (Westview, 1982).

Robert G. Wirsing. (PhD. Denver). Professor of International Studies at the University of South Carolina. He is a specialist on the international relations of South Asia and a frequent visitor to the area. His most recent book is *Pakistan's Security Under Zia, 1977-1988: The Policy Imperatives of a Peripheral Asian State* (St. Martin's, 1991). His *India, Pakistan and the Kashmir Boundary Dispute: The Search for Settlement* is forthcoming (St. Martin's, 1993).

Lawrence Ziring. (PhD. Columbia). Professor of Political Science and Director of the Institute of Government and Politics at Western Michigan University. He is President of the American Institute of Pakistan Studies and Academic Associate of the Atlantic Council. Professor Ziring is the author or editor of fourteen books and more than one hundred articles that have appeared in academic volumes or journals. His latest books include: *Pakistan's Foreign Policy* (Oxford, 1991); and *The Middle East Dictionary* (ABC-Clio, 1991).

Index

About the Book

Ever since the creation of Pakistan as an independent Muslim state in 1947, the country has struggled to integrate a diverse population and stabilize its borders. During its short but turbulent history, Pakistan has yet to achieve those goals, as political, economic, and social upheavals continue to challenge the world's ninth most populous state.

Despite the importance of Pakistan's status as a regional power and as a pivotal player on the global stage, relatively little timely, detailed analysis is available on the country. This book fills that gap by providing up-to-date analysis and information by leading scholars. The first in a biennial series, this volume interprets current developments in politics, economics, and foreign relations. In addition, special-interest chapters cover the 1990 general election, Islamization, health policy, and the intractable Kashmir conflict.

Scholars and general readers alike will find valuable insights and comprehensive coverage in this thoughtful collection of essays. A detailed chronology and glossary provide especially useful reference points.